India and East Asia

INDIA AND EAST ASIA
Culture and Society

Edited by
N.N. VOHRA

Introduction by
DR KARAN SINGH

SHIPRA

SHIPRA

INDIA INTERNATIONAL CENTRE

ISBN 81-7541-106-6

First Published in India in 2002

India and East Asia: Culture and Society

Published by :
SHIPRA PUBLICATIONS
115-A, Vikas Marg, Shakarpur
Delhi-110092 (India)
Ph. : 2458662, 2200954 Fax : 2458662
Email : siprapub@satyam.com.in

Laser Typesetting by :
R.S. Prints
New Delhi-110049

Printed at :
Choudhary Offset Process
Delhi-110051

CONTENTS

PREFACE

The India International Centre, established with the primary objective of promoting understanding between the different communities of the world, has been organising, for the past four decades now, a sustained series of programmes which seek to further this goal. These programmes have reflected on the genesis and evolution of various cultures, their efflorescence and civilisational impact through the centuries past, and the present and emerging cultural patterns and values. Side by side, the Centre has also been organising continuing debates and discussions focusing on political, economic, scientific and technological, environmental, security and other important issues in the national, regional and international perspectives.

Nearly five years ago, in early 1997, we decided to establish an IIC-Asia Project to enable structured exchanges among academics, scholars and experts to specially focus on the cultural, societal, religious and political bonds which have existed among the Asian countries for thousands of years. In this context it was consciously decided that these dialogues would eschew discussions on security related issues which receive adequate separate attention.

Under the aegis of the Centre's Asia Project, we have organised seminars on 'Religion, Politics and Society in South and South East Asia' (1997); 'Culture, Society and Politics in Central Asia' (1998) and 'Culture, Democracy and Development in South Asia' (2000). Thereafter, we turned our attention to our more distant neighbours and organised a seminar on 'India and East Asia: Culture and Society' (2001).

About two dozen scholars from China, Japan, Hong Kong, Mongolia, Korea, Taiwan and India representing universities and centres of specialised studies participated in the aforesaid India-East Asia seminar.

The seventeen papers contained in this volume reflect upon and seek to rediscover the invaluable heritage of Asian literature, art, painting, mythology, cultural values, deep-rooted historical commonalities and the interplay of co-existence and synthesis in the centuries past. All in all, the intensive discussions at this seminar reminded us about the glorious civilisational heritage of Asian countries and the shared cultures and values rooted in thousands of years of history which, if resuscitated, could lay the bedrock of an altogether harmonious future for nearly one-third of the world population which inhabits Asia.

We trust that this volume, like the three earlier Asia Project publications, would provide a useful resource for scholars and policy makers and, besides, generate interest among all those who are concerned with building a more peaceful and productive tomorrow.

I thank Sh. C.V. Ranganathan, who has enjoyed tenures of outstanding diplomatic service in Asian countries, for his invaluable contribution towards the organisation of the India-East Asia seminar.

The Asia Project would perhaps have faltered and faded away but for the vigorous direction provided by Dr Karan Singh who is a Life Trustee of the Centre and, besides, a noted scholar, thinker, philosopher, author, diplomat and parliamentarian. I record my gratitude for his sustained guidance and support.

For the timely publication of this volume, I thank Ms. Bela Butalia, Deputy Editor in the Centre's Publication Division, and Shipra Publications for their devoted efforts.

N.N.Vohra
Director

November, 2001
India International Centre
New Delhi

INTRODUCTION

KARAN SINGH

Asia being the cradle of civilisations, the birthplace of all the great religions of the world, without any exception, we decided to focus this series of seminars entirely on Asia. All the world religions are Asian religions. Even the religions which flourish today in other continents were born in Asia, which has been the home of great philosophies, science, technology, and of the most sublime literature. Colonial domination for 400 years has resulted in a fracturing and fragmenting of the relationship *inter se* between the Asian countries. We know more, individually, about countries in the West than we do about each other, and that has always been one of the major intellectual problems we face.

Let us take one example—the spread of Buddhism in Asia. Buddhism impacted almost all the countries of Asia—India, Nepal, Bhutan, Burma, China, and the countries of Southeast Asia. It went to Korea; it went to Japan. The great monuments that were built in Java—the Bhadra Vihar (Borobudur), the Param Brahman (Parambaran) temples—who were the people who built them? What were the sagas and the stories behind this magnificent efflorescence of art and architecture? These monuments were not built by the sword, unlike in the West which went conquering everywhere with the sword and destroying places of worship and putting up new ones. I do not think any place of worship was ever destroyed, but new ones were built. What were those kingdoms? Take Angkor Vat, the greatest Hindu-Buddhist temple in the world. It is neither in India, nor in China; it is in Cambodia. How is it that in Cambodia this tremendous efflorescence of art and architecture took place? How was the wealth generated? Who were the great leaders, who were the architects, who were the kings who had this great vision? None of this is known to us. In our history books we read all about European kings and princes, about their battles and marriages, their divorces but we know hardly anything about each other. We do not even know enough about our own countries, if I may say so.

Today, for the first time after Vasco da Gama in 1498, every inch of Asian territory is under Asian control. I think the last bit was Portuguese Macau. Now surely the time has come when our intellectual interactions must be re-established and be much richer and deeper than before. We decided as Trustees of the India International Centre that we should do something about this, and therefore we initiated this IIC-Asia Project. This series is specifically focused on civilisational contacts, not on security, nuclear or armament issues but on civilisational contacts, be it philosophy, religion, archaeology, iconography, dance, or music. What are the deeper layers of culture and civilisation that bind Asia together? We do not want to be exclusive, as we are all now partners of an emerging global society, but Asia does have a special ambience, a special contribution to make. We decided right at the beginning that we were not going to have any non-Asian participants in our seminars, and we took a decision that these seminars would be for Asians, by Asians and focused on Asia. The world of scholarship knows no boundaries or barriers but nonetheless we decided to confine our seminars to Asian scholars. As invitees were present in their personal capacities it was not necessary for them to articulate any official viewpoint.

There is a tremendous store of knowledge on East Asia and Asia's cultural artifacts. I can hardly comment on that, nor on the very quaint stories and the way these stories have travelled. One participant used the term 'Third World' a number of times. May I submit that this is an obnoxious term, it is a Eurocentric term. After having exploited and dominated Asia for four centuries, the Europeans appropriated to themselves the term 'First World'. They did not know what to do with the Communists, so they pushed them into the 'Second World', and all the rest of us have been lumped together as the 'Third World'. This is a phrase that I, for one, would ban from the vocabulary, particularly of Asians. In the earlier seminars it was asked as to why the seminars were exclusively male. We did try our best to invite women participants and this time we were able to get one woman, but unfortunately she fell ill and could not come. In the last seminar we did get one or two women. So gender inequality continues. Whether that is an Asian value or a European value, I do not know. But whatever it may be, that gender inequality continues is a fact.

Some ideas were mooted about academic linkages between certain East Asian and Indian academic institutions. There was a suggestion that the Chinese University of Hong Kong could perhaps have a link with the Delhi University and start some programmes and collaborative efforts. I strongly support that, because one of the ways in which the Asian identity will be able to assert itself will be in the interactions between the academic institutions. All of us have links with Western institutions; but *inter se* there are very few links. And areas like the research on the relationship between Hinduism and Shintoism, or Hinduism and Taoism, or Asian Christianity, are inter-disciplinary international Asian projects which can be taken up with great advantage. So I would like to suggest, particularly as there were three representatives from the Chinese University of Hong Kong and two representatives from mainland China, one from Taiwan, and two representatives from Mongolia and from Japan, that we should try and follow up these linkages. If there is anything we can do to facilitate this, we will do it.

This whole question of values is something that is really very interesting. Can we really say that there is such a thing as Asian values? And how do they work? That there can be a different approach in values, I would like to illustrate for you with two examples. Many years ago up in Kashmir a Caribbean group came to give a musical performance. It was a young group, they had guitars and a harmonium, and so on. The harmonium was lying on one side of the stage. As the group was starting the performance, one person started pushing the harmonium towards the centre of the stage with his foot. Now, in India touching a musical instrument with one's feet is something that is totally unacceptable. You may call it an Asian value or a Hindu value or what. Immediately, a girl ran out and picked up the harmonium with her hands and placed it at the centre of the stage. I remarked that I was certain that the girl must be a Hindu, and sure enough, when I enquired I learnt that this was in fact the case. Our generation has been taught that under no circumstances should either a book or a musical instrument ever be touched with the feet. It is something horrifying for us. This is something which is deeply embedded in our psyche. Perhaps you could call it a value.

I will give you another example. Many years ago we went to Los Angeles. Our elder son was getting his admission to the

University of Southern California. We thought we would buy him a small car, to make it easy for him to commute. So my wife and I went to a car showroom and asked the salesgirl the price of the cheapest car. We did not have very much money available those days due to restrictions on foreign exchange. The salesgirl asked us the purpose for which we wanted the car. I told her it was for our son who was going to college. She said, why do you want to buy him a car. Well, we said, he is going to college. She was genuinely astonished. Why can he not buy his own car, she asked. I said that we had just come from India. She said, no, no, in this country we would never buy a car for our son. He must earn his own living and then buy a car for himself. So it is a difference of perception. For us, the most natural thing in the world would be to try and buy one's son a car. But for her the idea that parents should buy a car for the son was something astounding.

I am not here making a value judgement in either case. I am just pointing out that values vary from civilisation to civilisation. Professor Chattopadhyaya talked about a hierarchy of values. Maybe these are behavioural traditions, as, for example when we do not touch a musical instrument with our foot. Or if a book were to fall on the ground, we would normally lift it, touch it to our forehead before putting it back on the shelf. The dancer who performed the Bharatnatyam dance at the end saluted the earth with her hands, asking forgiveness from the earth for having danced upon it. The earth is not considered to be just an inert clot of matter, it is itself a divinity. Therefore after the dance, she touches the earth and says I am sorry if I caused you any negative vibrations by dancing upon you. Maybe these are Hindu values, or Indian values, or Asian values, or maybe these are global values.

We are all global citizens apart from being denizens of our own country. My own view is now tending towards the idea that we have to try and adopt what we consider to be a positive, holistic and harmonious value system, for which we can draw from all civilisations. I do not think it is a question of being chauvinistic; that is, as these are Indian or Chinese values therefore we should only follow them. But there are differences. Dr Lokesh Chandra has performed a valuable service by pointing out that the Confucian worldview is in fact very different perhaps from the Hindu worldview, and the Hindu worldview is different perhaps from the Islamic worldview. The study of values is an area in which a lot of intercultural work is waiting to be done, and this is a challenge to Asian intellectuals.

The final point is the concept of multiple identities. That, to my mind is the key for us in the 21st century. The old idea of having a single identity is no longer valid, because we live now in a global society. Let me give you my own example. I can work out at least six identities of my own. Let me start with my linguistic identity. I am a Dogra. You may have never heard the word, Indians probably have. The Dogras are a small community in north India. They are an ethno-linguistic community. So, Dogra is my linguistic identity. Rajput is my caste identity. As a Hindu I have a caste identity, I am a Kshatriya. So I have been brought up with a caste identity. That is how the Kshatriyas are brought up. My religious identity is Hindu. Despite what some friends have said, Hinduism is a fairly well established religion so far and hopefully will continue to be so. So that is my religious identity. My national identity is of an Indian. I am an Indian, proud to be an Indian. I grew up here. I met Mahatma Gandhi. Jawaharlal Nehru was my political guru. I have been in the Indian Cabinet for many years. I have been a Member of Parliament. India is my national identity. Then there is my continental identity, as an Asian, which is perhaps the most tenuous of these identities. And then there is my global identity. By the definition global, I am a global citizen. I feel at home wherever I go on this planet. There is nowhere that I do not feel at home.

We have the concept not only of Bhavani Bharati, of India as a goddess, but of Bhavani Vasundhara, of the world as a divinity. Therefore wherever I go in the world, I am at home. So even in my own life my linguistic, my caste, my religious, my national, my continental and my global identity are all significant. These are my identities, apart from my identity as an academician or an educationist, or an environmentalist or a musician. We can no longer be satisfied with a single identity. However, what is essential is that one must have a centre around which these concentric circles can then revolve. If you do not have a strong centre, then you become eccentric. Instead of being harmonious, the identities clash and you become schizophrenic, neurotic or in some ways unbalanced. So as I see it from my own personal experience, the inner centre brings me back once again to the spiritual element. If you have a strong inner centre, then you can have a dozen different identities in concentric circles. But if you do not have a strong spiritual centre, then you get buffeted like a leaf in the wind, blown hither and thither, and you get disoriented because of the sheer multiplicity of identities which one now has to confront as a global citizen in the 21st century A.D. so that we can emerge as holistic human beings in a harmonious global society.

India and Asia : Parallels and Transmissions

D.P. CHATTOPADHYAYA

Grounds of Cultural Parallelism

Our cultural world is nested in and emerges out of the natural world. Nature is law-governed (*Ṛta-baddha*) and its influence on culture is bound to be deep, of course in an uneven manner. This unevenness is due to the freedom and creativity of human beings, the architects of culture and history.

Law-governed nature throws up a *finite number* of challenges to the concerned human civilisations. The problems and challenges faced by every civilisation are *limited in variety*. These limitations of variety are due to the natural rootedness of our cultural life. Because of the said limitation in the variety of problems, it has been possible for humans to solve or tackle them by discovering the underlying laws and appropriate techniques. *Natural challenge* and *cultural response* are the two key terms necessary for understanding parallelism and diffusionist contacts between different civilisations, between the products of the human mind embedded in art, science and technology. Also, these explain why similar philosophical ideas, religious beliefs, scientific hypotheses and technological inventions have been thrown up by geographically separate civilisations—Indic, Sinic, Semitic and Hellenic. I make a conscious distinction between what is Hellenic and what is Greek. The Eurocentric historians of civilisations, in their eagerness to highlight the European root of modern science and philosophy, include the east coast of the Mediterranean sea and the Aegean islands and somehow forget that mainland Greece is not to be confused with the larger Hellenic world, from where the great thinkers like Pythagoras, Heraclitus, Thales, Anaximander and Euclid hailed.

To illustrate my point I will refer only to a few important ideas which are found in different civilisations. Their exact origins continue to remain a matter of dispute among the experts. To start with, I will refer to the religious concept of Shaman. About the very origin of the word Shaman there is difference of opinion among the philologists. While some are of the view that it is a corrupt expression of the Sanskrit word *śraman*, there are several others who maintain that it is a Tunguso-Manchurian word. At.the very beginning one perceives the subtle phonological difference between (the Sanskrit) *śraman* (Manchurian) *săman* and its English form Shaman. If one looks into its wider geographical expansions—Siberian, Tibetan, Indian, Southeast Asian, Arctic, African and North American—one is bound to be struck by two things; the phonological difference and yet the spiritual affinity. The pronunciation of used words undergo changes, often beyond recognition, but their content retains a striking affinity.

A Shaman is a person endowed with spiritual power and healing capacity. The forms of sickness which a Shaman can heal may be mental or physical or both. Besides, a Shaman is believed to have a para-normal capacity of perception and communication. In different areas of Asia Shamanistic spiritualism has taken different forms. In some areas its ideological aspects have supervened over the technical ones. Techniques of healing spiritual and physical sickness have received uneven emphasis in different cultures. The Shaman is medicine man, priest and psychiatrist, a three-in-one. The most important function of the Shaman in all cultures is healing.

Long before the present, the wise men of India, China, Central Asia and West Asia did realise the deep relation between the psychic and the somatic causes of illness. Both in Ayurveda, Unani and Tibetan systems of medicine the importance of the soul factor, spiritual weakness, has been recognised as an important condition responsible for all sorts of human sickness. One who is spiritually or mentally weak is believed to be highly vulnerable to different types of diseases. Given spiritual strength, the healing capacity of the organic system as a whole improves. Therefore, the Shaman has been credited with para-normal (*alaukika*) powers and that explains why the office of the priest and that of the medicine man have been thought to be so kindred and socially respectable.

Because of his pre-eminent social usefulness he is supported by the society and accorded a very pre-eminent position. In the Hindu, Buddhist and Taoist traditions elements of Shamanism are evident. In all these religious traditions it is believed that the realised soul, the mendicant monk or *śraman*, like a true Brahmin, can help and heal the less developed souls and does perform a very important social role.

The *tantra* tradition which deeply informs Hinduism and Buddhism, exhibits very clear Shamanic influences both in the fields of spiritual exercise and medical practice. Megasthenes writes that this tradition was strongly influential in the east of India. The Vedic concept of *tāpasa*, ascetic, is close to the function of the *śraman*. He is not only wise but also spiritually powerful enough to heal the psycho-physical infirmity of others.

Parallel or Diffusionist Origin of the Symbol of Zero?

From a popular medico-religious concept of Shaman I would like to move to an abstract mathematical concept, zero or *śūnya*. The sense of *śūnya* in Sanskritic languages is manifold. It has been conceived as *binduḥ, pataḥ* and, ontologically speaking, both as *emptiness*, i.e. void, and *absolute*, i.e. fullness, not determined or negated by any attribute (*nirguna Brahman*, for example). In the English language the concept of zero has been influenced by the Arabic word, *cifr*, i.e. *cipher*. The words naught and nothingness are also associated with zero.

That in the ancient civilisations, in their numeral systems, zero as such has no place in itself is generally acknowledged by historians of diverse persuasions. The dispute is about the country or civilisation which should be credited to have first used the circular symbol for zero. Obviously it should not be a chauvinistic discourse but objective and evidenced. That Plato or even the pre-Platonic Hellenic thinkers, like Thales and Pythagoras, were not familiar with the circular symbol of zero is generally agreed upon. However, most of the historians of ethno-mathematics, mathematics and science like L. Conant, K. Menninger, and Carl B. Boyer are of the view (i) that indigenous techniques of making use of the zero for the purpose of counting and mensuration were known to the Indian, Chinese and the Semitic peoples, and (ii) that Hindus and Arabs should be given the credit of inventing the numerals of today. But it is also said that though there were separate symbols for 10 and multiples of 10, 20, 30, 40, 100, etc., but the systems could not understandably contain what is called place-value arithmetic. Joseph Needham tells us that the circular symbol of zero first appears on the Bhojadeva inscriptions at Gwalior, dated A.D. 870. The Chinese evidence of using it is dated as A.D. 1247. The first Arabic scholars who used Hindu numerals (from *Sindhind*) are Abu'l-Wefa (940-998) and al-Karkhi (or al-Kargi, c. 1029).

It is of interest to note that the symbol of zero is found also in some Indo-Chinese inscriptions and those of some ancient South American civilisations (Aztec, for example). The point which I would like to highlight here in this limited context is that similar scientific innovations are found to have emerged in different civilisations which are geographically widely separate. I must hasten to add here that even in ancient times, when the modern modes of human travel were not available, ideas and techniques did travel. How exactly it happened is an instructive story by itself. This brings me to the last illustrative point of my presentation, that is, the main routes of civilisational travel which carried not only merchandise but also philosophical, religious and scientific ideas.

* * *

The earlier we go back in the periods of history and pre-history the freer we find the flow of ideas and techniques between the peoples and their countries. The modern political notion of country, defined by a well demarcated boundary and guarded by armed posts, did not exist. Passports and visas for travel were not needed. Admittedly, differences between peoples and countries had been there but that did not interfere with the transmission of beliefs, customs and other characteristics of one culture to other cultures. It is true that political conflict and religious intolerance at times interrupted cultural flows but in most cases these interruptions proved temporary and gradually weakened.

Demographic migration and immigration were a way of life. Carrying language, myths, religions and various components of culture was an essential part of this way of life. It was *not* necessarily related to warfare. The heavy impact of political history on our mind leads many of us to believe today that international and inter-epochal exchange of ideas was primarily due to war, conquest, subjugation and imposition. This is only partly true. For the main truth in this area we have to look into the records of contacts and transmissions between cultures through intermediaries like ambassadors, travellers, traders, sailors, priests and, above all, ceaseless and silent human migration and immigration due to natural calamities, quest for hospitable climes and fertile lands, specially river basins.

When we look back into the history of India and its relation with the neighbouring countries of Asia, we are obliged to recall the land routes and maritime routes of India with countries like Central Asia, Far East, West Asia and Southeast Asia. Baghdad, Tashkent and Delhi formed a golden triangle of culture and transmission of material, intellectual and spiritual goods.

A vast and large canvas was there beyond this golden triangle. The Indus and the Gangetic Valleys of India had been well connected both with the Far Eastern and the West Asian countries. The two Silk Routes, the southern one and the northern one, which connected the Far East with East Europe and West Asia and passed through the north of India, had their direct extension through Khotan, Tashkent, Ferghana and Bactra to Taxila, Indraprastha (Delhi), Barbaricon (Sind), Ujjain, Pataliputra, Broach, Virapatanam (near Pondicherry), Tamralipta (Banga), Muziris (Kerala). The sea routes connected important ports like Canton (Kuangtung), Hanoi (Kattigara), Sabana (southern Thailand) and the coastal towns of India (already mentioned) with gulf ports like Hira and the Red Sea ports like Adulis, Berenice, Aelena and beyond, to Ghaza, Tyre and Alexandria. These land and sea routes are only the highways by which Indian, Chinese and Arabic-Semitic ideas travelled and interacted. Besides these highways, there were numerous side-ways and bye-ways. For example, India had close connections beyond the Himalaya with Yunnan, and beyond the Khun-Lun (mountain ranges) with the main Chinese cities. Contrary to popular belief, the Himalayan range, through its numerous passes, facilitated—though restrictively—transmission of ideas, religious and scientific, from India to China. There was also an active overland route between East India to Yunnan through Burma.

The relations between China and India were always marked by mutuality. Besides the well known Fa-Hsien and Hsuan-Tsang many other learned monks and travellers contributed to India-China relations. This point has been persuasively brought out, among others, by Professor Tan Chung in his comprehensive anthology, *Across the Himalayan Gap: An Indian Quest for Understanding China*. This quest is mutual and unending. The literature and the sources on the subject are vast. There is a definite scholarly opinion that China and India are not only two neighbouring civilisations due to geographical compulsion but also, perhaps more so, due to endless cultural contacts, exchanges and solicited enrichment. The history of

Buddhism across the Himalaya, the saga of gunpowder and the fine and long story of silk (Chinese *sera*, from which came the Indian word *sārī* and the English word sericulture) are well known. Joseph Needham and several other scholars have thoroughly studied and brought out this highly informative history to our notice.

What is yet to be done in a *really* comprehensive way is to study millennia-old and time-tested India-China relations in the light of recent researches—archaeological, philological, philosophical and scientific. To rewrite the long and extremely instructive history of a golden chain of civilisations, consisting of its Indic, Persic, Semitic and Hellenic linkages, is another Asian agenda. A collateral study needs to be undertaken tracing India's cultural linkages beyond Central Asia with Russia, and with the Slavic, Baltic and Nordic Europe. Let me repeat here once again what I have already said before: in the sphere of culture, the nation or continent knows no formidable boundaries. Geography and history are all cultural transmission belts. Cultural contacts and civilisational dialogues, unlike political episodes and upheavals, belong to the collective life-world and are therefore ceaseless and creative.

REFERENCES

Carl B. Boyer, *History of Mathematics,* John Wiley & Sons, New York, 1989.

L. Conant, *The Number of Concept: Its Origin and Development*, Macmillan, New York, 1933.

K. Menninger, *Number Words and Number Symbols*, MIT Press, Cambridge/ Mass, 1969.

IN SEARCH OF AN ASIAN COMMONALITY

PHILIP YUEN-SANG LEUNG

Introduction

In recent years 'Asian Values' have become a subject of much debate and discussion. Political leaders in Singapore, Malaysia, China, Korea and Japan have all expressed their opinions on the issue, while academics and scholars all over Asia have also contributed to the debate. Not only has the topic been hotly debated within Asia but many academics and intellectuals in the West have been following the debate closely and participating in the intellectual discourse as well.

What does the phrase 'Asian Values' mean? Does it refer to Chinese values? Or does it refer to Indian, Japanese or Korean values? The term is so elusive that no one seems to know the exact meaning. If we believe, as we usually do, that values ordinarily connote the core or axial elements of a culture, the traditional grounds on which rest a culture's most characteristic and enduring institutions, then here the phrase would mean 'traditional Asian' values. Even so, it is still unclear whether this means 'Confucian', 'Daoist', 'Buddhist', 'Hindu' or 'Islamic'. Even Professor William Theodore de Bary, a leading scholar at Columbia University who has studied Asian civilisations for more than half a century, found it difficult to define the notion. He said:

> When I was first asked by the National Endowment for Democracy (in the US) to speak on 'Asian Values' at a conference, the sponsors themselves admitted that they had only a vague notion of what Asian values were all about, and hoped I might give them a clue. Unfortunately, fifty years of studying, teaching, and writing about Asian civilisations and Asian humanities did not help much in answering the question. 'Asian Values' is a new concept in current political parlance, and one could not help wondering what this new usage was all about.[1]

We agree with Professor de Bary's opinion that the term Asian Values is vague and fluid, that its meaning changes from time to time and from place to place, and that the appearance of the term in recent books and newspapers is closely connected to political developments in contemporary Asia. In fact, the entire debate began in Singapore in the early 1990s when Lee Kuan Yew, after stepping down from the post of Prime Minister to become Senior Minister of the city-state, raised the issue as a challenge to Western democracy. The notion was immediately picked up by Prime Minister Mohamad Mahathir of Malaysia who endorsed the concept and used it to challenge the West. The debate then spread to other Asian societies such as Taiwan, Hong Kong and Japan, with allies of Lee and Mahathir lining up on one side and the supporters of Western democratic values rallying to the other. In other words, the debate on Asian values in the 1990s has to be understood within a specific political background.

We shall return to this debate in the latter part of this paper. But first and foremost, it is this paper's assertion that the current debate on Asian values does not arise solely from the political need of the two Southeast Asian states confronting Westernisation and democratisation. The drive to find an Asian commonality, as this paper attempts to show, has been a continuous effort of the Asian political and intellectual leaders in the last hundred years since the late 19th century. In this paper we shall examine several cultural and political movements in the last century which focused on common values as a means to foster common bonds and solidarity in Asia. This historical perspective, I hope, will enable us to better understand the current debate on Asian values.

Three cases of the 'Common Asia' concept are to be considered here. The first was the Pan-Asian movement launched by Rabindranath Tagore in early 20th century India. The second was the concept of the 'Greater East Asian Co-Prosperity Sphere' promoted by the Japanese in wartime Asia. The third was the Confucian project in Singapore in the 1980s which was directly connected to the 'Asian Values' debate in the 1990s.

This paper asserts that there has been a shared impulse among Asian leaders and Asian intellectuals to create an Asian commonality that would foster political identity and cultural solidarity in Asia. This impulse had been translated into intellectual and educational programmes such as Tagore's pan-Asianism and Visva-Bharati, and into social and cultural movements such as the Confucian Project in Singapore, or into political and military schemes such as Japan's 'New Order for East Asia'. However, all such programmes were developed as a response to the direct challenge of Western cultural penetration and Western economic dominance in the region.

India and the Pan-Asian Movement

When the announcement of Rabindranath Tagore's receipt of the Nobel prize in Literature was made in 1913, intellectuals in all Asian countries were filled with pride and excitement. In an era of rising importance of Western technological and capitalistic culture, an Asian writer-philosopher emerged as a refreshing star in the international writers' circle and as an 'alternative' cultural leader. Scholars and intellectuals in Asia began to pay more attention to this poet-philosopher who became the first Asian to be recognised by the Western world of intellectuals, scholars and writers. Riding on his newly acquired fame and popularity, Tagore had made two long trips to East Asia, visiting Japan and China in 1916 and in 1924 respectively. In his visits to Japan and China, he emphatically promoted Asian solidarity and the concept of Pan-Asianism. In the famous Bengali writer-philosopher's own words: 'I feel that Asia must find her own voice', he said. 'I do feel that if Asia does not find her own voice, humanity will not be saved. That was my message to China and Japan and they listened to me and I do hope that some good will come out of it.'[2]

What was that 'one voice' of Asia? What was that single thread that joins the cultures of Japan, Korea, China and India? What was that Asian 'voice' that could save humanity? Tagore's French friend, Paul Richard, describes this Asian voice as the combination of the various characteristics of Asia's different peoples. He said, 'A new soul is awakening in Asia which will contain within itself the best qualities of the various Asiatic peoples—the sensibility of Japan, the mentality of China, the spirituality of India. In this Soul of the Future will be gathered up the great Thought of Asia.'[3] Tagore's Pan-Asianism , as Paul Richard interpreted it, was the combined best of Asia, and these top qualities all pertained to the 'inner life' of humankind. Tagore's Pan-Asianism, therefore, seemed to stress the spirituality of the Eastern civilisation vis-à-vis the materialistic civilisation of the West.

According to Tagore, Western civilisation was political, mechanical, and commercial in character and was threatening to devour the spiritual civilisation of the East in the period of Western expansionism and colonialism. Tagore was very much concerned about the danger of this imminent threat and menace. He said, 'The political civilization which has sprung up from the soil of Europe and is overrunning the whole world, like some prolific weed ... is cannibalistic in its tendencies, it feeds upon the resources of other peoples and tries to swallow their whole future ... This political civilization is scientific, not human.'[4]

In order to promote a united front in Asia and to prevent its spiritual civilisation from being destroyed by the West, and to 'save humanity', Tagore embarked on a vigorous campaign throughout Asia to spread his idea of Asian spiritualism. He visited Japan in 1916 and again in 1927, delivering repeatedly the same message to the Japanese audience. His message to Japan: 'For centuries we did hold torches of civilisation in the East when the West slumbered in darkness.' He said, 'I cannot but bring to your mind those days when the whole of Eastern Asia from Burma to Japan was united with India in the closest tie of friendship, the only natural tie which can exist between nations.' He then continued, 'The lamp of ancient Greece is extinct in the land where it was first lighted ... But the civilisation, whose basis is society and the spiritual ideal of man, is still a living thing in China and India.'[5] He exhorted his Japanese listeners: 'Apply your Eastern mind, your spiritual strength, your love of simplicity, your recognition of social obligation, in order to cut out a new path for this great unwieldy car of progress, shrieking out its loud discords as it runs.'[6]

During his trip to China in 1924, Tagore reiterated the materialistic West/spiritual East theme. He said, 'There is one section of the youth in Asia which denies the value of ancient Asian civilization, and follows the ideas of western civilization, trying its best to absorb them. This is a great mistake ...Western civilization is simply interested in material things, and has many defects in its spiritual life. This point is obvious when we look at the bankruptcy of European culture after the World War.'[7]

Tagore's message of Asian spiritualism in Japan and China was not well received. The crowds gathering at his lectures were big, yet the number of real listeners and committed Tagoreans was small. Back in India after his first trip to Japan, Tagore put together his ideas of Indian spiritualism and pan-Asianism to form a plan of Visva-Bharati (world university or international university) where he could promote and inculcate in his students a balanced education from the cultures of the East and West. The formal inauguration of the university took place on 23 December 1921.[8] The brand of Asianism advocated by Tagore focused on the traditional cultures of India, China and Japan, especially the spiritual and moral values of these cultures. He saw the enormous destruction of Europe during and after the Great War, and hence realised the inadequacies of Western materialistic and technological culture. However, he was not altogether against modernity and the modern West. He and his followers at Visva-Bharati such as Tan Yun-shan were looking for the balance. But in an era of intensified imperialism, chaotic warfare and bitter struggles in all Asian countries, the message of balance and harmony was not well received and fell almost completely on deaf ears.

Japan and East Asian Co-Prosperity

If Tagore's pan-Asianism was somewhat idealistic, then the kind of pan-Asianism developed in Japan was driven by *realpolitik* and nationalistic concerns. In the first half of the 20th century the idea of a common Asian culture also gained considerable acceptance among Japanese intellectuals. Although most of the Japanese had a sense of uniqueness of their own nation and culture, they were not totally unfamiliar with the concept of pan-Asianism. In fact, a number of Japanese intellectuals in the last decades of the 19th century, such as Okakura Tenshin (1862-1913) and Tokutomi Soho (Lichiro, 1863-1957) were among the first Asians who supported the 'Asia is One' movement in the late Meiji period.[9] The early advocates of pan-Asianism in Japan were not isolated from the other pan-Asianists such as Tagore in India and Dr Sun Yat-sen in China. But the trend of pan-Asianism took a drastic turn in the inter-war years, when its emphasis changed from that of a common spiritual culture to the building of an Asian empire under the Japanese emperor. From the foundation of pan-Asianist ideas in Meiji and Taisho Japan, Prime Minister Konoye Fumimaro developed the concept of 'New Order in East Asia', in 1938, further developed into the concept of 'Greater East Asia Co-Prosperity Sphere' by Matsuoka Yosuke in 1940.

Historians are divided in their interpretations of the motives and ethics behind this Japanese concept. E. Herbert Norman, author of *Japan's Emergence as a Modern State* (1940), believed the concept was developed by expansionists as a deceptive and exploitative means to bring other Asians into a collaborative programme with Japan under its militarist rule.[10] On the other hand, scholars such as Marius Jansen believe that there was a genuine altruism in Meiji and pre-war Japan, arising out of a deeply felt sense of kinship with other Asians. They think that many Japanese sincerely wanted to help Asia in the wake of Western encroachment and imperialism.[11]

Recent studies show that Konoye Fumimaro's proclamation of the 'New Order of East Asia' might have originated from Nakayama Masaru, a professor of East Asian Politics at the Nation Building University (Kenkoku Daigaku) in Manchukuo. He was in Beijing when the invitation to draft the proclamation came from Fumimaro in 1938. Nakayama had attended the East Asia Common Culture College (To-A Dobun Shoin) in Shanghai in the 1910s and was believed to be influenced by Dr Sun Yat-sen (1866-1925), founder of the Chinese Republic. His idea of a common culture in East Asia and a new order in East Asia, therefore, resembled Dr Sun's 'Great Asianism' which asserted the basic superiority of Asian culture and virtues and called for cooperation among Asian nations in their struggle against Western imperialism. As explained by Marius Jansen, Sun saw the problem of pan-Asianism as a cultural problem of the conflict of the Occidental rule of Might with the Oriental rule of Right.[12] When Dr Sun delivered a speech on Pan-Asianism to the Japanese in Kobe in November 1924, the Japanese audience took Sun's speech as an appeal for Sino-Japanese collaboration for economic co-prosperity and joint security against the Western world.[13] In other words, in the late 1920s and early 1930s, the idea of 'Greater Asianism' had become trendy amongst some intellectuals in both China and Japan, who did not realise that a more vicious political program was being developed by the militarists under the pretext of Sino-Japanese collaboration.

The Greater East Asia Association was formed in 1932. Its Board of Trustees included Prince Konoye Fumimaro, Nakayama Masaru, Mitsui Iwane and others. So the concept of Sino-Japanese collaboration and Dr Sun Yat-sen's 'Greater Asianism' were not unfamiliar to these key figures. But it would be an exaggeration to say that their 'East Asian New Order'genuinely embraced Dr Sun's 'Greater Asianism', particularly the principle of equality between the two countries. The expansionists soon gained the upper hand in political influence and in the decision-making process in pre-war Japan. They adopted the concept of a 'New Order in East Asia' and further developed it into the plan for a 'Greater East Asia Co-Prosperity Sphere' in 1940. In the new conception of a 'Greater East Asian Order' they considered the other Asian states as mere satellites under various degrees of Japanese control. To establish this 'New Order', a Greater East Asia Deliberative Council was formed in March 1942 to give advice to the military government. Later that year, a Greater East Asia Ministry was formed to handle all overseas areas occupied by the Japanese except Korea, Formosa and Sakhalin. Under the new ministry, the Japanese government invited the 'collaborationists' from Asian countries to a much publicised assembly in Tokyo in 1943 where they came together to demonstrate Asian solidarity in their 'struggle against the West'.

In retrospect, we know that the 'Greater East Asia Co-Prosperity Sphere' was nothing but an ideology of false consciousness that served to advance the military interest of Japan and its dominance over other Asian peoples. But the call of 'anti-colonialism' and 'Asia for the Asiatics' worked with intoxicating effect on the minds of many Asian leaders who were struggling for liberation from European colonialism. Only later, when they saw the naked aggression and brutal military rule of Japan did they realise that the Japanese government was no real 'liberator' but a 'neo-colonizer' and that it was equally repressive if not more so than the colonial governments of Europe.

Singapore and Confucian Ethics

The current debate on 'Asian Values' has its origination in the tiny city-state of Singapore. But before 'Asian Values' became an issue in international diplomacy and intellectual discourse, Lee Kuan Yew had launched the Confucian Project in Singapore in 1982 when he was still prime minister. It would not be an exaggeration to say that Lee's talk on Asian values was a direct product of the decade-long Confucian movement in Singapore.

The Confucian Project, as it was referred to by Professor Tu Wei-ming of Harvard University, began in Singapore as part of the moral education reform efforts of the Ministry of Education, then under the leadership of Deputy Prime Minister Goh Keng Swee. Goh and other educational leaders of Singapore felt that the successful modernisation of Singapore's economy and the rising standard of materialistic culture had brought about some undesirable consequences, such as selfish and narcissistic values and immoral behaviour, especially among the young. One way of solving this problem of excessive materialism was to promote religious values through the Moral Education Program in secondary schools. At the end of 1980, a new moral education curriculum was prepared based on the various religious teachings of Islam, Hinduism, Christianity, Buddhism and world religions catering to the needs of Singapore's multi-racial society. Prime Minister Lee supported the change and remarked in 1980, 'However different various religions, the government is in favor of a man believing in something rather than in nothing. I would rather have a Muslim, a devout Hindu, than a permissive atheist.'[14]

At the beginning, only religions—Islam, Christianity, Hinduism and world religions—were introduced into the curriculum. But later in 1982 Confucian Ethics was also introduced into the curriculum by order of the prime minister. The addition drew enthusiastic response from the local community of which 77 per cent were ethnic Chinese. More important, eight world-renowned scholars were brought in to help promote Confucianism. They were professors of Chinese history and culture, teaching mostly at American universities: James Hsiung of New York University, Hsu Cho-yun of Pittsburg University, Tong Te-kong of New York City University, Yuan-li Wu of the Hoover Institution, Stanford University, Yu Ying-shih of Yale University (later transferred to Princeton), Tu Wei-ming of the University of California at Berkeley (later moved to Harvard University). A special writing team consisting of two groups (one in Chinese and one English) was formed under Dr Lau Wai Har, a former head of the Institute of Education to work out guidelines and formats for the Confucian Ethics textbook and reference materials. Professor Tu Wei-ming and Professor Yu Ying-shih were invited to serve as external advisers, and Dr Martin Lu and Dr Leung Yuen Sang (both were then at the National University of Singapore) as local advisers. But the Confucian movement had spread far beyond the schools and moral education curriculum. It became a hot topic in community forums and in the media. The Chinese-educated segment in the community embraced the movement as a 'renaissance' of traditional Chinese culture, while the government promoted some specific Confucian virtues for a variety of utilitarian purposes. For example, the concept of filial piety was promoted in connection with a housing program the government devised for three-tier families. Some critics of the Confucian project also suspected political succession (i.e. passing on power from father to son) was one of the motives behind Prime Minister Lee Kuan Yew's enthusiastic support for the movement.

In short, the Confucian Project in Singapore in the 1980s could be analysed at two levels. First, it could be seen primarily as part of the moral education reform meant to strengthen the moral fabric of society against the rising tide of Western, especially Hollywood, popular culture. Traditional Chinese virtues, such as filial piety, honesty, trust, sense of public good and community welfare were promoted to balance the concept of individual rights/gains and motivation for profit and success. Second, the Confucian Project could be seen as a social engineering or cultural engineering programme on the part of the Singapore government. It involved much more than the change in moral education curriculum and the teaching of Confucian ethics in the classroom. It went beyond education to include social and cultural policies such as housing and welfare for the aging, and political succession.

However, the Confucian Project in itself was not a total success. The project was launched in Singapore in 1982 but it was officially abandoned in 1989. The Moral Education Program was changed that year by returning to the Good Citizen curriculum and abolishing the Confucian Ethics text because of the rising tension among various ethnic and religious groups. The Confucian Ethics writing team was discharged and the course was cancelled. This signalled an end to the official Confucian campaign. However, much of the Confucian ideas and cultural values expounded in the Confucian Ethics texts have been preserved in the new textbook used for moral education and Good Citizenry. We may well say that the Confucian movement did not go away in 1990 but rather assumed a different shape in a new stage of development during which 'Asian Values' became the key issue.

The Debate on Asian Values and Its Implications

The debate on Asian values has been a recurring theme in the modern history of Singapore. Before the recent debate surfaced in the early 1990s at the end of the Confucian movement, Singaporeans had been discussing the relevance and validity of the concept of Asian values in a variety of ways and forms. In the sixties and seventies when Singapore leaders were debating about modernisation and modernity, some saw the need of preserving traditional Asian values as the 'cement' and 'cultural ballast' of the rapidly modernising society. For example, in a National Day Rally speech delivered in 1978, Prime Minister Lee Kuan Yew remarked:

> A person who gets de-culturalized—and I nearly was, so I know this danger—loses his self-confidence. He suffers from a sense of deprivation.... I may speak the English language better than the Chinese language because I learnt English early in life. But I will never be an Englishman in a thousand generations and I have not got the Western value system inside; mine is an Eastern value system.[15]

Here Prime Minister Lee used the phrase 'Eastern value system' vs. 'Western value system' to show the difference of Cultural Mentality (as indicated in his words 'inside' vs. 'outside'), which reminds us of the dichotomy of '*Zhong-ti vs. Xi-yong*' or 'Chinese essence vs. Western function' used by the famous Chinese scholar-reformer Zhang Zhidong of the late 19th century.

Goh Keng Swee, the Deputy Prime Minister and chief architect of the Singapore economy, also saw Western values and Asian values in polemic terms. He referred to 'undesirable Western values' as 'cults' such as 'hippism, permissiveness, student radicalism, ideologies of the welfare state and anti-establishment and anti-multinational company attitudes'. And in contrast, Eastern virtues included 'hard-work, thrift, honesty, self-discipline, regard for education, respect for enterprise and concern over family stability'.[16] On the other hand, S. Rajaratnam, then Foreign Minister of Singapore, had a somewhat different view of Asian values. He said, 'If it has any meaning at all it is merely a convenient way of describing the heterogeneous, conflicting and complex network of beliefs, prejudices and values developed in the countries which for geographical purposes have been grouped as being in Asia.'Rajaratnam not only raised doubts as to whether the term Asian Values has meaning but also argued that 'it is not so much Asian values as Western values that need to be critically reassessed, especially as these values are imitated by many Asians'. 'There is much in Asian values that [is] incompatible with modernization as there is also much in Western values which [has] become [an] obstacle(s) to modernization.'[17]

Recently Singapore's ambassador-at-large and law professor Tommy Koh also expressed a similar view: there are good and bad values in Asia and also good and bad values in the West, and that the Asia-West dichotomy is not a very useful concept in intellectual discourse.[18]

The 1990s debate on Asian values in many ways was a continuation of the debate of the past. But the Asian values debate of recent years did not focus entirely on domestic issues such as the relationship between cultural values and modernisation. It went beyond the Singapore context of industrialisation and social stability to include diplomatic and political issues such as Asian democracy and Asian solidarity. After stepping down from the prime minister's post in 1990, Lee Kuan Yew has continued to yield influence in Singapore politics as senior minister. Unlike the Confucian campaign during which much of the attention was directed toward domestic policies such as housing, bi-lingual and moral education, and political succession, Lee in the nineties talked about Confucian or Asian values more in the context of regional cooperation in Asia and political alliance against the West. One particular emphasis in his promotion of Asian values was that Asia has its own set of rules and values in pursuing political order and stability. Western liberalism and democratic values were not the most suitable or ideal type for Asian societies. To Lee, 'the exuberance of democracy leads to undisciplined and disorderly conditions which are inimical to development'. He remarked, 'What a country needs to develop is discipline more than democracy.'[19]

Tommy Koh also said, '... (some Asian leaders believe that) democracy... often leads to contention and political instability', and that 'an authoritarian but benign government could be a better vehicle to achieve development'.[20] Prime Minister Mohammed Mahathir of neighbouring Malaysia echoed the same concern by saying, 'Western thought.... fanatically focuses on the material as the basis of life. Values based on the spiritual, on peace of mind, and on belief in feelings loftier than desire, have no place in the Western psyche.'[21] Mahathir thus encouraged his countrymen to emulate Japan instead of following the West. He launched the 'Look East' policy in the eighties which could be seen as a strong assertion of Asian values.[22]

Studies on the campaign for Asian values in Singapore and Malaysia seem to suggest two principal motivations. First, these campaigns express the political need and concern for strong and steady leadership and government. Both Lee and Mahathir believed that strong leadership can keep communal peace, and that strong and authoritarian government would provide firm policy and social stability. Peace and stability, in turn, would be essential for economic growth. For example, in the words of William Theodore de Bary, 'the Singapore conception of Asian values has become identified with authoritarian rule and the two together brought into collision with modern human rights concepts and practices.'[23]

The economic motivation, explained by William Clark, Jr, in his Foreword to David I. Hitchcock's study entitled *Asian Values and the United States*, is as follows:

> With the economies of the West struggling against prolonged recession following the close of the Cold War, it is no surprise to find many of Asia's leaders questioning the West and placing greater confidence in their own methods of governance and democratic development. Consider only that on an individual basis, and in just 20 years, Asia's per capita income has quadrupled. As a region, East Asia now (1994) accounts for 20 percent of global gross domestic product, compared to 28 percent for countries party to the North American Free Trade Agreement, and 24 percent for the European Union. Thus, Asia's newfound wealth provides the basis for its new confidence in international politics. This confidence has led Asians to examine their values and cultures, to seek their role in the region's development, and to question Western influence.[24]

In other words, many Asians believe that their economic rise in recent decades was not merely an imitation of the West but deeply rooted in cultural values and work ethics such as frugality, high saving rates, diligence, patience, persistence, respect for leadership and learning, family support, and so on.[25]

The debate on Asian Values definitely has a political and economic dimension. But as Singapore's Kishore Mahbubani argues, it is also about finding a psychological equilibrium between East and West, and between tradition and modernity. It is not anti-West or anti-technology.[26] In fact, Singapore, Malaysia and many Asian countries have embraced modernisation and technology and the market economy as basic structures of their social and economic development. However, the notion of Asian values does have a defensiveness in the East-West dichotomy especially in the light of the theory of cultural confrontation made popular by Samuel Huntington in his book, *The Clash of Civilizations and the Remaking of World Order*.[27]

The debate on Asian values, therefore, can be put in a political, economic or psychological perspective. But, as this paper attempts to show, the search for an Asian commonality has a historical dimension, and the quest for that commonality took place in different parts of Asia, led by Indians, Japanese, Chinese, and Southeast Asians. The political motivation for each campaign might be different, but the frequent recurrence of the theme tells us that there is a sense of affinity and interconnectedness among the Asians to keep the search going. However, like a double-edged sword, the search for an Asian commonality promoted regional cohesion and cooperation on the one hand, and, at the same time, was manipulated and used by politicians for the advancement of their own ambitions and agendas.

NOTES AND REFERENCES

1. William Theodore de Bary, *Asian Values and Human Rights: A Confucian Communitarian Perspective* (Cambridge, Mass.: Harvard University Press, 1998), p.1
2. Cited from Stephen N. Hay, *Asian Ideas of East and West: Tagore and His Critics in Japan, China, and India* (Cambridge, Mass.: Harvard University Press, 1970), p.12
3. Cited from Stephen Hay, op.cit., p. 124
4. Ibid., p. 64
5. Stephen Hay, op.cit., pp. 63-64
6. Ibid., p. 65
7. Ibid., p. 148
8. Ibid., p. 133
9. Matsumoto Sannosuke, 'National Missions', in Marlene J. Mayo, ed., *The Emergence of Imperial Japan* (Lexington, Mass.: D.C. Heath and Company, 1970), pp. 59-67
10. For Norman's ideas, see Marlene Mayo, ed., *The Emergence of Imperial Japan*, op.cit., p. 47
11. Ibid., p. 55
12. Marius Jensen, 'Pan-Asianism,' in Marlene Mayo, ed., *The Emergence of Imperial Japan*, p. 58
13. Kimitada Miwa, 'Japanese Policies and Concepts for a Regional Order in Asia, 1938-1940,' in James W. White, Michio Umegaki, and Thomas R.H.

Havens, eds., *The Ambivalence of Nationalism: Modern Japan between East and West* (Lanham, New York, London: University Press of America, 1990), p. 139

14. Martin Lu, *Confucianism: Its Relevance to Modern Society.* (Singapore: Federal Publications, 1983), p. 71.
15. John Clammer, 'Culture, Values and Modernization in Singapore: An Overview', in Ong Jin Hui, Tong Chee Kiong, Tan Ern Ser, eds., *Understanding Singapore Society* (Singapore: Times Academic Press, 1997), pp. 502-503
16. Ibid., p. 503
17. Ibid., p. 504
18. Tommy Koh's comment in a Q&A session after his speech on 'Asia and Europe in the 21st Century' at Shaw College, The Chinese University of Hong Kong on 20 March 2000.
19. David I. Hitchcock, *Asian Values and the United States: How Much Conflict?* (Washington, D.C.: The Center for Strategic & International Studies, 1994), p. 1
20. Ibid., p. 2
21. Ibid.
22. Greg Sheridan, *Asian Values, Western Dreams: Understanding the New Asia.* (NSW, Australia: Allen & Unwin, 1999) p. 92
23. William Theodore de Bary, *Asian Values and Human Rights*, op.cit., p. 3
24. See William Clark's 'Foreword' in David I. Hitchcock, *Asian Values and the United States: How Much Conflict*? op. cit., p. vii
25. For a contrasting comparison of Asian and Western values, personal and societal, see the charts produced by David Hitchcock in his study, op.cit., pp. 40-41
26. See Greg Sheridan, *Asian Values, Western Dreams,* op.cit., p. 4
27. Samuel Huntington, *The Clash of Civilizations and the Remaking of World Order* (New York: Simon & Schuster, 1996).

Feudalism in China and India: A Comparative Study

MA KEYAO

Feudalism is a word with so many different meanings and different implications for historians. I would like to identify it with feudal social formation, feudal society and feudal mode of production. In this context I will make a comparison between ancient China and India.[1] In this short paper I cannot compare feudal institutions between China and India comprehensively and hence I will focus my attention on the peasantry. This is because, first, peasants are the main labourers in a feudal society and the peasant economy is the basic economic factor there as well. Second, I have noticed that in recent decades my Indian colleagues had a debate on the topic, 'Was there feudalism in Indian history?' which, as the title indicates, was mainly on the Indian peasant and the peasant economy in feudal society.

I

For a long time, oriental historians used west European concepts of feudalism as the models of reference. We are familiar with the notions of feudalism used by M. Bloch, F. L. Ganshof, G. Duby, etc., and by Western Marxist historians such as M. Dobb, R. H. Hilton, and P. Anderson. Most of our Western colleagues consider feudalism essentially as a political entity. Feudalism was a form of government in which political authority was monopolised by a small group of military leaders who were organised into lord-vassal relations with rights and duties to one another. The men who possessed political power also possessed the most important source of wealth, that is, land. Through land grant or surrender, the landed property in feudal Europe became tenure and was called fief. The fief was cultivated by the labour of dependent peasants. Every landlord was an independent ruler in his lordship and had the political and legal power and so the centrifugal was an inertial tendency in the Middle Ages.[2]

Marxist scholars allege that feudalism was one of the stages in the development of the mode of production. In this social formation, the essential means of production—land—belonged to the ruling class of landlords and the surplus was appropriated from the primary producers through non-economic coercion. But most Western historians, including Marxists, assume that feudalism was a distinctive phenomenon in Europe or even only in western Europe and there was no feudalism in such regions as Asia, Africa, etc. Bloch began to talk about Japanese feudalism in the 1940s. In the 1950s Coulborn and his colleagues made deliberate efforts to find feudalism in China, India, Japan, Iran, Babylonia and Egypt.[3] In the 1980s, Perry Anderson, a Marxist historian, expressed his disagreement with the application of the term feudalism to non-European regions. He said:

> The combination of large-scale agrarian property controlled by an exploiting class, with small-scale production by a tied peasantry, in which surplus labour was pressed out of the latter by *corvees* or dues in kind, was in its generality a very widespread pattern throughout the pre-industrial world. Virtually any post-tribal social formation that did not rest on slavery or nomadism, revealed in this sense forms of landlordism. The singularity of feudalism was never exhausted merely by the existence of *seigniorial* and serf classes as such. It was their specific organization in a vertically articulated system of parcellized sovereignty and scalar property that distinguished the feudal mode of production in Europe.[4]

Anderson's view is that 'pre-capitalistic modes of production cannot be defined except via their political, legal and ideological superstructures, since these are what determine the type of extra-economic coercion that specifies them.'[5] In my opinion, in any pre-capitalistic social formation, though extra-economic coercion is an important factor connected with economic infrastructure, it is not a constitutive factor. As P. Hirst said, Anderson's view 'means that there can be as many modes of production as there are distinct legal-political constitutions and forms of extra-economic sanction which follow from them.'[6] He deviated too far from economic analysis.

The historians of the Third World consider feudalism in their indigenous countries as a social formation inclusive of political, legal, ideological and economic aspects, and emphasize its economic substance, its productive force and the relations of production. Thus we can say that most of these historians agree that feudalism existed in their country as a historical stage. But when they take the essence of feudalism as a combination of large landownership with small peasant production, whose surplus was exploited by the landowners, they, intentionally or unintentionally, take all aspects of west European feudalism as a model. They then look for these aspects, such as seigniorial rights, scalar landownership, lord-vassal relations, serfdom, manor, autonomous cities and political parcellisation in their own history. Mukhia has pointed out that just as Sharma, in his *Indian Feudalism* made a point-by-point comparison with European feudalism,[7] most Chinese historians assume that there was a feudal society in Chinese history. Its characteristics were large landownership, small peasant production, centralised absolutist political authority, and the domination of Confucianism in ideology. They therefore emphasize the distinction of Chinese feudalism.

The late historian Shang Yue, in his *Outline of Chinese History,* conceived of Chinese feudalism as almost similar to west European feudalism. He dated its origins to the Wei (220-265) and Jin (265-420) dynasties and its decline in the 15th and 16th century. Shang Yue found some features of feudalism in China similar to the ones in Europe, e.g. barbarian invasion, natural economy, manor, and so on.[8] Shang Yue's model was hotly debated in the 1960s. Many scholars did not agree with him and pointed out that there was no manor in feudal China at all.[9]

The scientific model of feudalism originated from western Europe. All the related theories were established on the experiences and inspirations of western Europe. When feudalism of legal and political institutions grew gradually into a feudal formation and mode of production, more and more scholars were trying to enlarge it as a world system. The economic essence of feudalism—large land ownership combined with small peasant production was a universal category of pre-capitalism all over the world. It is both a loose and broad category because the universal law of historical development has to be very simple in order to be applicable everywhere. If one were to add its universal superstructures on it, these would be domination of monarchy and religious ideology. Under these generalisations, feudalism existed with its innumerable variants, regional, sub-regional and national.

European feudalism was one of these types of innumerable variants. Some of its factors were universal and some were distinctively Western. As a historian, especially as a historian from the Third World, one should distinguish between those which were universal and those which were Western. It is a pity that many scholars among us still take European feudalism as typical and base their comparative studies of Oriental feudalism upon this. I think this is one of the reasons why we have so many confusions and debates about Oriental feudalism. S. Reynolds points out that:

> The comparative use of feudalism in studies of non-European societies, although generally conducted in what is intended to be a Marxist sense, is gravely hindered by a tendency to bring fiefs and vassals into the discussion in the Cinderella's slipper-strategy of trying to fit one whole society into a conceptual model derived from a quite different one.[10]

The model of European feudalism is a curious synthesis. Its legal code came from Lombardy in the 12th century and its factual sources were selected arbitrarily and artificially from a small region situated between the Loire and the Rhine, between the 9th and the 10th century. That was an underdeveloped area in the Roman Empire. So some factors of its feudalism, such as vassalage, fiefs, manor and serfdom, etc., represented its backward districts and not 'the most developed form of feudal social organization'.[11] On the other hand, in western Europe, there were many regional variants of feudalism in France, Germany, England, Burgundy, etc. Maitland had complained that:

> Feudalism is an unfortunate word. In the first place, it draws our attention to but one element in a complex state of society and that element is not the most distinctive. . . . The impossible task that has been set before the word feudalism is that of making a single idea represent a very large piece of the world's history, represent France, Italy, Germany, England of every century from the eighth or ninth to the fourteenth or fifteenth.[12]

E. A. R. Brown challenged the use of feudalism in medieval western Europe and called it 'The tyranny of a Construct'.[13] The recent strong criticism given to the ideal type of Western feudalism was made by S. Reynolds. In her work she proved that vassalage and fiefs were marginal elements in medieval society and not the important ones. Feudalism was constructed by post-medieval scholars from the works of medieval academic lawyers and was not the reality of that society.[14]

In the Third World, some historians have expressed doubts about using the typology of Western feudalism to describe the reality of their countries. Mukhia criticised Sharma's conception of Indian feudalism and initiated a long discussion among Indian historians.[15] Some Chinese historians maintained that feudalism (Feng Jian) in China meant the formation of a principality, dukedom and county, etc., by the kings of the Zhou Dynasty (c. 1100-249 B.C.), and that from the Qin Dynasty (221-206 B.C.) onwards the separatist regime was destroyed and authority was centralised since there was no feudalism in China. They do not like to use the term *feudal society* when referring to ancient Chinese society.[16] I think they represent the awakening of the historians of the Third World, and the recognition that western European feudalism could not be a typical model for world history and it is better not to apply it to the study of their own societies. Post-tribal and pre-capitalistic societies all over the world had similarities in their means of production, relations of production, structures and infrastructures. We should research them one by one and then re-establish the law of development of feudal societies all over the world. The words feudalism and feudal society can still be used because they have been used for more than a hundred years and are not only familiar to scholars but also to the common people. It is not necessary to cast away a suspicious word but it is important to establish a new model, a new ideal type of the feudal society through our experiences, facts and sources, viewpoints and theories. It should be a real model synthesising all regional and national variants and should represent the reality of the world, neither Eurocentric nor Asiacentric. This is a great and urgent task for us, the historians of the Third World.

II

The basic economy of feudal society was agricultural production and the main producers were the peasantry. Economically, feudal peasants all over the world had their similarities. Their households were organised as economic units. They cultivated a small piece of land, belonging to them either in name or in fact, with the help of a labour force mainly recruited from their own families, and using their cattle and simple equipments, if any. Apart from agriculture, the members of a feudal peasant household did other work, such as animal husbandry, spinning, weaving, fishing, hunting and gathering. All of these occupations were taxed and rents charged on them by the landlord and the feudal authorities, and barely helped the peasants to earn more than their bare subsistence.

According to their wealth, feudal peasants were differentiated into richer, middle and poorer, but still they were a common class opposed to the ruling class, the landowners of feudal society. Feudal society was a hierarchical society. Everyone, including the peasant, had his own legal and political status. The identification of personal status had to be based on the law and customs of the country. Different nations have had different laws and different customs in different times. Is it possible, by looking into these laws and customs, to compare the peasants' status in feudal societies? In feudal times, the peasants of many countries could be stratified according to law and customs, from the highest to the lowest on the basis of rights, dignity and freedom, etc., appropriated by them. They might be named differently. Typical serfdom only appeared in medieval western Europe.

A serf was the lowest status among medieval peasants and originating from Roman slavery. According to the Roman law, men were divided into free and unfree. A free man possessed the rights of a citizen fully or partially whereas an unfree man did not have any rights at all. He was the chattel and could be disposed of arbitrarily by his master. In the Middle Ages, ancient slavery disappeared gradually but the demarcation of free and unfree survived in law. The notion that a serf was unfree persisted for a long period. He was the chattel of his master and his body (*corpore*) belonged to his master and his descendants belonged to him too. He could be scolded, beaten and disposed of (sold with or without his family, sold with or without the land) by his master, but his life and limb were protected by the kings' law and he could not be killed nor mutilated. These features differentiated the medieval serf from the ancient slave. His labour belonged to his master so that he had to work for him under his orders—labour service. He was lacking in freedom of mobility, freedom of marriage, freedom of disposing of his possessions and freedom of inheritance.[17] Thus we can say serfdom was in reality slavery that had deteriorated.

The uniqueness of the serfs' economic condition was that he should cultivate the lord's *demesne* and pay some rents in kind and in money which were obligatory for his subject status, and then he could work a small piece of his holding for his familys' bare subsistence. The forced labour rent is distinctive of the west European serf and some historians assume that labour rent is the serfs' label. If he serves a base service—labour service all the year round—he must be a serf.[18]

In feudal China, the basic demarcation of people was *liang* and *jian,* somewhat similar to free and unfree in medieval Europe. The *liang* had full legal rights and was protected by national law. The *jian* had the lowest status and lacked many of the civil rights of the *liang*. He could not take part in the civil service examinations and become an official. A *jian* was not permitted to marry a *liang* and, more importantly, legal penalties differed sharply according to the status of the offender. If a *liang* injured a *jian,* the punishment was lighter than when he harmed another *liang*; and if a *jian* injured a *liang,* the punishment was heavier than when the case involved two *liangs*.[19]

In the long period of feudal Chinese society, there were many sub-classes and levels of peasants with different names. Nubi and Buqu belonged to the category of *jian*. The Nubi existed in every dynasty of China and was a slave in status. According to the panel code of the Tang dynasty, the Nubi was a *res* or chattel in law and the property of his master.[20] His body belonged to the master and was dealt with by the master. He had no freedom of marriage and his descendants also belonged to his master. But his body and life were protected by the state and he could not be killed by the master. Usually the Nubi had his family, his possessions and his independent economy and was different from the Western slave who was fed and clothed by his master. The Nubi worked for his master in the fields and workshops, took part in trading merchandise, and most of the Nubi served in the master's family as servants or concubines. Their economic and legal conditions were better than those of the west European slaves and their role in social production was not as important as in Greece and Rome. Most Chinese historians assumed that the Nubi represented the descendants of ancient slavery and was not an integral stratum in feudal society.

The Buqu constituted another kind of subject category of persons in feudal China. Originally they were subject men, used as war retainers by their masters. Their status gradually deteriorated and was as low as that of the *jian* in the law of Northern Zhou (A.D. 557-581). In the Tang penal code Nubi and Buqu are often said to be in the same category and not treated as *liang*. The Commentary of the Tang penal code says clearly that the Buqu had been homeless from a young age and had commended themselves to their master for subsistence. The master treated them as slaves. They did not have their own separate household registers in the census but were attached to their masters' household. They still had the right to possess property that was acknowledged by the state law.[21] The legal status of Buqu was close to that of the west European serfs. They were used for agricultural production, particularly in the northern and southern Dynasties (420-589), but their number was so small that they were not counted as important.

The third category of subjected peasants in feudal China were the Ke. They appeared very early in the beginning of the first millennium A.D. and were labourers, subjected to a master due to poverty. Their number grew steadily in time and reached its peak during the Song dynasty (960-1279). According to the state law the Ke were like the *liang* and registered in the state census but in many local customs, they were harshly treated, often similar to the *jian*. We can sum up their characteristics as follows:

1. They were often registered by the local authorities in the masters' family register and did not have their own household register.
2. They had personal dependent relations with the master, and sometimes could even be sold and transferred by the master. In the Song dynasty, the custom of selling the land together with the Ke living on it still survived.
3. The master not only enslaved the Ke but his wife and descendants as well. Even the marriage of the widow and the children of the Ke needed the permission from the master and the payment of a fee.
4. Provided by the master with seeds, plough, oxen and a hut, the Ke cultivated the land of the master and had to pay rent, often in *metayage* form. Hence the master was concerned about the Ke's performance and would supervise it closely.
5. The Ke did not have the freedom to leave the master. They were important labourers in the Song villages. Their status has been discussed for a long time by historians and some of them have assumed that the Ke, at least in some regions, were serfs. They have based their augments mostly on local

> customs. But according to the state law, the Ke was a *liang*, not a *jian*. The Song law certified that anyone who killed a Ke was to be punished as it was a crime to kill a *liang*. The Ke had the freedom to leave his master after the harvest.

In general, a Ke was not a serf but a dependent peasant in feudal China.[22]

We do not know if there was a demarcation between the free and unfree (*liang* and *jian*) in ancient Indian law. But there were the Arya and the Dasa. They were different ethnic groups in the Rigveda period and then the Dasa were subjected and enslaved as a slave class.[23] That is to say, the institution of slavery still existed in ancient India. Manu mentioned seven kinds of Dasas: a captive of war; a son of a female slave; one purchased for money; one condemned to slavery for committing an offence, etc.[24] Slaves were defined as men dependent on other men and even referred to as farm animals. The Dharmasastra laid down rules for the inheritance of slaves together with other properties of the deceased. A slave could be sold, pawned and lost over a game of dice. The Arthasastra gave some improvements in the slaves' condition and allowed him to earn, own and inherit property. His kinsmen had the priority of claim on his property over the master. The chastity of female slaves was guarded even against the master.[25]

Indian slavery had its characteristics and it was not as rigid as in Greece and Rome. The slaves were treated with kindness and in the context of the caste system, we can hardly differentiate slaves (*dasas*) from hired laboureres and the lowest caste Sudra. They were used more in domestic service as cooks, washermen, nurses, dancers and concubines, and less in agricultural and industrial production. Magasthenes said once that there was no slavery in ancient India at all. Thapar believes that because Indian slaves were expensive, it was preferred to use a hired labourer to work in the fields as this was cheaper than buying a slave.[26] The institution of slavery, with its Indian features, never was a major factor in production, but its role was by no means negligible. It existed for a long time until the consolidation of Muslim rule when it even demonstrated some growth and development.

From the Gupta period onwards slavery gradually declined and the Sudras, hired labourers and other dependent workers were listed as cultivators through land grants.[27] Can we call these mass peasants serfs? Yadava said that the fact that agricultural labourers were subjected to restrictions on their mobility and were involved in the relationship of dependence from generation to generation cannot but be regarded as somewhat close to serfdom. They may be regarded as semi-serfs.[28] Sharma, relying on the evidence of epigraphic and Chinese monks' records, considered that after the land grant, mass peasants, including Vaisyas and Sudras, were obliged to serve as ploughmen or tenants for land grandees. They could not leave freely but could be evicted by the master. They were hence the serfs in feudal India.[29]

The problem is whether we can find serfdom in Asian countries like China and India. What is our definition of serfdom? How can we use the western European medieval conception of serfdom in regions that were very different in many aspects from the West? As I have noted above, European serfdom originated in the custom of slavery. The enslavement of man arose in primitive societies. The first enslaved peoples were captives of other tribes and clans captured in the war and which had not been killed. They became the properties of their master. Their body, labour and their life were entirely in the hands of their masters too. They worked in their master's homes under his orders and supervision. They were fed and clothed by the master if he wished. They had no property and were the property of their master so they could be dealt with by the master by any means whatsoever. This has been the universal conception of a slave, a conception employed by historians all over the world. Hence the sets of legal ideas of European unfree, Chinese *jian* and Indian *dasa* obviously had something in common and their economic conditions had something in common too, although both Indian and Chinese slavery was not as rigid as the European one.

Slavery metamorphosed and deteriorated into serfdom in western Europe. But this did not happen in India and China. Serfdom was a distinct phenomenon in Europe. I think we cannot understand serfdom as compulsory attachment of the peasants to the soil only.[30] The essence of European serfdom was a survival of slavery legally and a kind of labour-service economically. Labour-service was the important label of serfdom, as I said before. In the medieval West, extensive farming was the main cultivation method. The cultivated land in the manor was divided into the *demesne* and the peasant holdings, and the form of rent there was mainly labour service. The labour of serfs towards the lord and for the peasant himself was divided in space and in time. It was necessary that the lord himself or through his bailiff conduct the production, otherwise sabotage and slowing down could greatly damage the lord's economic interests. Hence it was also necessary for the lord to impose personal subjection, pre-economic coercion and serfdom. The manor, the serfdom and the labour rent constituted a tripartite combination in the medieval West. In recent decades, our Western colleagues were of the view that serfdom might not have been so important as their predecessors had assumed and the number of serfs in the production may not have been as many as calculated before.[31] But they believed that it still was a base element in society.

In feudal China and India, the method of cultivation was intensive farming. The land was tilled minutely every year. Fertilizers, irrigation and advanced equipments were used in agrarian production. The form of rent was mainly rent in kind, *metayage,* or a fixed amount. The producers were given more freedom and independence, and the supervision over them was unnecessary in most cases. Hence serfdom was not needed here. Only some minority people like the Buqu in China held a status very close to that of serfs but serfdom was never an important factor in production. Could we call some of the agrarian producers in feudal China and India free peasants? That depends on our definition of the term free peasant.

In medieval Europe, a free peasant was one who was not an 'unfree' peasant. He had not the duties or the services of the unfree; mainly he did not do the labour-service for the lord but still had to pay the rents in kind or in money because the land he cultivated belonged to his lord and he usually was tied to the manor by the lord. He had the legal and proprietary/dependent relations with the landlord.

In feudal China, we can say that there were two categories of peasants, first the dependent peasant which included the Ke, the Buqu, etc., and then the independent peasant or state peasant. The dependent peasant was subject to a master, worked in his fields, had obligations to him and did services for him. Usually he was not registered in the government census and had no obligations to the government. The independent peasant owned a small piece of land and sometimes it was an allotment grant to him by the government, or it was rented from a landlord. He was registered in a neighbourhood administrative system and was prohibited from moving freely. He had obligations of taxes, *corvee* and military service to the government and had to pay rents in kind. He owed some obligations to the landlord too if he was a tenant. The taxes and forced labour of the independent peasant were heavy and he often had a miserable life and sometimes even went bankrupt. But in name he had all his legal rights and was protected by state law.

In feudal India, just like in China, we have two categories of peasants, the dependent peasant and the independent peasant. The dependent peasant had dependent relations with intermediaries through the land grant of the state, had no freedom of mobility and was forced to do some labour-service for his master. But what was the condition of the independent peasant? He was taxed and restricted by the state, lived a life of mere subsistence and lacked freedom of mobility. As some Chinese monks recorded, he cultivated a small piece of land and paid rents in kind of one-sixth the harvest. But there were no neigbourhood administrative records in India and the peasants were controlled by the caste system.

In feudal China, the state peasants existed in large numbers. We do not know how many there were in feudal India. Yadava says that the dependent peasants' 'number must have far exceeded that of the free peasants,'[32] and therefore the independent peasants in India must have been a minority. Sharma was of the view that dependent peasants in feudal India were the product of the land grants. But to determine the extent of peasant population working in the land grant areas and of those in the other areas was a problem too difficult to solve.

The independent peasant in feudal China and India was different from the free peasant in the medieval West. Those in China and India had no dependent relations with a master and were directly controlled by the feudal authority, but the free peasant in the medieval West usually had a lord too. As for the freedom of mobility, in the Ming-Qing dynasties (1368 - 1911), the Chinese independent peasant had the freedom to leave his landlord if he had no debt to him but could not move freely under government control. The Indian independent peasant seemed to have no freedom of mobility under the caste system control. In feudal society, the peasant was attached to the soil because of the nature of the economy, and particularly due to the weakening of the household economy. It shows in the infrastructure that usually he was attached by legal and political regulations to the land and to the landlord as well. In the medieval West, the freedom of mobility of a free peasant meant that he had no charge of *chevage*, he did not do labour-service but paid rent in kind or in money, but actually he could not leave his lord freely because of his dependent relations with him.

Can we understand the feudal free peasant to be one who had the freedom to control the process of production, e.g. he had the freedom in the activity of cultivation, and could decide the act of cultivation freely and independently? The feudal peasant economy was a small household peasant economy; its characteristics were that the peasant acted freely in his activity of cultivation and ran his small farm independently either as an independent tenant or as a serf. Bracton, a lawyer in 13th century England, had noted that if some one did not know what he would do from the next morning to the evening, he should be a serf. It seemed that a serf did not have the freedom in his cultivation activities. But historians did not agree with Bracton. They said that the lords' *demesne* was scattered in the form of strips in every field and the cultivation in the manor generally was according to the customs of the manor so that the serf in the evening knew as a rule what he would do the next morning. The labour-service did not obstruct the freedom of action of the serf. The control of his process of cultivation could not be a good criterion to judge the status of the peasant.

The conception of the feudal peasant, just as the conception of feudalism, can only be applied to various regions of the world in a very broad sense, and in most cases in economic terms. If we go too far in stressing the legal connotations of these conceptions, we meet many difficulties in deciding what is universal and what is not. It is preferable that we call the peasant controlled by the state in the feudal Orient an independent peasant rather than a free peasant. That is my point.

NOTES AND REFERENCES

1. Chinese historians usually do not use the term Middle Ages to define one of China's historical periods. My Indian colleagues use *medieval* to indicate Muslim ruling period in India, but I prefer to use 'ancient' here.
2. M. Bloch, *Feudal Society*, London, 1962; F. L. Ganshof, *Feudalism*, London, 1951. For a concise summary of the concept of feudalism see J. R. Strayer, 'Feudalism in Western Europe', in R. Coulborn (ed.), *Feudalism in History*, Princeton, 1956, pp. 15-25
3. R. Coulborn (ed.), *Feudalism in History*, Princeton, 1956
4. P. Anderson, *Lineages of Absolutism States,* London, 1986, p. 408

5. Ibid., p. 404
6. In C. H. Wickham, 'The Uniqueness of the East', in J. Beacher *et al.* (eds.), *Europe and the Rise of Capitalism*, New York, 1988, p. 70
7. H. Mukhia, 'Peasant Production and Medieval Indian Society', in T. J. Byers and H. Mukhia (eds.), *Feudalism and Non-European Societies*, London, 1985, p. 235
8. Shang Yue, *Zhongguo Lishi Gangyao* (Outline of Chinese History), Renmin, 1956
9. Deng Guangming, 'Was there the manor in the Tang and the Song dynasty?' *Lishi Yanjiu (Historical Research)*, 1963, p. 6
10. S. Reynolds, *Fiefs and Vassals*, Oxford, 1996, p. 3
11. H. Mukhia, op.cit., p. 266
12. F. Pollock and F. M. Maitland, *History of English Law before Edward the First*, Cambridge,1923, Vol.1, pp. 66-67
13. E. A. R. Brown, 'The Tyranny of Construct: Feudalism and Historians of Medieval Europe', *AHR*, 1974
14. S. Reynolds, op. cit.
15. Some articles are collected in T. J. Byers and H. Mukhia (eds.), op.cit.
16. Ri Zhi, 'The problem of "Feudalism",' *Shijie Lishi* (World History), 1991, p. 6
17. M. Bloch, *Slavery and Serfdom in the Middle Ages*, Los Angeles, 1975; P. R. Hyams, *Kings, Lords and Peasants in Medieval England*, Oxford, 1980.
18. R. H. Hilton, "Freedom and Villenage in England", *Past and Present,* 31, (1965)
19. Qu Tongzhu, *Zhongguo Falu yu Zhongguo Shehui (Chinese Law and Society)*, Beijing, 1981, pp. 220-22
20. *Tanglv Shuyi (The Exposition of the Tang Penal Code)*, Vols. 4 & 6.
21. Ibid., Vol. 20
22. Zeng Qiongbi, 'Ke's Subjective Status in the Song Village', *Collected Papers on the Song Dynasty*, Shanghai, 1982, pp. 89-103
23. S. Jaiswal, 'Stratification in Ṛgvedic Society', *Indian Historical Reveiw*, Vol. 56, 1989-1990, pp. 14-15
24. *Manusastra,* Chap. 8. p. 415
25. D. D. Kosambi, *An Introduction to the Study of Indian History*, Bombay, 1985, p. 231
26. R. Thapar, *From Lineage to State*, Oxford, 1994, p. 83
27. R. S. Sharma, *Indian Feudalism*, Delhi, 1980, pp. 49-51; also R. Thapar, *Interpreting Early India*, Delhi, 1993, pp. 130-31
28. B. N. S. Yadava, 'Problem of the interaction between the Social-Economic Classes in the Early Medieval Complex', in D. N. Jha (ed.), *Feudal Social Formation in Early India*, Delhi 1987, pp. 76 - 77, 202 - 203
29. R. S. Sharma, *op.cit.*, pp. 46 - 47; 96 - 97, 217-19
30. R. S. Sharma, 'How Feudal was Indian Feudalism?' in T. J. Byers and H. Mukhia (eds.), op.cit., p. 32
31. R. H. Hilton, *Bondman Made Free,* London, 1980, p.61
32. B. N. S. Yadava, op.cit., p. 203

New Evidence on Wang Xuance's Missions to India

BANGWEI WANG

Nearly a century ago, the French scholar Slyvain Lévi published in *Journal Asiatique* his study on the missions of Wang Xuance (Wang Hiuan-ts'e), a Chinese official envoy sent by the Tang Emperors to India in the 7th century.[1] In another paper in *T'oung Pao* he again discussed this issue.[2] Lévi's disciple, P. C. Bagchi, dealt with this in a whole section in his book *India and China*.[3] In between and particularly since the middle of the eighties some Chinese scholars have also discussed Wang's missions or mentioned him in their papers and books. More important, in recent years some new materials relating to Wang and his missions have been discovered by Chinese archaeologists. Since he was a contemporary of the well-known Chinese pilgrim Xuanzang (Hiuan-tsang), Wang Xuance undoubtedly played a role in the lengthy Sino-Indian contacts in history which cannot be neglected. It is appropriate to discuss his missions to India once more in the light of this new evidence.[4]

How Many Missions to India?

The question of how many missions Wang undertook to India has been dealt with in various ways by scholars. S. Lévi maintains that Wang visited India four times. Bagchi follows Lévi's conclusion while Feng Chengjun, a Chinese professor at Peking University in the thirties, says Wang had undertaken only three missions.[5] In my book *Da tang xiyu qiufa gaoseng zhuan jiaozhu* (Annotated biographies of the prominent monks [who] went to the West in search of the Dharma during the Great Tang) I am inclined to agree with Feng.[6] My basic arguments on this matter are from *Fayuan zhulin* (The forest of the jewelleries of the Dharma), a Buddhist encyclopedia edited by Daoshi, who was Wang's contemporary and a Buddhist monk scholar. Daoshi not only collected his materials from different sources but he also edited and classified them under various subjects, adding his own observations to these in his book.

He personally knew Wang Xuance and the latter was one of his informants. Several passages in Daoshi's book are related to Wang Xuance, of which three explicitly mention how many times Wang travelled to India.

> 'The Tang ambassador Wang Xuance has been there (India) for three times. When I met Xuance, he told me this.'[7]

> 'The envoys of the Great Tang, Wang Xuance and the others, went to (India) for three times and not only one saw this.'[8]

> 'The late Great Tang Emperor Taizong Wen (Taizong wenhuangdi) and the present Emperor ordered the *Chaosan dafu weiwei sicheng shanghujun* Li Yibiao and the vice-ambassador, the former Chief of Huangshui county of Rongzhou, all of them are of twenty-two, to go to the Western Region. Totally speaking, they went there three times.'[9]

And Wang Xuance says the same in one of his own reports to the emperor:

> 'Since Buddhism arose in India, I, the servant (of your Majesty), have been sent there for three times and I saw and heard a lot.'[10]

The reason why Lévi and Bagchi believe that Wang Xuance was sent to India a fourth time is attributed to a book, *Da tang xiyu quifa gaoseng zhuzn* (The biographies of the prominent monks [who] went to the West in search of the Dharma during the Great Tang), written by the well-known Chinese Buddhist pilgrim Yijing (Yi-tsing). Yijing went to India by sea from Guangzhou in South China, in the winter of the second year of Xianheng (A.D. 671) and arrived in East India two years later. In the second year of Tianshou (A.D. 691) he wrote the book while he was in Srivijaya, then a kingdom in present-day Sumatra, Indonesia, when on his way back to China. This occurred a little after the time of Wang Xuance. In his book Yijing gave whole accounts of the experiences of over fifty Chinese Buddhist pilgrim monks in India. The first one in Yijing's account is Xuanzhao (Hiuan-chao). Xuanzhao went to India twice, first soon after the fifteenth year of Zhengguan (A.D. 641). Yijing tells us that when Xuanzhao was staying in India, Wang Xuance, after returning to the imperial court, praised the merit of the former in his report to the emperor. The emperor thus ordered (Wang Xuance or someone else?) for Xuanzhao to be brought back to the Chinese capital. In Yinjing's account, however, it is not clear who was sent by the emperor. From the context it is unlikely to point to Wang Xuance, as Lévi and Bagchi seem to have understood, because not only were there only three missions related to Wang Xuance, but Wang himself also mentions that he had been to India three times.

Dates and Routes of the Missions

As regards the dates of the first two missions there are no major divergences in views among scholars. Wang Xuance was initially sent to India by the Emperor Taizong as the assistant to the imperial ambassador Li Yibiao. The delegation went to India through Tibet and Nepal in the seventeenth year of Zhengguan (A.D. 643) and came back to China in A.D. 645.[11] They met King Harsa in Magadha and paid respects to a number of Buddhist holy sites. This was Wang's first visit to India.

Wang visited India again after one or two years, but this time as the head of the delegation, in the nineteenth or twentieth year of Zhengguan (A.D. 646 or 647) and was back to the imperial court in the twenty-first year of Zhengguan (A.D. 648). The details of the dramatic happenings during this mission can be seen in Lévi's articles and in Bagchi's book. The route is still via Tibet and Nepal.

On the date of the third mission of Wang Xuance there have for long existed differences of opinion. Lévi and Bagchi maintain that he started for India, similarly via Tibet, in the second year of Xianqing (A.D. 657), while other scholars think this happened in the fourth or the fifth year of Xianqing (A.D. 659 or 660). Although from one quotation in the *Fayuan zhulin* we know Wang was back in Luoyang in the early spring of the first year of Longshuo (A.D. 661), nothing is mentioned about the starting date of Wang's mission. Fortunately for our study a recently discovered inscription provides new and important evidence on this matter.

Recent Discoveries

In June 1990 in the county of Skyid-grong of Tibet, Chinese archaeologists discovered a rock inscription directly related to Wang Xuance's third mission to India. This is undoubtedly an important discovery throwing new light on the research on Sino-Indian relations in this period. The inscription has been seriously damaged, particularly in its lower part. It is 81.5 cm wide and the surviving upper part is 53 cm high. The remaining upper part holds a total of 222 characters, placed in 24 lines of which some are not recognisable. However, according to the photograph taken, and the report of the archaeologists, we can still recognise the title and the main contents of the inscription. The title of the whole inscription reads, 'The epigraph of the Great Tang envoy to India *Datang tianzhu shichu ming*.' Of the remaining part the most important sentences read :

(Line 1) ... composed by the clerk Liu Jiabin, the clerk ...

(Line 2) ...scribed by..., scribed by He Shouyi ...

(Line 3) It is in the sixth month of the third year of Xianqing when the Great Tang rules the world ...

...

(Line 7) bringing (?) rations and going across the mountains and seas, India is nearby ...

.....

(Line 9) great ... *Zuoxiaowei changshi* (an officer's title) Wang Xuance proclaims...

(Line 10) Liu Renkai had chosen six *liangiia zi* (sons from good family) from (the district of Guanzhong) ...

.....

(Line 12) The voice goes so high, over the Snow Mountains, to the Hill of Gçdhrakåta and ...

(Line 13) In the fifth month of the summer of the year of... have arrived at the west of *Xiao Yangtong* ...[12]

.....

(Line 23) Being at the end of the territory, inscribed on the good stone by the hill Gçdhrakåta ...

(Line 24) the son of the envoy, Wang Lingmin ... The nephew of the member of the envoy ...[13]

Though the damage prevents us from understanding the entire contents of the inscription we still can concur on the following points which were previously not so clear concerning Wang's third mission: First, the emperor sent Wang and his entourage to India in the sixth month of the third year of Xianqing, that is, in c. A.D. 658. Second, in the fifth month of the summer of some year, the delegation arrived somewhere, which probably is just the place where the present inscription was discovered. Logically, this must have happened in the fourth year of Xianqing, that is, A.D. 659, the year following the one in which they left the imperial capital. Third, in the inscription we discover some new names of the members of the delegation, which were unknown before and may provide some new clues for further study.

Last, the delegation went to Nepal and India via the route through Skyid-grong, not through Glya'-lam as some scholars have suggested. The inscription is also of help in identifying the location of Xiao yangtong, which is the name of a district or a once existing kingdom in Tibet. Its location has been a controversial question for a long time. The place where the inscription was set up is to the west of Xiao yangtong. From the inscription we can roughly decide where Xiao yangtong was. It should be to the east of Skyid-grong and between Skyid-grong and Lhasa.

Last, we may mention another inscription related to Wang Xuance and discovered not long ago at the well-known Longmen Grotto in Luoyang. It mentions a donation by Wang Xuance in the second year of Lingde (A.D. 665). In this year he constructed a Maitreya image as a donation for the southern cell of the Pingyang Grotto:

> 'Wang Xuance ... (here seven characters have been damaged) ... on the fifteenth day of the ninth month of the second year of Lingde, for (every life of) the lower Dharmadhatu respectfully constructed a set of statues (of Maitreya).'[14]

Although this is not of much help in reconstructing the history of Wang's missions to India, still it helps as it acquaints us with his pious belief in Buddhism, which is not an insignificant detail. It helps us to understand his religious background at the time when he was chosen by the Chinese emperors to undertake this important task.

NOTES AND REFERENCES

1. 'Les missions de Wang Hiuan-ts'e dans l'Inde', *Journal Asiatique*, vol. 15, March-April and May-June 1900), pp. 402-468.
2. Wang Hiuan-ts' e et Kaniùka, *T'oung Pao*, vol. 13 (1912), pp. 307-309.
3. *India and China*, Calcuttta: Asraswat Library, 1981, pp. 96-99.
4. This paper was written quite early, in 1997, originally for a *Festschrift*, but as far as I know has not yet been published anywhere. After that only one reference note was added—9 March 2001.

5. Feng Chengjun, 'Wang Xuance shi ji' (Collected materials about Wangxuance), in his *Xiyu nanhai shidi kaozheng lunzhu Huiji* (Collected papers on the history and geography of the Western Region and South Sea), Beijing: Zhonghua Book Company, 1959, pp. 102-128.
6. Published in 1988 by the Zhonghua Book Company.
7. *Taisho Tripitaka* 53, No. 2122, p. 310b.
8. Ibid., p. 559b.
9. Ibid., p. 703c.
10. *Taisho Tripitaka* 52, No. 2108, p. 461c.
11. Not in A.D. 647 as Bagchi says in his above-mentioned book, p. 96. And the date that the Chinese envoys were sent to India is 643, not 634 as in Bagchi's book. But this discrepancy I feel was possibly due to a misprint.
12. *Xiao Yangtong*, which in Chinese means 'Small Yangtong', is believed to be the Chinese name or a part of Zhang zhung mentioned in Tibetan literature. Cf. Seigbert Hummel: *On Zhang-zhung*, Dharamsala: Library of Tibetan Works and Archives, 2000.
13. See Huo Wei, '*Da tang chushi Tianzhu min jiqi xiangguan wenti de yanjiu*' (A study on the epigraph of the Great Tang envoy to India), in *Toho Kakuho* (Journal of Oriental Studies), Kyoto, No. 66 (1994), pp. 270-253. Also *Xizang zhizhiqu wenguanhui wenwu puchadui* (The investigative team of the administrative committee of cultural relies of the Tibet Autonomous Region), '*Xizang Skiyad-rong xian faxian tang xianqing sannian da tang tianzhu chushi min*' (The newly discovered Epigraph of the Great Tang envoy to India of the third year of Xianqing in Skiyad-rong county of Tibet, in *Kaogu* (*Archaeology*), 1994, No. 7, pp. 619-23.
14. Wen Yucheng, '*Longmen suojian zhongwai jiaotong shiliao chutan*' (A preliminary study of the materials concerning the history of relations between China and foreign countries discovered in the Longmen grottos), in *Xibei Shidi* (The history and geography of the North-West Region), 1983, No. 1, p.62. The second year of Lingde is 665.

CHINA'S TRADITION OF RESEARCH ON INDIA[1]

GENG YINZENG

What are those factors that had been conducive to promoting the contacts between two ancient civilised nations: India and China? As we all know, both China and India have been the cradle of human civilisation. At the dawn of history, the Yellow River civilisation and the Indus Valley civilisation started off in the eastern part of the globe. During the 5th-6th century B.C; Buddhism was founded in India. At the same historical moment, Confucius and his thought made headway. Founded in the two great civilisations, Buddhism and Confucianism conceived a splendid thought culture and made a remarkable influence on the growth of human society which is evident in the present world as well.[2] According to a stipulation of the UNESCO, both China and India have figured first in the ranks of cultural relics and heritage of the world.[3] The contribution of both the countries to the development of human civilisation is immense. As both the countries are repositories of immense information on civilisation, Chinese scholars could perseveringly and consistently pursue their research on India.

The towering peaks of the Himalaya and the deep gulfs of the southern ocean were never an obstruction to the growth of a bilateral interface between the two countries. From very early times, there existed land and sea routes as links between the two nations. Since the Western Han times (206 B.C.-A.D. 25) there were two principal overland routes between the Chinese and Indian peninsulas. One was known as the western path, while the other was known as the Yunnan-Burma route. The former route flourished day by day after the famous visit of Zhangqian (?-114 B.C.). The world famous silk road, which sprang from Asia to Europe, is also on this route. Information about the later route came when Zhangqian, in the course of his visit to Bacteria (presently in the eastern part of Afghanistan) found to his great surprise some bamboo sticks and cotton materials from the south-western provinces of China and upon enquiring learnt that they had been brought by Indian merchants through north India and Afghanistan. After returning back to China in 126 B.C., he gave a report to the imperial court. Henceforth, many envoys were sent to the western region to gather more information on this route, but they could never get accurate information about this path. However this route existed in reality for mutual trade and the commercial activities between the local people of the region. In the 7th century, during the period of the Tang dynasty (A.D. 619-907), there sprang up one more route which passed through Tibet and Nepal and finally connected to north India. In the last decade of the 20th century an inscribed tablet has been found in the Tibetan region, which mentions the Tang envoy, Wang Xuance, who visited India while passing through Tibet.[4] Hence in the first millennium A.D., these three overland routes played a pivotal role in fomenting direct communication between India and China.

With the progress in maritime transport in the Indian Ocean and the South China Sea, merchandise activities between India and China showed increasing growth. During the western Han period, there was a sea route which originated from Leizhou in China, and passing through the southern peninsula of Myanmar reached Conjeevaram (Huang Zhi Kingdom), which is now on the eastern coast of the Indian peninsula.[5] In the period following the Tang dynasty, Chinese sailors could directly sail up to the Arabian and Persian Gulf passing through the Gulf of Bengal and Siam.[6] Since the beginning of the Song dynasty (960-1127), Quilon, which is on the western coast of the Indian peninsula, became the junction of the Chinese sailors who frequently travelled along western Asia and Africa.[7] The opening of the sea route across the Indian Ocean turned into a very convenient channel for promoting the relations between the two ancient civilisations.

The significant point to be noted is that the mutual visits of the envoys of the two ancient civilised friendly nations have been widely recorded in Chinese historical documents. They started in the 2nd century B.C., when Zhang Qian sent his envoy to India, and during the Han period when the Han empire and the Kashmir region (which is known as the Ji Bing kingdom in Chinese sources) were frequently visited by the envoys of the respective nations. These episodes continued till the 6th year of the reign of Qing Emperor Guang Xu (1880) and the process never ceased, no matter whether China was in a state of unification or bifurcation, as one dynasty succeeded the other.[8] However, these friendly contacts came to a halt when the Western colonial powers subjugated the Eastern nations. But they were unable to completely obstruct the traditional friendship between the two nations, which had been shaped by the ancestors of both nations.

The above-mentioned factors with cultural connotations and conducive communication facilities, friendly relations and topographical and climatic advantages, and coordination among the people of both the countries presented the pre-requisites to the Chinese for research on India. There has been a continuous history of more than 2,000 years since the Chinese started doing research on India, which can be categorised under the following headings:

1. Buddhism as the central force for research on India in the first millennium.
2. After the 10th century, the commercial and merchandise activities between the two nations which fostered the relationships.
3. The advent of the Western colonial powers and the subjugating of the Eastern world and the Chinese concern for Indian society and polity. Therefore, in the latter half of the 20th century, Chinese research on India made considerable progress.

A brief account of the whole process is given in the following paragraphs. Buddhism, founded in ancient India, spread over the central plain of China through the western region (central Asia) in the first century A.D. during the Eastern Han dynasty (25-220). Most of the scholars are in agreement over this. Towards this alien religious teaching ancient China did not adopt a hostile attitude. On the contrary, it was discussed, explored, absorbed and finally assimilated by them. In the higher ranks of society the rulers supported it while in the lower rungs the masses started having deep faith in it. By the time of the Tang dynasty, the Chinese people had established their own sect of Buddhism. This demonstrates the prospering of Buddhist thinking in China. The Chinese had achieved remarkable success in their research on Buddhism in the interim between the Han and Tang dynasties, of which the most outstanding achievements are reflected in the translations of the Buddhist scriptures and of the marvellous records of travels of the Chinese monks while touring the Buddhist country.

The translation of Buddhist scriptures started during the later period of Eastern Han by An Shigao (1st century). This received a momentum during the Wei and Jin dynasties (220-589), and was at its peak during the Sui (581-618) and Tang dynasties, gradually declining by the time of the Northern Song (960-1127). According to later research, it is learnt that there were more than 150 scholars who were directly involved in translating these scriptures over a span of more than 1,000 years and during this period about 71 monks visited China from India. Under the joint efforts of these monks from both countries, it is now confirmed that China has preserved more Buddhist scriptures than the original country—India—having more than 5,700 volumes under 1,500 different titles.[9] The translated Chinese Buddhist scriptures and Tripitakas constitute an unparalleled record of Buddhist thought and are one of the most precious cultural legacies of human society.

Along with the translations of the Buddhist scriptures, there began a pilgrimage of Chinese monks to the western world to embark on Buddhist soil. Undaunted by the sufferings during the travels, one monk followed the other, as they were countless in number. This has been well recorded in *Liang Gao Seng Zhuan* (Biographies of Eminent Monks of the Liang Dynasty), *Tang Gao Seng Zhuan* (Biographies of Eminent Monks of the Tang Dynasty) and *Song Gao Seng Zhuan* (Biographies of Eminent Monks of Song Dynasty). Among them the most outstanding pilgrim monks have been Faxian (337-422), Xuanzang (602-664) and Yijing (635-713). From 399 to 412, Faxian toured across the length and breadth of India (known as Tian Zhu in ancient Chinese documents) and on his return, he wrote a travelogue known as *Fo Guo Ji* or *Faxian Zuan* (Account of the Buddhist Country or Autobiography of Faxian).

Xuanzang studied in India and travelled throughout the country between 627 to 645. He was warmly received by Harshavardhan, the king of central India and his ally, King Bhaskaravarman of Kamarupa (Assam in eastern India). On his return, he also wrote a travelogue, *Da Tang Xiyu Ji* (Record of the Western Countries During the Great Tang Dynasty). In 671 Yijing started off for India by a sea route and till 695 he travelled widely, collecting a huge number of Buddhist documents. On the way back, he stopped over at Srivijaya kingdom (Sumatra Islands in Indonesia) and then compiled two books in 691 on the social, geographical and political situation of India and the southern ocean region, which are known as *Da Tang Xiyu Qiufa Gaoseng Zhuan* (Biographies of the Eminent Monks in Search of Dharma to the Western Countries During the Period of the Great Tang) and *Nanhai Jigui Nei Fa Zhuan* (An Account of Dharma

Brought from the Southern Ocean). In 962, one of his disciples brought them back to Changan (Xian). These books are not only the main resource material for researching ancient India, they are incomparable and their research value has been widely acknowledged and appreciated by scholars all over the world. Hence it can be said that the translation of the Buddhist scriptures and the records of the Chinese monks were the most remarkable achievements of the Chinese people's research on India during the first century of the first millennium A.D.

After the 10th century, under the remarkably conducive factors of progress in maritime activities in the Indian Ocean and the development in commercial and trade activities, the commercial interface between the two great ancient civilised nations grew by leaps and bounds almost on a daily basis. To supplement the evidence let us discuss the discovery of some monuments in both the nations. Quanzhou of Fujian, China, was an important port during the Song (960-1127) and Yuan (1271-1368) dynasties, and was also a famous international port during the classical medieval period. During that time, merchants from various countries of the Indian Ocean congregated here and even now we can find traces of a Hindu temple at this place.[10] We also find some tombs of merchants here, and some of them have the Tamil language inscribed on it, which proves that merchants from the Indian peninsula traded at this place. The eastern coast of the Indian peninsula was also the meeting point of the merchants during the Song period. We find a Chinese mud tower in Najiabad, which is located 48 km east of Tanjore in Tamilnadu, with Chinese characters carved on the bricks which read as follows, 'built in 8th month of the third year of Xian Chun era'. The third year of Xian Chun means the year 1267. The building of a Chinese tower certainly shows that many Chinese merchants must have been visiting the Indian peninsula during that period. This surviving tower of three storeys had a total height of 30 meters in 1846. However, in 1867, unfortunately with the consent of the British government, the Jesuits of Najiabad destroyed the tower.[11]

We have many literal documents to prove the existence of the above-mentioned monuments and some of them also record the trade and merchandise activities of the Indian peninsula. For instance, Wang Dayuan (1311-?), the Indian Ocean maritime expert of the 14th century has in his book *Dao Yi Zhi Lue* (Brief Accounts of the Islands and their Barbarians), which he wrote in 1439, mentioned the various cloth and cotton products of the Indian peninsula. He mentions the cotton fabrics of the Punjab, the silk of Seripattanam, the cotton of Da Badan (a place north of present-day Calicut whose identification has still not been properly made), the fine silk of Mala[ya]Bar (and the super fine clothes of Somnath (Ahmedabad region). These cotton products were also exported to various countries. The sailors of those times, when they reached the eastern African coast (present-day Malindi in Kenya), reported that local people there clad themselves in Indian made clothes and skirts.[12] During the Ming dynasty in the fourteenth century, the famous Chinese navigator Zheng He (1371/75-1433/35) sailed the Indian Ocean with his fellow countrymen. He authored some books including *Yin Ya Shen Lan* (The Overall Survey of the Ocean's Shores), *Xing Chuo Shen Lan* (The Overall Survey of the Stars and Planets), and *Xiyang Fan Guo Zhi* (The Records of Various Countries of Western Ocean Region). These books not only reflect the social life, local customs and human behaviour of the various places along the eastern coast of the Indian peninsula but its most valuable part, meticulously detailed and seeming like a life-like sketch, records the dealings during the commercial and trade activities of those times, for example the weights, measurements, coins, and the currency and revenue system in existence. This encounter expresses the other aspect of Chinese research on India, and it also demonstrates that the Chinese people's understanding of India entered a period of newer heights.

By the end of the 15th century Western colonialists started penetrating into the Eastern countries. The Portuguese, the Dutch, the British and the French colonialists, one after another, made inroads into India and after a series of wars the British expelled the other Western powers from the soil of India. By the 19th century India was completely subjugated by the British. During the same time, on the pretext of opium trade, the British colonisers were involved in the opium war with China. Both the ancient civilisations faced the unfortunate invasion from the Western powers simultaneously. After the fall of India to the British, the court and the common people of China were shocked and highly concerned about the situation of India. They intensified their research on the country. Some academicians and scholars are known to have pointed out that, there was not only a need for supporting India in its anti-imperialistic independence movement, but it was also important to learn a lesson from the Indian suffering. It would be useful to discuss at this juncture the exquisite ideas and understandings of the progressive intellectuals of that time.

On the basis of modern scientific knowledge, the Chinese people started acquiring an accurate understanding of India. The famous thinker Wei Yuan (1794-1857) edited a voluminous book, *Hai Guo Tu Zhi* (Records and Illustrations of Oceans and Countries) which was based on metereological and geographical accounts. Thus the Chinese people learnt about the latitude along which the Indian continent lay. In one part of the book, *Wan Guo Dili Quan Tu Ji* (The Complete Geographical Map of World Countries), the position of India has been mentioned as 6.5 to 35 degree as its latitude from north and 65 to 95 degree as its longitude from east; the total area of the country is mentioned as 3.84 million sq. *Li*, and the population as being 134 million. The most important thing, however, was that forward thinking intellectuals, after research and analysis, acquired a deeper perspective on the social conditions of India and guaged the genuine nature of colonial policies. They pierced the truth with a single pertinent remark: 'what the Britons [were] saying in the name of commerce was not true and their main aim was that in the name of commerce [to] gradually subjugate India, Malacca, Burma and some other Asian countries'.[13] A diplomat, Zhang Zhengyi, after visiting Britain came to the conclusion that after invading India, in 200 years they had conquered more than three-fourths of the total land of the nation.

The British army officers stationed in India were 3,011 in number, soldiers being 66,578, while indigenous soldiers totalled 122,346. The Indian British government collected heavy taxes every year as the customs duty for import and export. The annual income from all kinds of taxes, including import-export, land, property, forestry, poll, post, communication, rail, automobiles and salt raised from Bombay and other 7 cities was 192.5 million silver *taels*. Apart from that, the agricultural tax raised from the 9 places under British rule was 13,634,845 million silver *taels*, hence the total revenue collected was almost 1,938,634,845 million silver *taels*.[14] The colonial wild of the Britons in India prompted the Chinese to realise the necessity of 'anti-barbarians'. The most famous of them was Wei Yuan, who analysed the whole situation of the Indian peninsula, the conflict among the colonisers and their barbaric aims and then further accounted on the prospect of the cooperation between India and China in their anti-colonial struggle.[15] The barbaric Western rule certainly fomented Sino-Indian relations after the Europeans subjugated India, as China also grieved for India's pain and supported the Indians. During this period of subjugation of India, sympathising with the sufferings of its denizens and supporting its freedom struggle became the mainstream trend of Chinese research on India. A war poem composed by the then Canton Governor, Zhang Zhidong (1837-1909) well reflects this spirit:

> The whole globe and the countries are like tiger and leopard,
> With the militant soldiers trying to subjugate the nations
> Our country would be feeble and subjugated if we don't defend and foreigners
> Would crack and sarcasm on us,
> If we don't strengthen ourselves, it might be depleted
> Look, India is not a small country
> But it is under the control of western shackle.[16]

By describing the Indian calamity Chinese scholars insinuatingly cautioned their own people about the barbaric nature of the colonisers. At the same time, the Chinese people also pointed out the existing social backwardness of India, for example the weak social status of the woman, sati practice, etc.[17] In 1902, Zai Zhen was going to Britain as a Chinese envoy. In the same ship he met a minister of the Sindh province who was also going to Britain to participate in a ceremony held in honour of the British queen. The Sindh minister was full of arrogance, carrying an entourage of more than 20 servants, and there were other two Indian chiefs going to Britain too for showing off their wealth, each taking another boat of gifts. Zai Zhen made remarks on their swaggering posture and forgetting the real tribulations and calamities of the nation remarked, 'Ah! So those are Indians.'[18]

Modern Chinese scholars not only pointed out the social backwardness and existing malpractices in India but also the hope of India's people. This was well represented in an article by Zhang Taiyan in the daily newspaper *Min Bao* (People's Paper). In Japan Zhang Taiyan met Balbinder Singh and other Indian revolutionaries and advocated for 'co-operation between China and India'[19] as well as 'mutual support between the two countries'.[20] Many articles in *Min Bao* advocated the 'Unity among the Asian nations' and 'cooperation between China and India' so that the European and American countries could not colonise the Asian countries, and the countries of Asia could restore their freedom.[21] It further pointed out that China and India would form an alliance and Asia could keep peace forever.[22] These thoughts reflect deep insights even today and can be termed as far-sighted ideas. This was the representation of the advanced Chinese scholars of those days and it was also the conclusive theory of the Chinese people after research on India for a few centuries since western colonialists subjugated India.

When the world stepped into the 20th century, wide-ranging changes started to take place all over the world. In the first half of the century, China was also caught up in the tornado of internal civil war. However, despite that the Chinese continued to do their research on India. I would specially like to point out some thinkers of China of this period. The famous educationist, Professor Cai Yuanpei (1868-1940) while serving as the chancellor of Peking University, initiated a course for the first time on Indian philosophy in the university. This was also the earliest course started on India in any of the contemporary Chinese universities and it has been continuously followed till date. In the forties when Hu Shi (1891-1962) took over as the president of Peking University a new department, Oriental Language and Literature, was established in the university. Sanskrit and Pali were the main languages being taught in this department and the teachers were Professor Ji Xianlin, who studied in Germany and Profesor Jin Kemu, who had returned from India very recently. By the fifties, apart from Pali and Sanskrit, Hindustani languages like Hindi and Urdu were added in the curriculum of this department. Peking University turned into a major centre of research on India in the 20th century. It also played a big role in upbringing and fostering research on Indian studies. The article *Beijing daxue de Yindu Xue Yanjiu: Bashi Nian de Huigu* (Research on Indology in Peking University: Eight decades in retrospect)[23] by Professor Wang Bangwei has earlier deliberated on this and I will not repeat it here. In the following paragraphs, I would like to briefly describe the status of research on India by Chinese scholars in the latter half of the 20th century, particularly after the reforms and opening up of the country.

Research during this period further grew on the solid foundation of earlier concrete works. I would like to talk about the three venerated master scholars of this period, Professor Tang Yongtong

(1893-1964), Professor Ji Xianlin (1911-) and Professor Jin Kemu (1912 - 2000). All three have Chinese and foreign expertise and are experts in Sanskrit, Pali, Chinese and other languages and worthy of being called the founders of research on India in the 20th century. Now, let us discuss their major achievements, which include three aspects: first, there emerged authoritative works, for example, the books written by Tang Yongtong, *A Brief History of Indian Philosophy* (published by Chongqing Independent Publication House in 1945, reprinted by Zhonghua shuju, Beijing in 1960 and 1988); books written by Ji Xianlin, *A Brief History of Sino-Indian Relations* (published by Peoples Publication in 1957), *Collection of Some Chapters on Sino-Indian Relations* (published by Sanlian Book House in 1982) and a *History of Sanskrit Literature* (published by Peoples Publication in 1964) by Jin Kemu. These authoritative works have been widely appreciated in the whole academic world and are considered to be the classics on Indian studies.

Second, the translation of the classical texts of India. After translating the great literary works, *Shakuntala, Panchatantra* and *Uravshi*, in the fifties and sixties, during the very tortuous period of the 'cultural revolution', Ji Xianlin translated the classical Indian religious epic the *Ramayana* in Chinese. From 1980 to 1984, the Peoples Publication House, Beijing, published this mega work in seven parts with eight volumes. It is enthralling to note that the other classical epic the *Mahabharata*, is currently being translated by the disciples of Professor Ji under his supervision. Apart from that, the mega work *Zhonghua Dazang Jing* (The Chinese Buddhist Tripitakas) is being published with new annotations and a new ordering. *Faxian Zhuan* (The autobiography of Faxian), *Da Tang Xiyu Ji* (An Account of Western Region during Great Tang Dynasty), *Da Tang Xiyu Qiufa Gaoseng Zhuan* (The Biographies of Eminent Monks who Visited Western Region in Search of Dharma During Great Tang Dynasty) and *Nanhai Jigui Nafa Zhuan* (An Account of Dharma Brought from Southern Ocean) have been republished recently with new annotations.[24] These annotations reflect and are based on the recent research works and new ideas of annotators.

The great classical work, *Da Tang Xiyu Ji*, has been annotated again and published by Zhonghua Shuju in 1985, under the supervision of Professor Ji Xianlin and the combined efforts of many scholars. The whole book has almost 630,000 characters with the original text, preface, annotations and explanations. It reflects the new heights in the field of research on India by Chinese scholars.

The third aspect I am going to discuss is the research and investigation on India made in the fields of the polity, economy, culture, and so on.[25] The most outstanding among these works is the publication of *Collected Works of Gurudeva Tagore* in the year 2000 with more than 10 million Chinese characters. The South Asia Institute of Sichuan University, Chengdu, has carried out remarkable research on contemporary India. Minutely observing the social and economic developments of India and learning from its experiences became the hot topic of research on India by Chinese scholars.

Now I would like to talk about my personal view of the characteristics of the tradition of Chinese research on India. Accumulation and dissemination are the main characteristics of Chinese research on India. Records on India in the Chinese official history books are fully commensurate with this point. From the *Book of History* composed in the first century A.D. to The Official Documents of Qing Dynasty (*Qing Chao Xuwenxian Tong Kao*) composed in the 20th century, we find the records of Shendu (India), Tianzhu Guo (India), Chola Kingdom (9th to 12th century), Malabar, Bengal and Bangladesh. The continuity in the records on India has been remarkable. If we arrange them in order of the mutual visit of the officials and envoys, geographical communication, Buddhist relations, it is expressed in one continuous form which is rarely seen in other records of historical materials. These records also reflect the fact that the research carried out by the Chinese people on India over the past 2,000 years gradually popularised and continuously deepened.

The Official History of Liang, composed in A.D. 636, not only noted that India was a prosperous country, but it says that it was a highly cultured and civilised nation. It has depicted well the marvellous paintings and carvings on the palaces, beautiful dresses and fascinating music and has mentioned about 16 Mahajanapadas of 5th century B.C. like Vatsa, Kasi, Vajji, etc. *The Official History of Song*, composed in 1345 A.D., has recorded in detail the social and political conditions of the Chola kingdoms, which were in power from the 9th to the 13th centuries, and their 31 tributary states. It also discusses the laws and punishments of the country. 'There were life sentences, being beheaded or crushed under the feet of an elephant if found of serious guilt, small punishments for minor offences were beating for 50 to 100 times.' Till date, these literal recordings in Chinese historical documents have become major sources for the writing of Indian history.

Paying more attention to investigation on the spot has been the other characteristic of Chinese research on India. The writings and recordings of Faxian, Xuanzang and Yijing have been documented on their own experiences and whatever they have written has been witnessed by themselves personally. These sources are obviously quite reliable, and their historical value is very high. It goes without saying that these sources were also very scientific in nature and based on facts. It reflected the spirit of hardships and efforts of the Chinese scholars. Faxian set out for India in A.D. 399 at the ripe age of sixty-five years. He crossed the high mountains and passed the dreary deserts, all the way tramping on the skulls and bones of the dead in the Gobi desert. He conquered unimaginable tribulations and finally reached the Buddhist country. After repatriating to his country, he wrote his travelogue, *Records of Buddhist Kingdom*, which is based on real personal experience. Professor Jin Kemu studied in India from 1951 to 1945. While working in a newspaper he simultaneously carried on his research work and also simultaneously studied Hindi, Sanskrit, Pali, Buddhism, Indian philosophy and literature. He made great achievements in the academic field and his recently published book *Fan Zhu Lu JI* (including *Fanyu Wenxue Shi*, *Tian Zhu Shiwen, Fan Fo Tan*) demonstrates this.

In the course of research on India, Chinese scholars attached great attention to the trends of the times. The records reflect the features and needs of the era. *Da Tang Xiyu Ji* of Xuanzang is a good example of this. The social conditions of India is more than Buddhism in the book. The reason is that Tang court at that time wanted to understand comprehensively the turbulent situation of the western region. In the second year after Xuanzang's return to China, Emperor Tang Taizong personally met him in order to understand the actual situation of the western region and gave him an assignment to compose a book about his travels and then read the book personally. So, if we call this book a mirror of the actual situation in the western region of those days it will not be an exaggeration at all. When the Western colonialists subjugated the Eastern world in a barbaric manner, the Chinese intellectuals of those days realised this vividly and protested vehemently. Among the subjugation of the eastern nations, the first to be noted was the fall of India to the British and the Chinese tried to learn a lesson from this. This also proves the actual benefits of the research on India by the Chinese people.

China and India are both ancient civilisations of the world. The Chinese people learnt from the experiences of India, glorified their own civilisation and in this way also further developed and enriched the civilisations of the whole world. The process of more than 2,000 years of research on India by the Chinese people is an unparalleled event in the world. Since the advent of Buddhism into China, translating Buddhist scriptures became the fervent love of the Chinese people and the study of the Sanskrit language also enriched the linguistic and phonetic aspects of the Chinese language. The philosophical ideas of Buddhism influenced the formation of the philosophy of Song and Ming China. The three major carvings and paintings in the stone grottos of China, named Dunhuang, Yungang and Longmen have been deeply influenced by the Gandhara art of India and have then flourished in their unique style.

The research of present-day Chinese scholars on India is also identical to that of the old days. Professor Ji Xianlin used comparative language and linguistic research methods and came to the conclusion that the early translated Buddhist scriptures of China were not only based on Sanskrit but they were based on both the Tocharian language of the western region and the Indian language.[26] This helped greatly in determining the period of original Buddhist classical texts being translated before the Sui dynasty. These types of true explorations had a far-reaching influence on the research and translation of Buddhist scriptures into the Chinese language.

With the beginning of a new millennium, I am confident that the Chinese research on India will continue to grow on the basis of earlier research. Chinese scholars would achieve sparkling success in their research on India. I believe that in the age of information technology today the Chinese people, with the help of high-tech scientific methods, will further enrich and give new dimensions to Indian studies. This is probably also the common aspiration of the scholars of both countries.

(Translated by Yukteshwar Kumar, Lecturer, Visva-Bharati, Santiniketan, presently doing research on Sino-Indian ties as Nehru Fellow at Peking University under the guidance of Prof. Geng Yinzeng.)

NOTES AND REFERENCES

1. In the late seventies of the century that has just ended China stepped into a period of reform and opening up and subsequently it witnessed the spring of thought culture in the country. Under the able guidance of noted Professor Ji Xianlin, I engaged in a research project, tracing and collecting the records on India from ancient Chinese documents. After an arduous scramble of eight years, I collected material from Chinese official history books, Buddhist scriptures, ancient geographical books and various other literary sketches, in addition to editing two volumes of a book, *Collection of South Asian Historical Materials from Chinese Sources* (where 90 per cent of the records are on India) and also authored another book, *Historical Data of South Asia from Chinese Sources*. The first book has been reviewed in India in *India Historical Research* and the *Statesman. India Historical Research*, Vo1.18, nos. 1 & 2 July 1991 - January 1992, *The Statesman*, 26 July, 1996
2. There had existed a great tradition of research on India among the Chinese people since a very long time. It began with the advent of Buddhism in China and has continued without interruption for more than 2,000 years.
3. According to latest reports India has 22 while China has 27.
4. Da Tang Tianzhushi chuming *Archaeology* (*Kaogu*), 1994, no. 7, pp. 619-623.
5. *Book of Han. Chapter on Geography* (*Han Shu. Dili Zhi*)
6. *Book of New Tang, Chapter on Geography* (*Xin Tang Shu, Dili Zhi*)
7. *Lingwai Daita, Waiguo Men*
8. Geng Yinzeng, 'Ancient Friendly Relations between China and South Asian Nations' (*Zhongguo he Nanya de Youhao Guanxi Yuanyuan Liuchang*), *South Asia Research* (*Nanya Yanjiu*), no. 2, 1982.
9. Huang Xinchuan, *Yindu Zhexue Shi* (History of Indian Philosophy), Shangwu, 1989, p. 169
10. T.N. Subramaniam, 'A Tamil Colony in Medieval China', *South Indian Studies*, Madras, 1978. Wu Wenliang, *Quanzhou Zongjiao Shike*, Kexue,1957, pp. 41-59
11. *Dao Yi Zhi Lue*-Tu Ta; 'Nagapatlinam he Quanzhou yi Xiaoshi de Simiao', *Haijiao Shi Yanjiu*, 1995, vol. 2
12. *Dao Yi Zhi Lue*- Ma Na Li
13. WangYi, *Yu Ying Lu Zhi*, vol. 2
14. *Yi Shu Qi*, vol.6
15. Hai Guo Tu Zhi, vol. 19
16. *Qing Chao Xu Wenxian Tong Kao*, vol. 199
17. Ibid.
18. Zai Zhen, *Yingyao Riji*, vol. 3
19. Zhang Taiyan Quan Ji, vol, 4, p. 367
20. *Zhang Taiyan Wencao*, vol. 5
21. Ibid.
22. Zhang Taiyan Quanji, vol. 4, p. 368

23. *Beijing Darue Xuebao* (The Journal of Peking University) , 1998, vol. 2
24. *Faxian Zhuan* was published by Shanghai Guji Chubanshe in 1985 while the annotated copies of *Da Tang Xiyu Qiufa Gaoseng Zhuan* and *Hanhai Jigui Neifa Zhuan* by Wang Bangwei have been published by Zhonghua Shuju in 1985 and 2000
25. See Zhang Minqiu, 'Indian studies in China', Prof. Tan Chung (ed.), *Indian Horizons*, vol. 43, special issue nos. 1-2, 1994.
26. Ji Xianlin, 'Lun fanwen t and d de yinshi' (The phonetic detail on t and d of Sanskrit), in *Zhongyin wenhua Guangxishi luncong*, Renmin, 1957

INDIA AND CHINA : THE BEYOND AND THE WITHIN

LOKESH CHANDRA

Chinese Alphabet for Buddha

The last twenty-three centuries have seen a continuing cultural interflow between the Western Paradise that is India and the Celestial Kingdom that is China. The rustling breeze of Buddhist fragrance has awakened the mindscape of both countries, endowing them with the web of thought, the harmony of art, the magnificent colour of murals and sculptures, incarnating a new life and sinking into the sensitivities of our people's deep-reaching muscles of mystery, draped in the intimacy of the mind. The first contacts were made by Buddhist scholars from India who appeared in the Chinese capital in 217 B.C. under the Tsin dynasty. Contacts during the Tsin dynasty are a fair possibility as the Sanskrit word for Cathay is *China*, as such was the dynastic name Tsin heard by the Indians.

Voltaire (1694-1778), the unrivalled French writer and philosopher, was impressed by the 'sublime ideas' of the Indians about the Supreme Being. His enthusiasm for Asian civilisation and Eastern wisdom was shared by Sir William Jones. Jones followed the standards set by the French philosopher, and read his works assiduously. Voltaire admired the political organisation of China and her ethics based on Reason. He found in China a great civilisation which owed nothing to the Graeco-Roman or Christian tradition. The Chinese managed their affairs of state more rationally and without Christianity. The German philosopher Leibnitz too had established the Berlin Academy to open up interchange of civilisation between Europe and China. The more the Europeans investigated China the more they found India to be its roots, in fact the Greece of Asia, the birthplace of philosophical ideas and the overwhelming influence in art and poetry.

The *chinoiserie* of the 18th century led to revealing the fabulous bonds of China with India. In their study of China, French scholars started to unravel Central Asia and India. Jean Pierre Abel-Remusat published a history of Khotan in 1820 and his French translation of the travels of Fa-hian through Central Asia, Afghanistan and India appeared posthumously in 1836. By his labours, it became evident that Chinese sources were fundamental to the understanding of Indian history. In fact the Indian pronunciation of this first great Chinese pilgrim's name derives from Abel-Remusat's transcription, like that of his illustrious successor Hiouen-thsang. The travels and biography of the latter were again translated by another French scholar Stanislas Julien in 1853-58.

The biography of Hiouen-thsang after his return to China as summarised by Julien 132 years ago is still our main guide. Indian scholars rarely have access to this French work and are thus deprived of detailed knowledge of the academic achievements of Hiouen-thsang after his return home. Julien was again the first to point out that Sanskrit literature had been translated into Chinese on a gigantic scale for a thousand years. In his Sinico-Sanskrit concordance of Buddhist works, published in 1849, he gave the Sanskrit titles of Chinese Sutras from a Chinese catalogue of 1306. Thus he injected a new dimension into Indic studies.

Names of Indian savants and sages, deities and divine beings, titles of works and toponymns abound in Chinese chronicles, hagiographies, canonical texts and other historical treatises. Complete Sanskrit texts of hymns are also extant in Chinese transcriptions. These hymns have sunk their roots deep into the lipping adoration of the Chinese. To decipher Sanskrit from them, Julien wrote *Methode pour dêchiffrer et transcrire les noms sanscrits qui se rencontrent dans les livres chinois* in 1861. Even after the passing of 130 years it remains our only guide, though in dire need of updating and enlarging.

Silk Across the Sands

Roman ladies of rank, draped in see-through muslin cottons of India and in shining silks and brocades of China were the eyeful rage of Imperial Rome. Silk was imported from China, where its production began as early as the New Stone Age. The oracle bone inscriptions of the Yin dynasty contain Chinese characters for mulberry, silkworm, thread and woven fabric. The consort of Emperor Huang Ti (2640 B.C.) made sericulture fashionable by herself cultivating mulberry trees, raising worms and reeling silk. The Nihongi states that this fabulous fabric was introduced in Japan around A.D. 300. The Roman empire at Rome and later at Constantinople realised the potential of silk. Emperor Justinian had two Iranian monks, who were living in China, smuggle silkworms to Constantinople in the hollows of their bamboo canes in about A.D. 550. In the 19th century steeped in Classical antiquity, it was but natural that a German geographer termed the ancient way from Hsian to Rome the *Seidenstrassen* or the Silk Route. This Eurocentric nomenclature emphasized the commercial aspects of the route. After all, the Greek work *serikos* for 'silk' is derived from *seres* 'Chinese', that is, the Chinese fabric. As children, we saw the Chinese cycling around the streets of Lahore and peddling silk. China and silk were interlinked in our minds. To my father, Professor Raghu Vira, however, the Chinese were a symbol of the Confucian Classics, great artists and architects, painters and sculptors of exquisite Buddhist icons in the flat and in the round, bearers of the profound thought of Buddhism, a vast segment of the world's cultural heritage, and a people who had preserved thousands of Buddhist *sutras* whose Sanskrit originals had been lost in India, the land of their origin. The Chinese paintings in our home and the Shanghai and Taisho editions of the Chinese Tripitaka covering a whole wall of the residence left a deep impression on my growing mind. In later years when I took up the study of Central Asia, silk and *sutras* came to mind again as two characteristics of the Chinese and of the Sutra Route.

To the Chinese, it was the way to the Western World of India. Across the vast stretches of desert, in the void of the self, they heard the echoing of 'I am the Truth.' Travelling and traveller became one, one with the eternal. The waterless deserts were the void of the self. The traveller trod not with his feet, but with his heart on wings.

Courage tore the terror of the terrain, and despair turned to hope in the supreme quest of a beyond without shores. The drop 'departed from its native home', found a shell and became a pearl. The desert and oasis became an embodiment of Buddhist teaching, according to Takayasu Higuchi. The desert symbolises hell and the oasis paradise, or in the broader perimeters of Buddhist philosophy 'everything flows and nothing is permanent.' I-ching speaks of the hardships and perils that had to be braved to reach India:

> No doubt, it is great merit and fortune to visit the Western Country (India) in search of the Dharma but at the same time it is an extremely difficult and perilous undertaking... Many days have I passed without food, even without a drop of water. I was always worried and no spirit was left in me... If, however, a monk happened to reach India after such perilous journey, he would find no Chinese monastery there. There was no fixed place to settle down. We had to move from place to place like a blade of grass swept by the wind.

The monk Hsuan-k'uei, who could not come to India as he suffered from illness, wrote: 'My heart goes to the sacred land of Buddhist temples. I dream to move in the land of the Buddha. Will that auspicious day ever come, when with the help of a cup or bowl only I shall be able to cross and reach India? Shall I be able to witness the magnificient flow of Dharma in India?'

Heavenly Horses

Though the route has been named the Silk Route by the Europeans, it was not opened by them as a communication system for silk. At the end of the second century B.C., the Han emperor Wu-ti sent Chang Ch'ien to Hsi-yu, the Western World. His return to Ch' ang-an in 126 B.C. was the opening of a regular road, as the Chinese realised the importance of other cultures. Xenophobia and the concept of Barbarians underwent change. Nomadic tribes traded silk with Central and Western Asia. The main purpose of the journey of Chang Ch'ien was defence; to find the whereabouts of the Hu barbarians who had been a major menace to Han-period China. The thoroughbred 'heavenly horse' (*tien ma*) was imported from Dawuan to improve the breed of horses during the Han dynasty. Chang Ch'ien was amazed to see in Bactria staves or walking sticks made of bamboo of Kiung and cloth of Shu, both from Sechuan. The

Bactrians had purchased them in India. This subsequently led the Chinese to the discovery of Yün-nan. An ancient trade route ran from Sechuan through Yün-nan into northeast India, thence to northwest India and then to Iranian lands. Silk-horse barter was a feature of Western Han times. The Han Emperor Wu-ti twice despatched troops under the command of General Li Guangli to obtain fine horses across the Tienshan mountains from the west. The new breed reinforced the military capability of China to such an extent as to eliminate the Huns and to expand its power as far as Korea.

The Imperial Mausoleum of Western Han in Yangjinwan has thousands of clay figures of war horses. Kasyapa Matanga, the first Indian teacher in China in the first century A.D., stayed at the Poma-suu or White Horse Monastery. The word 'white' can refer here to the colour of the horse or the horse of the 'white' people. The ethnicon of Kucha was `white' and *śvetadvipa* `White Land' refers to an area beyond northwest India. The white horse is at the base of the modern economic miracle of Japan. At the end of the Second World War, General MacArthur rode the sacred white horse of the Emperor of Japan to seal the newly won victory, and offered the equivalent of Marshall Aid to Japan. The Japanese responded: `No aid, only trade. We will work hard and grow rich.' The white horse became the heavenly horse that led Japan to unprecedented economic heights.

Music, Milk, Paper, Rice, Fruits

In 138 B.C. Chang Ch'ien, the envoy of the Chinese Emperor, took back musical instruments and Mahatukhara melodies from India to the Chinese capital Ch'ang-an. The son-in-law of the Emperor Wu-ti wrote 28 new tunes based on this melody which were played as military music. Along with Buddhism, the Tokharians of the route introduced milk to China. The Chinese ideograph *lo*, pronounced *lak* in ancient times, which meant various kinds of fermented milk products, was a loan from Indo-European (Latin, *lactic*). The peach and pear reached India in the reign of Kaniṣka. Cotton cultivation had been introduced from India to China in the second century B.C.The Japanese word *uruchi* is derived from the Sankrit *vrihi*. It seems to have arrived via northwest India where Greek and Roman influences were dominant. Rice is *oruza* in Greek and Latin (*oryza*), both derivatives of *vrihi*. The knowledge of rice came to Greece from the expedition of Alexander and the mention of *oruza* by Theophrastus (c. 320-300 B.C.) dates almost from the lifetime of Alexander who died in 323 B.C. The Japanese is so close to the Greek form that its origin can be connected with a variant of *vrihi* that was prevalent in northwest India, from which the Greek and Japanese forms are derived. The golden peach was introduced into China in the reign of Emperor T' ai Tsung of the T'ang (A.D. 629-49) from Sogdiana. The peach and the apricot were introduced to Rome in the first century A.D. through Iran, via Armenia, Greece and Rome. In A.D. 647 the king of Gandhara in northwest India sent the 'Buddha-land vegetable' to the Chinese court.

Graeco-Roman Elements

The three Tathagatas of the past, present and future in China and Japan are: Dīpaṅkara, Śākyamuni, and Maitreya. Hsuan-tsang localises the cult of Dipankara the Tathagata of the past at Nagarahara (modern Jalalabad in Afghanistan). His names, translated into Chinese by various pairs of characters meaning 'Constant Light', 'Universal Light', 'Blazing Torch', show proximity to the Iranian light cult. The sitting posture of Maitreya, with his feet hanging down the seat in European fashion, are a feature of northwest India, where Iranians, Greeks, Romans, Scythians, Kushans, and Tokharians jostled with the Indians.

The continued political presence of the Achaemenians, Parthians, Seleucids, Indo-Greeks, and Kushans had a far-reaching impact on the cultural hegemony of northwest India. It saw the osmosis of Iranian and Hellenistic ideas into Buddhism. The king-cult or emperor-worship was prevalent in Iran, Greece and Rome. The deification of kings was a solemn act of legislation in Greece even before Alexander crossed over into Asia. It was transplanted into Rome. Images of deified kings were installed in temples in live physical dimensions or in heights of multiples thereof to express greater loyalty. The loyalty of the provinces to Rome was gauged by the veneration which they felt for the person of the Emperor, whom they were prepared to treat as a god. The practice of offering divine honours to Augustus began in the East soon after Actium and in the course of his reign penetrated to all parts of the Empire.

The term *jen-chung hsiang* has been a puzzle to Japanese, Chinese and European scholars. They were personalities (*jen*), (*chung*), (*hsiang*) in statues. These were life-size sculptures, made to the breadth of the donor's finger (*aṅgula*). There are several instances in the Buddhist world. The proportions of a Tibetan Buddha are those of the Prince of Shalu (Zhva.lu) or the image of an Avalokitesvara has the same size as Sontsengampo, the first emperor of Tibet. These portrait-statues of the royalty were an expression of sanctified power. The Sanskrit word *pratimā* means a portrait-statue done to (*prati*) the measures (*mā*) of the donor. The Daibutsu, larger than life-size, were an extension of this principle: the colossal Maitreya statue at Darel seen by Fa-hsien, the two images at Bamiyan, the 27 metre high standing Maitreya at the Binglingsi caves are royal enterprises. They remind one of the colossi in the Graeco-Roman world. The colossus of Apollo astride the entrance of the harbour of Rhodes was the most celebrated in Greek antiquity, 120 feet high, made by Chares in 250 B.C. Colossal statues of deities and emperors were erected all over the Roman empire to impress the might of Rome on the people. Zenodorus was summonded by Nero to Rome and there he made a statue 106 feet high to represent the emperor but dedicated to the Sun. In the 8th century Rocana of Nara symbolised impirium. Emperor Shomu ordered, in A.C. 743, the construction of the gigantic statue (*daibutsu*) of Rocna, 16 metres in height, at the Todaiji monastery, in his attempt to unify the nation in an awareness of its power, to consolidate the sovereignty of the nation in a harmony of the emperor and his people on the deeper spiritual levels of a shared awareness: it was a 'Grand National Temple'. Portrait-statues or colossi in China and Japan go back to northwest Indian prototypes which were cognate to Roman concepts of imperial power expressed as cult images.

The portents of sweating, weeping, shaking, light-emitting images from the Chin (A.D. 265-420) to the Northern Ch'i and Northern Chou (A.D. 550-81) dynasties are sensitive not to individual worshippers but to the body politic. Their forerunners were the state cults of Greece and Rome. The Roman historian Livy records sympathetic sweating while Hannibal was in Italy at a critical stage of the Second Punic War. Livy and St. Augustine cite that Apollo of Cumae lamented publicly when the Greeks were worsted by the Romans in three successive wars of the second century B.C. Just as the safety of ancient Troy depended on the statue of Pallas, the Buddhist images in China were also palladia. It is an indication that the Greco-Romanised peoples of northwest India were active intermediaries not only in the trading of silk, but also in the transmission of the *sutras*. The role of the Graeco-Roman world in the conditioning and in the transferring of Buddhism across the Sutra Route deserves a close study.

Jade Beauties to Flying Devis

The Chinese were fascinated by jade beauties and by the music and dances of the Central Asian peoples. The Chou (1027-256 B.C.) got music of the Western Barbarians and played it on special occasions to vaunt their political might. The first three masters of Buddhist psalmody (*bombai*) in China were Kuchean, Scythian and Sogdian. In A.D. 384 Lu kuang brought music from Kucha as triumphal booty.

The Mogao Caves at Tun-huang and the Yulin Caves have extensive representation of flying goddesses, some of whom hold musical instruments. Beginning with Northern Wei (386-534) they come down to the Yuan dynasty (1271-1368). They emerge from the Pool Seven Jewels in the Pure Land of Sukhavati.They dwell in heaven and refrain from taking meat and wine, but collect the sweet nectar of different flowers and scatter blossoms from the sky to make the world fragrant. With no robes above the waist, they fly in the air in their flowing scarves.The flying celestials at Tun-huang with long silk scarves trailing out gave rise to the 'Scarf Dance'. Their hand and body postures are strongly reminiscent of the Indian style of dancing.

In 568 Emperor Wu-ti of the Northern Wei married a Turk princess of the A-she-na family. The princess brought in her train the musicians of Kucha. Since then we find the music of Kucha, Kashgar, Bukhara and Samarkand in Northern Chou.

'The concupiscent statues of goddesses at Nav Bahar in Bactria established the equation 'ideal beauty: Buddhist image' in the East Iranian world. Even when Buddhism had faded away, early Persian poetry continued to cultivate abstract mental forms poignantly recalling ideas of the grace of Buddhist statues. Ayyuqi writes of his beautiful heroine that 'she was. . . a Buddhist statue in a temple full of offerings'. Further on, we find the crescendo in stanzas 2138-42 where she is addressed as *Bot* (Buddhist statue), then *lo'bat* (statuette), and finally as *nowbahar*, the Buddhist monastery which was well-known for its graceful statues in Iranian literature up to the time of Yaqub in the 13th century. No wonder that the metaphor of the *Bot* 'Buddhist statue' is constant in early Persian poetry.

The Annals of the Sui and T'ang dynasties record Iranian dances and musical instruments. Prosperity flowed into the T'ang capital Ch' ang-an, an international centre of politics, trade and culture, as it was the easternmost terminus of the trans-national Silk Route. Chinese poets speak of citizens of Ch' ang-an enjoying wine served by Barbarian women in the taverns. Some of the finest murals at Tun-huang are of dancing goddesses in the joyous tenderness of their vibrant movements. These dancing angels are Indian for they wear no raiments above the waist. Tun-huang caves show three types of female dresses: the flowing drapery of Chinese ladies, the tight wear of Central Asian beauties and the sensuous elegance of the bare bodies of Indian belles who bid the onlooker to accompany them into worlds of luminous beauty.

In the reign of Kaniṣka, bilateral relations entered a new phase in the economic, political and cultural domains. Kaniṣka as the greatest of Kushan emperors symbolised his international status by the adoption of four titles: Devaputra or Son of Heaven from China, Shaonana Shao or King of Kings from Persia, Kaisara or Caesar from Rome, and Maharaja of India, signifying the imperial dignity of the four superpowers of the time: China, Persia, Rome, and India. He played a major role in the dissemination of Buddhism to China. The policy of cultural internationalism enunciated by Asoka found its prime efflorescence in the reign of Kaniṣka. Hsuan-tsang relates that Kaniṣka defeated the Chinese in Central Asia and Chinese princes were sent as hostages. Territories were allotted to them in Punjab which were known as *Cina-bhukti*, an area that Hsuan-tsang visitied in the 7th century. Now it is a village Chiniyari near Amritsar, and Chiniot from *Cinakota*. The Chinese princes introduced two new fruits to India: The peach and the pear. They came to be known respectively as *cināni* and *cinarājaputra* which means 'Peach the Chinese Princess' and 'Pear the Chinese Prince'.

Paper had been manufactured out of cotton in India, and out of silk in Han China. With the introduction of Buddhism cotton also became a component of paper, as is evident from the old lexicon entitled Ku-chin tzu-ku where the silk radical of the character for paper is replaced by the radical for cotton. Cotton cultivation had been introduced from Kashmir and Bengal to China as early as the second century B.C.

The Yuechi rulers presented Sanskrit texts to the Chinese court in 2 B.C. The first historically owned Buddhist masters arrived in

China in A.D. 67. The Han Emperor Ming-ti dreamt of a golden person. On enquiry from his courtiers he learnt that He was the Buddha. He sent ambassadors to the West (i.e. India) to invite Buddhist teachers. They returned with Dharmarakṣa and Kāśyapa Mātaṅga. They arrived on white horses laden with scriptures and sacred relics. The first Buddhist monastery was built for them on Imperial orders and it came to be known as 'The White Horse Monastery' (Poma-ssu). They wrote 'The Sutra of 42 Sections' to provide a guide to the ideas of Buddhism and to the conduct of monks. This monastery exists to this day and the cenotaphs of the two Indian teachers can be seen in its precincts.

The translation of the first Sanskrit sutra into Chinese is by An Shih-kao in the middle of the second century. He was a Parthian Prince turned Buddhist monk. He had abdicated the throne in favour of his uncle to take up the robes. A number of his translations survive. He founded a school of translation of Sanskrit texts into Chinese, which was hailed by the Chinese literati as 'unrivalled'. Among his associates were *bhiksu*s from Sogdiana (corresponding to modern Samarkand and Bokhara) known as Uttarapatha or 'Northern India' in Chinese historical works. The name of Khang Seng hui from Sogdiana stands out as a master of Sino-Indian literature and as one who preached in South China in a systematic manner. He translated even a short Ramayana into Chinese.

Kumarajiva, born of an Indian father and a Kuchean princess, educated in Kashmir and Kashgar, was a scholar of great reputation. He reached Ch'ang an in 401 and worked till A.D. 412. He translated 106 works into Chinese. Most outstanding is his Chinese translation of the Sanskrit text entitled *Saddharma-pundarika-sutra*, known for short as the Lotus Sutra. He is one of the most outstanding stylists of Chinese prose. He is the only Indian whose Chinese diction has been hailed over the centuries by Chinese men of letters.

The Lotus Sutra is at once a great work of literature and a profound religious classic, containing the core and culmination of Buddha's ageless teaching of compassion and the way to achieve liberation from suffering. For more than fourteen hundred years, it has been a rich source of themes for art. Generations of monks, nuns and lay believers confident in the Sutra's promise of spiritual reward for those who revere it and pay it homage, have made opulent transcriptions of it, fashioned lavishly ornamented caskets for its preservation, and commissioned votive art depicting its narratives and religious teachings. The range of artistic expression inspired by the Lotus Sutra is astonishing.

The Path of the Sutras

This route is first and foremost the pathway of texts and translators, of *sutras* and schools of thought, of the triumphs of Buddhism as the mental and material culture of East Asia. The development of Buddhist temple architecture, new stylistic features in Chinese that arose from translations of Buddhist texts, the Buddhist plurality of inhabited worlds as opposed to the Chinese earth-centred world view, and various elements of cultural transmission, opened up Sinocentrism to wider horizons. The several people inhabiting the route participated in the cultural exchange for a millennium. The earliest and most celebrated of the masters was the Parthian An Shih-kao who organised the first translation team, after his arrival at Loyang in A. D. 148. An Hsuan (A. D. 181), Than ti (A.D. 254), An Fa-hsien, An Fa-chin (A.D. 281-306) are other Parthians who translated Sanskrit works. From Gandhara came Jnanagupta who translated the Avalokiteśvara chapter of the Lotus Sutra (A.D. 561-578).

Kubha or Kabul the capital of modern Afghanistan, sent the largest number of scholars whose Chinese translations are found in the Tripitaka. In A.D. 383, Gautama Sanghadeva arrived at Loyang. Vimalaksa was another teacher of Kabul who was a gereat master of Vinaya. He was a teacher of Kumarajiva at Kucha and he came to China in A.D. 406. Sanghabhuti from Kabul translated three works in A.D. 381-85. In A.D. 404 Punyatara of Kabul translated the Sarvastivada-vinaya, together with Kumarajiva. Buddhayasas (A.D. 403-13), Dharmayasas (A.D. 407-15), Buddhajiva (A.D. 423), Dharmamitra (A.D. 424), Gunavarman (A.D. 431) Buddhatrata, Buddhapala (A.D. 676), Prajna (785-810) were from Kabul who took part in the translation of Vinaya, Vaipulya and other texts. The Chinese monk Chih-yen went to Kabul to obtain Sanskrit texts. He was a companion of Fa-hsien on his journey to India. The brahmana Wu-t'ao of Lampaka (Lamghan in Afghanistan) translated a dharani of Amoghapasa in A.D. 700.

From Udyana or Swat, Vimoksasena came to China in A.D. 541. He was a descendant of the Śākya family of Kapilavastu. Narendrayaśas (A.D. 557-68), Vinitaruci (A.D. 582), Meghaśikha (A.D. 705), Dānapāla (A.D. 980) were from Udyana. Dānapala translated 111 works, which are found in the Tripitaka.

Dharmanandin (A.D. 384) and Mitraśānta (A.D. 705) were monks from Tukhara. I-tsing saw a Tukhara monastery in Eastern India, which had 'been built long before by the people of that country for the accommodation of the Buddhist monks from Tukhara. The monastery was very rich and had an abundant supply of all necessities and comforts of life. No other monastery could surpass it in this respect'.

The Yüeh-chih were the earliest non-Indian translators of Sanskrit texts into Chinese. Lokakṣema came to Loyang in A.D. 164 and worked till A.D. 186, and has left 12 translations including the longer Sukhāvati-vyuha and Akṣobhya-vyuha. He is the third translator of *sutras* after Kāśyapa Mātaṅga and Dharmarakṣa. He was followed by a Yüeh-chih householder Ch'ien in A.D. 220 who taught the heir apparent of the Wu dynasty.

The Tripiṭaka has 49 works by him, which include the Prajñāpāramita of 10,000 verses, the longer Sukhāvatī-vyūha and Vimalakīrti-nirdeśa. The greatest of Yüeh-chih masters is Dharmarakṣa whose family had lived at Tun-huang. He was born around A.D. 230 at Tun-huang. He came to Loyang in A.D. 266. He translated several *sutras* of the Vaipulya class for the first time. Ninety of his works survive in the Tripiṭaka. He was called the 'Bodhisattva from Tun-huang', and he contributed the most in the conversion of China to Buddhism, and made Chang-an the foremost Buddhist centre in China. A tireless itinerant preacher and ingenious translator, he integrated Buddhism in the intellectual and spiritual life and gave China its classics of Maḥayana. He translated the Lotus Sutra for the first time, which later became the most venerated and fundamental scripture. He got Sanskrit manuscripts from Kashmir, Kucha and Khotan. His collaborators included two Kucheans, a Yüeh-chih, a Khotanese, a Sogdian, and Indians. Various nationalities on the Sutra Route climaxed in his person. In A.D. 373 a Yüeh-chih householder Shih-lun translated four works.

The first Kuchean monk who translated *sutras* at the White Horse Monastery in A.D. 257 was Yen. In A.D. 307-312 came Śrimitra who translated the Mahamayuri. Towering over all is Kumarajiva whose translation of the Lotus Sutra is a marvel of transcreation. He translated a number of Prajñāpāramitās. Sanskrit manuscripts used to come to China from Kucha, for instance, the Avaivartika-cakra-sutra was brought to Dharmarakṣa by a Kuchean envoy. Sujiva, a member of the royal house of Kucha, came to China in A.D. 568

and introduced the seven keys of Indian music: sādhārita, kaisika, ṣaḍja-grāma, ṣaḍja, ṣāḍava, pancama, and vṛṣabha.

The Sogdian K'ang Chü translated a *sutra* at Loyang in A.D. 187. In the next decade came another compatriot K'ang Meng-hsiang who translated at Loyang six works, including a life of the Buddha, in A.D. 194-99. Half-a-century later K'ang Sang-k'ai Saṅghavarman translated some works at the White Horse Monastery in Loyang in A.D. 252. K'ang Seng-hui, the eldest son of the prime minister of Sogdiana, came to the capital of the Wu kingdom in A.D. 241. In 251 he began his work of translation. In A.D. 396 K'ang Tao-ho translated a *sutra*, which is lost.

I-tsing gives a bio-sketch of Saṅghavarman of Sogdiana who came to China around A.D. 656. He was ordered by Emperor Kao-tsung to go on a pilgrimage to India. In Chinese texts Sogdiana is a part of northern India, Uttarapatha in Sanskrit, or its Chinese translation 'Northern Route' which extended from NW India up to Sogdiana. This usage was common in India and China. Northern India in Chinese texts refers to NW India and regions beyond, in fact to the dominions of the erstwhile Kushan empire or Kusansahr.

While the Sogdians and their language has disappeared, European expeditions have discovered fragments of Sogdian texts near Tun-huang and in the Turfan depression. They reflect Chinese Buddhist literature from which they are predominantly translated. Majority of the translations date from the T'ang dynasty's domination in Central Asia (about A.D. 650-750).

I-tsing speaks of the nobility and purity of the monk Ch'ang-min in the following words: ' He sacrificed his life for the good of others. He was pure like a mirror, he was priceless like the jade of Khotan'. Khotan was famed in China for its jade and sutras. In the eloquent panegyric of Visa Samgrama Khotan is called *Ratna-janapada*, 'The Land of Jade'. Chu Shih-hsing, the first Chinese to leave his country in quest of sutras, chose to journey to Khotan, famous for Sanskrit originals. He undertook this arduous journey in A.D. 260 and succeeded in locating the Sanskrit text of the Prajnaparamita in 25,000 verses. He had a copy made at Khotan. In 282 he sent his Khotanese disciple Punyadhana together with the Sanskrit manuscript to China. Written on birch bark leaves it was preserved in a Chinese monastery till the sixth century. In 291 the Khotanese Moksala and the Indian layman Chu Shu-lan started its translation. It was given the title Fang Kuang Ching 'the sutra of the emission of light'. True to its name, it was to play a dominant role in the formation of Buddhist thought in East Asia. In A.D. 296 the Khotanese Gitamitra arrived at Ch'ang-an with a copy of the same scripture. In A.D. 401 the Chinese pilgrim Fa-hsien spent three months at Khotan and speaks of the flourishing community of Mahayana. In the beginning of the fifth century Chih Fa-ling found the text of a shorter recension of the Avatamsaka sutras at Khotan. It was translated by Buddhabhadra in A.D. 422. In AD 689-91, the Khotanese monk Devaprajna translated six works. Siksananda of Khotan rendered several works, of which 16 are found in the Tripitaka. Empress Wu Tso-t'ien (684-705) sent a special envoy to Khotan for the Sanskrit text of the Avatamsaka and took part in its translation along with Siksananda for five years (A.D. 695-99). In A.D. 721 Chih-yen, a son of the king of Khotan, translated four works. Khotan was in the forefront of the transmission of Sanskrit sutras to China.A bilingual Sanskrit-Khotanese conversation roll, the only one of its kind, was discovered at Tun-huang. The conversation has the following sentences:

> 'Have you equipment for the road or not?'
> 'I do not like equipment for the road. A horse or two and I shall go.'
> 'Have you books or not?'
> 'I have some.'
> 'What is the book?'
> 'Sutra. Abhidharma, Vinaya, Vajrayana.'
> 'Among these what book (i.e. title) is there?'

This conversational piece is a clear indication of the frequent transmission of Sanskrit sutras from Khotan in China.

The standard Chinese expression for travelling monks means that they went primarily 'to obtain the doctrine'. The oldest Sanskrit manuscript of the Lotus Sutra in existence today, the so-called Kashgar manuscript, is a manuscript from Khotan and it has a colophon in the Khotanese language giving the names of donors. History lives. We also know that Hyecho, a famous Korean monk of Silla returned from India via Ansi near Tun-huang in A.D. 723.

Khotan established its hegemony over the southern Central Asian states in the first century A.D. by breaking the power of Yarkand (So-chu) and extended its authority up to Kashgar. Yarkand is mentioned in the Kasika commentary on the Sanskrit grammar of Panini. It had brilliant academic traditions. Kumarajiva was initiated into Mahayana by Suryasoma, the royal prince of Yarkand. Kumarajiva confessed that when he studied the Hinayana texts he considered stone to be wonderful and had not recognised gold.

Tao-an, the great master of 'Fundamental Non-being' (pen-wu), was fully conversant with the concepts of emptiness versus phenomenal existence, or the relation between 'Absolute Truth' and 'Worldly Truth' as expounded in the Prajnaparamita. It reminds us of the convergence of the spiritual and the secular, or better their symbiosis, in the ideas of President Ikeda-san. They are the live hues of sensibility of the dawning century of an open society. Tao-an used to explain the entire text of Moksala's *Fang-kuang ching* twice a year at Ch'ang-an. To enable him to complete and correct his understanding on many points, he obtained a Sanskrit original of the Astasahasrika from Turfan in A.D. 382. Turfan introduced systematisation of Abhidharma, till then unknown in China. The king of Turfan sent his royal priest and Abhidharma-expert Kumarabodhi to Ch'ang-an in A.D. 382, as a member of a tribute mission to the Chinese court. The pilgrim I-tsing mentions two monks of Turfan. Pi-an and Chih-an, who boarded a ship to India. They fell sick on board and died.

China has many grottoes that rival Ajanta in their synthesis of Indian suppleness, Hellenic elegance and Chinese grace. The Yun-kang Caves were excavated between 414 and 520 under Wei rulers. Fifty three caves remain till this day and contain over 51,000 statues. It is one of the largest groups of stone cave temples in China. After the first Wei capital, Tatung, was transferred to Loyang in 494 work commenced on Lungmen. Sculpting went on for 400 years till the Tang dynasty. It has around 100,000 statues; the highest is 55 feet high. It is a treasure-house of China's heritage of sculpture.

Mogao Caves

On the ancient Han frontiers, in the vast deserts of Inner Asia lies the sandy city of Tung-huang, the 'Blazing Beacon'. In this tiny oasis are the sacred grottos of Chien Fo Tung or 'Caves of the Thousand Buddhas', carved into a rocky cliff rising aside a meandering rivulet. The walls of these Caves are covered by murals of surpassing beauty, with the largest array of authentic paintings extending over several dynasties: a task of sixteen centuries. It has ever been the sacred oasis, one of the glories of Buddhism. A stone tablet of the Tang dynasty states that the first 'Cave of Unequalled Height' (Mogao-ku) was constructed by an Indian monk in 366 A.D., increasing up to 460 caves as faith continued to inspire radiant visions.

The Sutra Route is an age-old witness to the mingling of many ancient cultures of the Chinese, Iranians, Tokharians, Graeco-Romans, and Indians. The outstanding achievements of manking are strewn along this path which culminates at Tun-huang, with its golden sands and blue skies. The first town was established here as a midway stop of the travel route in the first century B.C. at the time of the Han dynasty. It has seen Chang Ch'ien the Han ambassador to befriend the tribes of the west, Hsuan-tsang the prince of pilgrims to procure sutras, Marco Polo on his return to Europe, and others too many to specify. Ancient ballads tell the sad and lonesome life of Chinese soldiers on these remote borders of the west. The prosperity and stability of the country under Emperor Wu (A.D. 265-290) favoured the development of international trade and cultural exchange with improved agricultural teahniques and irrigation. In the middle of the third century it became a main commercial centre with a mixed Chinese and barbarian population.

At the grottos of Tun-huang Paul Pelliot went through 16,000 manuscripts crouched in a tiny space, working by the light of a candle or in his own words, 'a philologist travelling at the speed of a racing car'. He selected all the rolls that were of any importance for their contents or for their antiquity authenticated by dated colophons. The Pelliot Collection at Paris is a repository of historical data that will be under investigation for another century. Local legends in Central Asia claim that three hundred towns lie buried beneath the desert with great treasures protected by demons. The number 300 reminds of the *tri-ratna* of Buddhism. The Buddhist past of Serindia obliterated by the onslaught of Islam and abandoned to the all-devouring sand is being brought to light by a devoted band of scholars in the world. The hand-written notes of Pelliot have been translated into Chinese at the Tun-huang Institute: such is their importance. The photographs of the chapel interiors taken by the Pelliot Mission have formed the principal basis for the international study of Tun-huang art.

Tun-huang was the occidental bastion of China, the gateway to the Indo-Iranian and Roman worlds. It was the sentinel of a trail whence China gave the pear and peach to India, orange, rose, peony and chrysanthemum to the West. The first ever moveable printing types were found by Pelliot at Tun-huang and are dated by him to about 1300. The discovery is so momentous that even *Webster's New International Dictionary* records it under the entry 'Type'. Paul Pelliot's *Notes on Marco Polo* are a mine of information on historical geography and on the etymologies of place-names which reveal lost dimensions. For instance Bokhara, with its modem Turkman form Buhara, is derived from Sanskrit *vihāra* through its Sogdian, Uighur and Monogolian form *buqar*. It was a city whose skyline was dominated by the spires of Buddhist monasteries and hence this name. The city retained its sanctity and importance even after Islamisation. It was here that the first of the seven Sunni Imams, known as Imam Bukhari (810-70), was born in the 9th century. His collection of 7,000 hadith constitute the *Sahih* or true compilation which is regarded as the most authentic book of traditions by the Sunnis, held sacred only next to the Quran. What a dissembling coincidence that the Imam of Delhi is Imam Bukhari.

Divine musical instruments are played to which heavenly angles or apsaras dnace in Sukhavati the resplendent Western Paradise of Amitabha. The flying goddesses from cave 321, which belongs to the golden age of Early Tang (618-741 A.D.) are unique. The sensuous tenderness of the body, the delicate flowing lines of drapery, the joyous colours, garments vibrating with the rhythm of space, mirror the vigorous culture of Serindia. Bearing in their hands trays of fruits and flowers, arrested as it were in their stately flight for a moment, they seem to bid the onlooker to accompany them into worlds of luminous beauty.

Ch'an Buddhism

Ch'an was carried to China by Bodhidharma, the youngest son of a king of Kanchi and a follower of Prajnatara's eminent line. Palmleaves inscribed by Prajnatara have survived in Japan. Bodhidharma reached China early in the sixth century after long peregrinations. He had an audience with the noted patron of Buddhism, Emperor Liang Wu-ti (502-550) of South China. He pointed out to the Emperor the futility of establishing monasteries, copying *sutras* and supporting monks. The historicity of Bodhidharma has been controversial. The first mention of Kanchi is in the 'Record of the Transmission of the Lamp' compiled in 1002.

The Ch'an tradition says that their doctrine was transmitted by an uninterrupted succession of twenty-eight Indian patriarchs. Bodhidharma handed down the doctrine to Hui-k'o (traditional dates : 487-593), and from him through four other Chinese patriarchs to Hui-neng (639-716). Bodhidharma finally transmitted the 'Seal of Mind' to Hui-k'o, who had cut off his arm to express the deep sincerity of his resolve. In the Kozanji ink scroll of the Six Patriarchs of the Bodhidharma lineage, Hui-k'o kneels down in front of him. Blood gushes forth from the stump of his left arm, and the knife and the cut-off arm lie next to him on the ground. According to late accounts Bodhidharma crossed the Yangtze on a reed, and spent nine years in meditation in front of a rock wall at the Shao-lin monastery.

Bodhidharma had said that Tao-fu had acquired the skin, the nun Tsung-ch'ih the flesh, and Tao-yu the bone, and that Hui-k'o had penetrated into the marrow (the essence) of the doctrine. Like this statement, mist surrounds the evolution of the legend of Bodhidharma, which is as controversial as he himself must have been in life. The tradition is consistent in pointing out that he was a prince of Kanchi. His association with Tamil-speaking Kanchi is confirmed by the Japanese form of his name : Bodai-daruma, shortened to Daruma. The Tamil form is Bodi-daruma. A modern painting at the Kanchi seminar on Dhyana and Tantric Buddhism held on 10-15 March 1986, had the caption *Bodi-daruma*. The Japanese name *Daruma* goes back to an ancient popular name of the master. Moreover, the tradition that the doctrine was transmitted from Mahakasyapa to Bodhidharma appears to have a basis. It seems that the modern Kacchapesvara Temple at Kanchi was a Buddhist sanctum in ancient times dedicated to Mahakasyapa the first patriarch of Dhyana Buddhism. To this day there are some Buddhist sculptures in this temple. The tradition of twenty-eight patriarchs of Dhyana Buddhism is of Indian origin.

There are three basic scriptures of Ch'an (i) Lankavatara-sutra (ii) Vajracchedika Prajna-paramita and (iii) the Hymn to Nilakantha Lokesvara. Bodhidharma took Gunabhadra's translation of the Lankavatara-sutra as the scripture, as it was the only available Chinese version at the time.

The 'Record of the Succession of the Dharma-treasure', a history of Ch'an Buddhism discovered from the Tun-huang Caves, says that the first patriarch of the Lankavatara as representing the Dharma-treasure was Bodhidharma who revealed the inner meaning of the Sutra. The connection of Bodhidharma and Lankavatara is thus intimate. Lankavatara can refer to Kanchi. It is stated in the life of Hsuan-tsang by Hui-li: 'Kanchipura is the sea-port of South India for Ceylon, the voyage to which takes three days'. Further, subtle nuances point to Kanchi as the native place of Bodhidharma and as the home of Ch'an. The tea ceremony ends with the banging of the lid on to the teapot. When I enquired of my Japanese host, Prof. Chikyo Yamamoto, he said: 'Master Bodhidharma used to slam the lid in times of yore'. How Indian! I was sure once again: It must go back to Bodhidharma.

Ch'an adepts reject the written word and claim an unwritten doctrine, transmitted from mind to mind, where the heart of man directly sees into its own nature. Yet, when Hui-neng was invested as the Sixth Patriarch, the corridor was painted with scenes from the Lankavatara, besides the paintings of the Five Patriarchs Transmitting the Robe of Bodhidharma and the Dharma as a testimony for future generations. Bodhidharma had sanctioned the lineage of five Chinese Patriarchs of Ch'an in a *gatha* that ran: 'one flower with five petals is unfolded'.

In its earlier phases Ch'an Buddhists were mainly a kind of Lankavatara sect. The teachings of pratyatma-gati-gocara of the Lankavatara provide a philosophical basis for the transcendental intution of Ch'an . In the Lankavatara Buddha tells Mahamati to attain a state of inner realisation (pratyatma-gocara) and when one has pratyatma-jnana one is enlightened. The Lankavatara is unique in emphasising that life is experiencing truth: seeing must be living and living seeing. The Lankavatara certifies the existence of the Buddha-mind in each of us and provides Ch'an its doctrinal base. The Lankavatara forbids meat-eating and recounts eight reasons for abstaining from meat. To take the lives of animals and eat their flesh is like eating our own. Eating meat is spiritual pollution. To this day, food in Ch'an monasteries is vegetarian. While Ch'an stands on its own, the Lankavatara confirms it and is also its philosophical essence.

The Lankavatara was highly philosophical and abstruse to the Chinese. During the time of the Sixth Patriarch Hui-neng the emphasis shifted to the Vajracchedika which was more understandable than the recondite Lankavatara. Besides meditation, painting was the other forte of Ch'an. Prajnaparamita lent itself admirably to the tenor of Ch'an painting. Th Ch'an masters of Mid Tang were distinguished by their non-conformist techniques of painting. Wang Mo 'Ink Wang' painted landscapes starting from configurations of ink splashes, the manner of Ch'an painters who delighted in expressing their sincerity in trans-logical forms like a 'one stroke' Bodhidharma (Jap. Ippitsu Daruma by Shokai Reiken 1315-1396). The dictum *rupam eva sunyata sunyata eva rupam* of the Vajracchedika inspired Ch'an art which vanished into nowhere, with its diaphanous water colours and empty spaces interfering with the coherence of thought and form. A painting shimmered in meditation. Ch'an was deeply steeped in the Prajnaparamita philosophy of sunyata.

Protection of the State

The Mahaprajnaparamita-sutra is called 'the king of *sutras* which protect the state'. Sutras have been copied, chanted and expounded with the belief that the merit of these acts would stop calamities in the state and secure peace and security.

The fifth chapter of the Jen wang ching is entitled 'protecting the country'. Tathagata says : 'You, sixteen Great Kings, must practise the Rite of Protecting the Country, and you must keep, read and explain this *sutra*. If in future ages the kings of countries wish to protect their kingodms and to protect their own bodies, they too must act in the same way'.

The Tang dynasty established an extensive empire and under it Buddhism reached its apogee by the induction of Vajrayana texts. The grandeur of their ritual ensured unprecedented popularity in the Imperial household, in the great families of the realm as well as among common people. Sutras were used for 'the benefit and advantage of the state'. The logistic problems involved in distant military campaigns in Central Asia were resolved with success through Vajrayana rituals. It would suffice to cite the strategic military role of Vajrayana rituals of Vaisravana who was venerated in China and Japan as a god of war. Amoghavajra gives a *dharani* entitled 'Dharani of Devaraja of the north, Vaisramana, who watches over armies for protecting the Dharma' : if one pronounces this *dharani* before an image of Vaisravana—which represents the Devaraja under his terrible aspect,. . . he sends his third son Nada to the side of those who direct their troops for the protection of their country; or still, if one covers the armour plate of his image with the powder of gold and offers him perfumes, flowers and other offerings while pronouncing the *dharani* a hundred thousand times, he himself takes the command of his celestial troops and goes to support his devotee, to whom he assures victory; or furthermore, if one recites non-stop day and night he delegates his heir-prince Dokken at the head of celestial troops; or still one can suspend his image on a staff and carry it as a banner fifteen paces in front of the army which will render the enemy ineffectual.

The Vaisravana-kalpa by Amoghavajra, specifically consecrated to Nada, adds in the colophon that during the 'grand troubles of the Five Kingdoms', one tried in vain during eight months all sorts of other ceremonies. Only the rite prescribed in this text proved efficacious for stabilising the country. It refers to the troubles which burst forth in Central Asia at the end of the reign of Hsuan-tsung during the Tang dynasty and by the 'Five Kingdoms' are intended the five foreign people who besieged the city of Anhsi. The incident is reported in details in the 'Ritual of Vaisravana' by Amoghavajra:

> In AD 742, the Five Kingdoms of Seiban—Tibet, Daiseki] Arabs, Koko, Sogdians—and others besieged the city of Anhsi. On the second day of the second moon, a report was presented to the Emperor demanding relief troops. The Emperor said to master I-hsing: 'Master! the city of Anhsi is besieged by Arabs and others and it requires troops. But as it is situated at a distance of 12,000 leagues, it will take eight months for my troops to arrive there and I do not know what to do'. I-hsing replied: 'Why does Your Majesty not invoke to your aid the Devaraja of the north, Vaisravana, with his celestial troops'.—'How can I invoke him?'—'By the intervention of the Serindian monk Amoghavajra'.—The Emperor sent word to this monk who invited him to provide an incense-burner and follow him to the monastery. The monk pronounced a dharani from the Jen wang ching (tr. by Amoghavajra) 27 times. The emperor then saw hundreds of soldiers in arms and the monk explained to him that they were the troops of Dokken the second son of Vaisravana, who had come to take charge before departure for Anhsi. In the fourth month he received a report from Anhsi, declaring that, on the very day of the ceremony they saw appearing in the north-east of the city, the envelopings of an obscure haze, of giants dressed in armour plates of gold. They heard an uproar of drums and of horns, and experienced a

violent trembling of the earth. The troops of the Five Kingdoms, frightened, retired to their camps, where rats of gold gnawed the strings of their bows and of their traps. A voice in the sky enjoined to spare the old and the feeble, who could not flee away. Then Vaisravana manifested himself in person on the northern gate of the city. They drew his image which was appended to the report addressed to the Emperor.

The first T'ang Emperor Kao-tsu (A.D. 618-627) received from Fu Yi his seventh memorial in A.D. 626 requesting a ban on Buddhism. His Councillor P'ei Chi reminded him :

> O your Majesty! formerly when you raised the righteous armies, you promised before the Three Jewels that you would open the doors of the profound school (Buddhism) if you were enthroned. Now, the world has come under your benevolent administration and you possess the wealth of the four seas (i.e. world). If you want to accept the words of [Fu] Yi, it will affect your past virtues and foster what is evil in you.

Thus, profundity of Buddhism lay embedded into the very foundations of the T'ang state. A natural consequence was the quest for Tantric texts in India and elsewhere, their translation into Chinese and the efficacious utilisation of their ritual. It led to the progressive development and continuous spread of Tantras in China, spurred on by periodic Chinese reverses in Central Asia.

In A.D. 629, or the first month of the third regnal year of Emperor Tai Tsung (A.D. 627-649), an Imperial edict ordered Buddhist monks to recite the Jen wang ching in the national capital on the 27th of every month to pray for the welfare of the nation. The government undertook to supply all the materials for the ceremonies.

Armies, manuscripts and scholars were allies in China. In the beginning of the seventh century after a military expedition to Champa, the Chinese army returned with a rich booty of 1,350 Buddhist manuscripts among other things. They were all of Indian origin.

During the T'ang dynasty Indian astronomers served on the Imperial Board for the purpose. Three Indian astronomical schools of Gautama, Kāśyapa and Kumara were known at Ch'ang-an in the seventh century. More accurate calendars were prepared anew by

Indian astronomers. Sanskrit mathematical works were translated into Chinese which are lost.

In the seventh and eighth centuries, scientific works were known as 'brahmana books' in China. Books with the prefix 'brahmana' dealt with astronomy, calendrical science and mathematics. Unfortunately, since all were subsequently lost, one cannont now estimate what they contributed. It is certain, however, that during these two centuries brahmana scholars were employed in the Astronomical Bureau at the Chinese capital. Kasyapa Hsiao-wei, who was there shortly after A.D. 650, was occupied with the improvement of the calendar, as were most of his later Indian successors. The greatest of them was Gautama Siddha who became President of the Board. It seems that these brahmanas brought an early form of trigonometry, a technique which was then developing in India.

Though most of their writings failed to survive, something more should be said here of these Indian astronomers and calendar-experts of the Sui and T'ang. The story begins with the books of brahmana astronomy such as the P'o-lo-men Tien Wen Ching, mentioned in the Sui Shu bibliography, but long lost. These must have been circulating about A.D. 600. During the following two centuries we meet with the names of a number of brahmana astronomers resident at the Chinese capital.

The first was Gautama Lo, who produced two calendar systems in A.D. 697 and 698, but the greatest was Gautama Siddha who compiled the Khai-Yuuan Chan Ching about A.D. 729, in which a zero symbol and other innovations appeared. It is a work of great importance often mentioned. In any case the paradox remains that we owe to the brahmana Gautama Siddha the greatest collection of ancient and medieval Chinese astronomical fragments.

Vajrayana masters, Subhakara, Vajrabodhi and Amoghavajra, arrived in China and translated the major texts of their school into Chinese during the reign of Emperor Hsuan-tsung. Hence it is important to evalute the varied dimensions of his glorious rule.

Himself a poet, the Emperor welcomed poets like Li Po (701-762), and Tu Fu (712-770). Existing forms of poetry were brought to the highest perfection in the period. The T'ang dynasty was to be most famous for its poetry 'Poets and painters contributed to the elegance of his magnificent court ceremonial'. The T'ang lyric poetry was inspired by the cosmic reverie of Taosim and the universal impermanence of earthly things, evoked by Buddhism. It is very apparent in the poems of Li Po. A clear prose style of the essayists developed. 'New forms of sentences make their appearance in prose writing, with new pictures and similes brought from India through the medium of Buddhist translations'.

In the domain of painting lay the principal achievement of T'ang. The six fundamental laws of painting laid down by painter Hsieh Ho were drawn from the Indian sadanga canons. Central Asian monks were continually pouring into China as decorators of Buddhist temples. The famous T'ang painter Wu Tao-tzu was strongly influenced by Central Asian techniques. As a pious Buddhist he painted pictures for temples. In such an environment the mandalas must have been welcome as new visual types of a complex and hence advanced idiom in Buddhist painting. Sculptures in stone and bronze, excellent fabrics, finest lacquer, high quality porcelain had the active encouragement of the Emperor.

The blue and white jar of Emperor Xuande who ruled China from 1426 to 1435. It has a Sanskrit *mantra*, all over, as well as at its bottom. The visible portion reads:
hrim kham
divā svarti svastī madhyandine
am hrim kham

The administration was strong, and schools were established in every village. Fond of music, the Emperor founded a music school in 714 to train musicians in the fashionable foreign-influenced music. The Emperor selected an elite of 300 best musicians and trained them personally in the Agreeable Spring Court of the imperial Pear Garden. The Emperor is honoured as the patron saint of the theatre. The members of the Left Chiao Fang school were dancers, those of the Right were singers. The Buddhist scenes of song and dance at Tun-huang evoke memories of foreign dancers who are bare on the upper portion of the body: 'Women ceased to veil themselves as of old'.

A few hundred Indian teachers went to China from the first to the twelfth century. They have bequeathed a legacy of about 3,000 works translated from Sanskrit into Chinese. We may mention a couple of them: Gunavarman, a prince of Kashmir who reached Nanking in A.D. 431; Buddhabhadra, born at Nagarahara, claimed direct descent from Amrtodana, the uncle of Lord Buddha. Nagarahara is modern Jalalabad. He died in China in 429. Bodhiruci was from south India. A Chinese envoy came to the Chalukya court in A.D. 692 to invite Bodhiruci. He reached China in 693 by sea and translated Sanskrit works. One of the last outstanding Indian teachers in China was Dharmadeva of Nalanda. He was received by the Chinese Emperor in 973.

The Chinese pilgrims to India like Fa-hsien, Hsuan-tsang, Wang Hsuan-tso, I-tsing, and others have bequeathed historic records which are invaluable for the understanding of the cultural and political history of India. I-tsing has left short bio-sketches of 60 eminent Chinese monks who visited India. In 964, three hundred Chinese monks started for India, to pay Imperial homage to the holy places. They set up five Chinese inscriptions at Bodhgaya. One of the inscriptions ends :

> I now make use of the eulogy of the marvellous excellence of the three bodies and the sculptures that I have executed of the extraordinary acts of the Thousand Buddhas, in order to secure the prosperity of the glorious sovereign of my country and to offer to him for many years a holy longevity.

Edouard Chavannes brought to light these five Chinese inscriptions at Bodhgaya, the only ones in India. They were erected in the 10th and 11th centuries to pay Imperial homage of China to the holy places of India in moving language. Unswallowed by devastating centuries, they are with us still : alas! cenotaphs to the splendid creativity of a millennium smothered by fundamentalism. Chavannes translated into French the lives and voyages of over sixty Chinese pilgrims to India written by I-tsing. His translation of the voyage of Song-yun to Udyana and Gandhara (518-22) and of the itinerary of Wu-k'ong (751-90) are primary sources for Indian history. For wider dissemination they deserve to be translated into English. The four volumes of his *Cinq cents contes et apologues*, running to over 1600 pages, are a treasury of Indian story literature, extracted from the Chinese Tripitaka. It is a *sine qua non* for the history of our literature and for our folklore. Like several other French classics on Indology and allied disciplines, it needs to be done into English.

Indian scholars were honoured guests as late as the Ming. Pandita Sahajasri led a twelve-member Indian Buddhist delegation to China. He was received tby the Yuan and Ming emperors in 1363 and 1371. He was from a ksatriya family of Kapilavastu. His status and privilege placed him in a position to soften the autocratic temper of the emperor. Recently a blue and white jar of the Xuande period (1426-1435) has been discovered with Sanskrit mantras all around : *diva svasti svasti madhyandine...* It seeks good fortune by day, by midday, by night: at all times.

The long and time-honoured contacts have been mature time, reverberating in a subtle interweave of thought, ritual, legend and art. They are symbolic of the deeps of hearts that have never been too subtle for habitation. India and China were linked by a route of thought, the way of cultural exchange, the Sutra Route and not only the Silk Route. Ideas, impirium and emporia; intellectuals, generals and traders; monks, marshals and merchants; cassocks, armour and silk were all pilgrims on this route bringing together many races in companionship. Fabrics, fruits, vegetables, and technologies enriched life. This spirit of an 'open society' was the bridge of dreams floating under an open sky.

Re-discovering Cultural Heritage Through Studies on Local Religion

TAM WAI LUN

Asian culture consists of two foci—the Chinese and the Indian. They are the oldest and most influential civilisations in Asia. Both cultures have their own indigenous religious traditions, the study of which has been dominated by a Western origin of the whole discipline of religious studies, and bears a deep imprint of Western religious mentality, especially that of Christianity. A normative west European Christian viewpoint of religion is that monotheism is an absolute value; the locus of a religion is in its sacred texts and its focus is on faith and ecclesiastical structure. It also involves an understanding that the goal of religion is transcendence. The forcing of such Western assumptions and categories on non-Western traditions may artificially create labels that do not correspond to observable reality. Classic examples are 'Hinduism' in Indian and the 'three religions' in China.

When Belgian scholar Thierry Verhelst interviewed an Indian intellectual from Tamil Nadu, he recorded the following interchange:

> Q: Are you a Hindu?
> A: No, I grew critical of it because of casteism... Actually, you should not ask people if they are Hindu. This does not mean much. If you ask them what their religion is, they will say, 'I belong to this caste.'[1]

In this connection, Wilfred Cantwell Smith goes so far as to use 'false conceptualization' to describe the inadequacy of the term Hinduism to represent the richness of Indian religious tradition.[2] What Smith means is that in postulating Indian religion as a single religious tradition known as Hinduism, we distort the complexity and diversity of the Indian religion. The term 'Hindu' is the Persian variant of the Sanskrit *sindhu*, referring to the Indus River, and as such was used by the Persians to denote the people of that region.

Although the use of the term by Hindus themselves can be found as early as the 15th and 17th centuries, the description of Indian religion as Hinduism is a Western-inspired abstraction. Applying a postcolonial point of view, a scholar like Richard King has argued that the homogenisation of Indian religions under the rubric of Hindusim characterised by essentialism was a modern construct contributed by Western colonisation and was heavily informed by the Judeo-Christian presuppositions of Orientalists and missionaries.[3] The construct was subsequently adopted by Hindu nationalists in their quest for home rule (*swaraj*) and in response to British imperial hegemony. This modern construction of Indian religion, under the influence of Protestantism with its emphasis on scriptures, tends to locate the core of Indian religiosity in certain Sanskrit texts. The result is a double process of textualisation and Westernisation of Indian religion. Romila Thapar has described the process aptly:

> (New form of organization or syndicated Hinduism) seeks historicity for the incarnations of its deities, encourages the idea of a centrally sacred book, claims monotheism as significant to the worship of deity, acknowledges the authority of the ecclesiastical organization of certain sects as prevailing over all and has supported large scale missionary work and conversion.[4]

Modern construction of a unified Hinduism, supported by the scholarly brāhmana caste, focuses upon the Sanskritic and brahmanical forms of Indian religion, the high culture of the brahmins. It represents the triumph of universalised, brahmanical forms of religion over the tribal and the local. There is an obvious tendency to emphasize Vedic and brahmanical texts and beliefs as central and fundamental to the essence of Hinduism. Attention is also drawn specifically to various brahmanical schools of the Vedanta, the Advaita Vedanta, that generated an intellectual and textually based Hinduism, which is then read back into India's religious history to represent the whole of Indian religion. Other prototypical features of Hinduism as a single religion include the worship of deities such as Śiva, Krsna, and Ganesa, temple worship, the practice of *puja* and brahmanical concepts of *dharma, samsara, karma, advaita*, etc. But as pointed out by Ferro-Luzzi, 'The prototype of a Hindu might be a person, who worships the above deities, visits temples, goes on a pilgrimage and believes in the above concepts. Undoubtedly, such persons exist but they are only a minority.[5]

To see Indian religion as 'Hinduism', that is, as a unified all-embracing and independent religious entity with its origin in the Vedas, therefore, may err in two ways. First, it may distort the complexity and religious diversity of Indian religious culture. Second, the oral and popular aspects of Indian religious tradition as well as the non-brahmanical and non-Vedic elements are ignored. We pay due respect to the reinterpretation of the Indian religious tradition by outstanding Indian figures who had reinterpreted them precisely towards the direction of a unified, all-embracing and independent whole since the second half of the 19th century.[6] We, however, make a call to represent more accurately the heterogeneity of human experience and to open up new directions of research on not only the Indian religion but also the Chinese religion to which we now turn our attention.

In a similar fashion to Thierry Verhelst's interview, Valerie Hansen has observed:

> I had assumed Chinese people would categorize their own religious beliefs much as we did...All Chinese, I had reasoned would similarly be Buddhist, Taoist, or Confucian. To my surprise, none of the people I met identified themselves as such. And, as far as I could tell, they all attended the same Buddhist, Taoist, and popular religious temples.[7]

The earliest reference to the idea of three teachings is attributed to Li Shiqian, a prominent Chinese scholar of the 6th century, who wrote,'Buddhism is the sun, Taoism the moon, and Confucianism the five planets.'[8] To represent Chinese religion as the 'three religions' is, however, Western-inspired, There is no traditional Chinese linguistic equivalent of the word religion. The now standard translation *zongjiao* was borrowed first by Christian missionaries from the 19th century Japanese translation in the beginning of the 20th century. Late 16th and 17th century Jesuit missionaries created an image of Chinese religion based on the concept of three teachings, an image which has since dominated the Western perception of Chinese religion. As noted by Jordan Paper, the three religions do not apply to the dominant mode of Chinese religiosity involving most religious behaviour: the state, clan, and family sacrificial complex going back well over four millennia.[9] To subsume several thousand years of Chinese religious experience under the term of 'three religions', *sanjiao*, in effect excludes the vast majority of

Chinese religious behaviour. In reality, only a few elites oriented their lifestyles to the Buddhist or Taoist concepts of transcendence. An overemphasis on the intellectual and spiritual world of the scholarly official, the gentry and the literate elite overlooks the religious practices and beliefs of the ordinary people, the peasants and the labourers who make up the majority of the Chinese population.

By pointing out that there has been a domination by a normative paradigm of religion based upon contemporary Western understandings of the Judeo-Christian tradition in the studies of both Indian and Chinese religions is not to promote a xenophobic ideology. To go beyond a Christian missionary interpretation of both Indian and Chinese religions that perpetuates Eurocentric values is to broaden the range of our understanding and appreciation of both religious traditions. It also parallels a post-structuralist agenda of looking beyond images of homogeneity and univocality in the study of humankind. By expanding our horizon from globalised, highly abstract and univocal systems of thought, to domestic, localised, oral and non-elite mentalities, we are striving to represent more accurately the heterogeneity of human experience. The proper acknowledgement of the heterogeneity of Indian and Chinese religions opens up the possibility of new direction in scholarship and overcomes the cultural and political elitism supported by homogenising and hegemonic discourses. For these reasons, we call for a re-discovering of our cultural heritage.

Rather than explicitly discussing methodology, this study presents an approach through the example of the study itself. The approach we take may be called a local approach that seeks to look at Chinese religion in and on its own terms and for its own sake, apart from Western categories and logic and not from a pan-nation approach. The following is an attempt to reconstruct Chinese religion from the perspective of such an approach.

A Village Based Analysis

The basic unit in Chinese society is the village. Despite modernisation, this structure of villages remains. In 1991, there were 479 cities in China which represent 12.7 per cent of the whole area of China. In other words most of China today belongs to a village setting. About 73.63 per cent of the Chinese population still lives in villages. The village, therefore, remains the proper context to describe any aspect of Chinese civilisation. Based on the recent fieldwork study by my research partner John Lagerwey and myself in three adjacent provinces in South China,[10] I will show how a different picture of Chinese religion emerges when we adopt a local approach and study it without the label of three religions.

Local History and Lineages[11]

We must distinguish two kinds of villages in China. The administrative village, divided by the modern Chinese government today, is composed of two or more natural villages which had developed naturally over history. Each natural village may consist of one or more lineages with which our study must begin. In the past, a group of villages formed a circumscription, *bao*, which sometimes corresponds to today's administrative village. All these terms changed constantly over time. The basic unit is a group of natural villages which usually occupy a valley. At the confluence of two streams at the valley's water exit, there is often an earth god mound or a temple guarding the water exit. As a rule, all lineages in the villages of South China were immigrants from the North. Most claimed to have come during the Song dynasty in the 10th century, but their lineage genealogy records trace them back only to the Ming dynasty in the 13th century. Their lineage foundation legends follow a pattern and always have to do with geomancy. The first settler of the lineage, usually a scholarly official, passing by the area, sometimes during his official trip to the South, was attracted by the good geomancy and decided to settle down. Sometimes the carrying pole broke when the migrating lineages entered the area during their search for new settlement spaces. In other cases, the founder of the lineage received instructions in a dream from a local deity to settle down while he passed by the area.

The foundation legends of lineages arriving after others have settled usually take the form of herding ducks. A lineage founder could be a servant of the other already settled lineage and, led by the prodigious laying of eggs by the ducks, an indication of good geomancy, the founder built the first hut on the site from where the lineage developed. The site might also later become the ancestral hall for the lineage. Another oft-encountered story was that the founder of the lineage came as an indentured servant on whom a geomancer took pity because a wealthy employer had slighted him. The geomancer then told the founder the best site to build his first hut. The lineage therefore later developed into a strong lineage because of good geomancy. The ancestral hall built for the lineage founder and other ancestors is an importat focus of religious culture in Chinese villages. Since ancestor worship has already been well documented, we will turn our attention to other less studied aspects like local village gods.[12]

Village Gods

When we come to the religion of the village, local gods dominate the scene.[13] Based on field observation, Lagerwey classifies village gods in south China hierarchically in three groups: (1) those with neither open-air altar nor temple; (2) those with an open-air altar; and (3) those with a temple.[14] Deities of rocks, fields, trees, or bridges that are called Bogong belong to the first kind. Sons and daughters with bad health are sold contractually to tree or stone gods. Some may even be given names with the character of 'trees' or 'stones'. Elsewhere, sons and daughters are contracted out to Gyanyin (Avalokitesvara) or other local deities. Parents of such adoptive children usually have to worship the divine foster parents along with the child annually and 'ransom' the child when he or she reaches the age of sixteen.

Gods with open-air altars are usually called 'Duke-king, Gongwang, or 'Big King', Dawang. Very often they are the protectors of a village with their altar situated at and guarding the water exit. At the start of a new year, villagers pray for good fortune, *qifu*. In the winter, solstice, they thank the god, *huanshen*. Children are contracted to him and there may be a medium, called the lad, to be possessed by him.

Gods with a temple are generally speaking higher-level gods. There are two main categories for temples, *tan miao* and *si guan*. Different places use slightly different terms but the broad division remains the same. The different terms for temple illustrate well the interpenetrating of the 'three religions' and the local cults in China. In the gazetteers, for instance, there are usually sections on (1) altars and temples (*tan miao*), and (2) cloisters and monasteries (*si guna*). The first category, *tan miao*, consists of three types, altars (*tan*), temples (*miao*), and shrines (*ci*). *Tan* are altars for local gods. The *miao* are temples for gods like the City God the renowned Empress of Heaven (Tianhou) and King Guan (Guandi). These temples of higher-level gods are likely to be found in townships rather than villages. The *ci* are shrines for historical worthies and meritorious officials reflecting Confucian ideology of righteousness and state loyalty. The second category *si guan* refers to Taoist cloisters and Buddhist monasteries. They are frequently established in the surrounding hills and normally occupied by monks, nuns or vegetarian mothers (*zhaima*). They perform both village funerals and communal sacrifices called *jiao* rituals. More often another group of ritual specialists or local Taoists, who remain at home, perform the *jiao* ritual. We will return to an analysis of one of the most important and elaborate religious activities in the Chinese villages.

Ghosts

The account of village gods would be incomplete without mentioning their opposite, the ghosts, *gui*, the other possible translation of which is demons. If gods occupy different vital points in the villages, the ghosts, their opposite, are not tied to a single spot. They wander and make unwonted appearances in solitary places. By definition, ghosts are the spirits of those who are not the ancestors. They either do not have any offsprings or, because of violent death, they are unable to receive offerings from their descendants.[15] One of the main purposes of the *jiao* ritual is precisely to subdue wandering ghosts of the area. A sacrifice is first offered followed by the driving away of any uncooperative ghosts.

The Jiao Ritual

One of the most important local religious activities in China is no doubt the *jiao* ritual. The Chinese word *jiao* means offering but it is used specifically as the technical term for the large-scale ceremonies, lasting several days, performed by Taoist priests in Chinese communities on behalf of the people of these communities. According to Poul Andersen:

> The whole event may be characterized as a 'definitional ceremony'. It is the means by which a Chinese community defines itself on the religious level and renews its contract with the gods. A *jiao* may function as a kind of redressive action (following major calamities, such as epidemics, drought, fires, and the like), but it also serves as a periodic restatement of the identity of a community.[16]

A classical *jiao* is a Taoist ritual and is presided over by a Taoist priest of the Zhengyi tradition (which originated at the foot of Mt. Longhu in Jiangxi), who is hired for the occasion.[17] The result of our field studies, however, challenges this view. To illustrate the case we will quote a *jiao* ritual we observed recently in a village called Paishang about half an hour's drive from the Huangpu township in Northern Guangdong.[18] As we will see, the *jiao* ritual, rather than a pure Taoist ritual, is a local ritual interpenetrated by both the Buddhist and Taoist traditions.

A small local temple dedicated to the local gods including the Great King of the Seven Old Men (of the Luoliu), Qigong daiwang,[19] was recently rebuilt at the *shuikou* or the mouth of the stream flowing to the village. To mark the event, the local leaders organised a five-day *jiao* ritual performed by three old local Taoists, locally known as *shigong* or *yanggong*, and sometimes called *shiyelao* in their ritual manuscripts, assisted by their two young acolytes. To differentiate local Taoists from formal Taoists of Taoism, we will refer to them as ritual masters in this paper. This was the first opportunity since 1949 for the community to perform a *jiao* ritual. The ritual was held in the lineage hall of the strongest local lineage *Cao*. The ritual masters were either in their sixties or seventies and some of the manuscripts they used dated back to 1896 (twenty-second year of Guangxu). Therefore we believe that, based on fieldwork, we may still have a glimpse of the 'little tradition of the village society in medieval China'.[20]

Our discussion of the *jiao* ritual will focus on the analysis of the wen, 'civil', as opposite to the *wu*, 'military', components of the *jiao* ritual, two categories used by the local ritual masters themselves.[21] By using fieldwork notes and a study of the ritual manuscripts collected in the field, we will show that although the *jiao* ritual is usually understood to be basically a Taoist ritual, a substantial part of the ritual, in fact, comes from the Buddhist tradition. This is evident in the civil part of the *jiao* ritual when we examine the pantheon to whom the memorials are presented. The Buddhist elements are also clear in the *baichan* and *banshe* or the penance rituals, literally the ritual for redemption of sins by prostration and chanting. In the *Mengshan* or the deliverance of the homeless ghost ritual, *tantric* Buddhist ritual components are obvious. Even in the military part, despite the fact that it is fundamentally Taoist, the Buddhist components are not absent when we examine closely the pantheon involved in the ritual.

The Record Book of the Ritual and the Programme

Much basic information of the *jiao* ritual can be found in the Record Book. This book was handwritten by one of the acolytes of the ritual masters. It contains a statement of the purpose and content of the ritual as well as the name of the performers, which constitutes the basic content of most memorials used in the ritual. It also carries a record of the names of the ninety-six organising committee members, *Huishou*, and their families who sponsored the ritual. The record book is to be read aloud during most sections of the ritual. At the beginning, the book gives the altar name (*tanhao*) of the ritual masters as the Altar of Complete Buddho-Taoist Practice, *Fodao zongchi fatan*. The title of the chief ritual master is known as 'the disciple of Buddho-Taoist and Emperor Yu (who has received) the teaching handed down (by the Buddha) and who has received a (Taoist) register', *Fodao yuwang menxia chuanshou yijiao zhilu dizi*. When asked, 'What kind of religion do you belong to?' (*nimen shishenme jiao*)—The chief ritual master replied 'We are a religion' (*women shi zongjiao*)—When we refined our question as 'Are you the same as Buddhist monks or Taoist priests?'—They replied, 'We are Buddho-Taoist' (*women shi fodao*).

The Buddho-Taoist character of our ritual masters can also be shown through the couplets they hung over the lineage hall where the ritual took place. With the help of a retired secondary teacher, our local guide who lived in Huangpu, the ritual masters hung eight pairs of couplets over the lineage hall. The couplets were copied from the ritual manuscripts and were arranged in two rows hanging on a long rope tied over the hall. Each of the back row of couplets started with the Chinese character *fo* or Buddha and read :

The **Buddha** is the great saint in the West Heaven
The **Buddha** cultivated a gold elixir for his sixteen feet body
In front of the **Buddha** are five hundred Arhats
Behind the **Buddha** are three thousand numerous (*gati*?) gods
The land under the **Buddha** mountain is forever in spring
Buddha! We now pray respectfully for
The descending of **Buddha** into the altar to witness our ritual

The front row, on the contrary, were all Taoist in content and read:

Tonight we send out the soldiers after offering them a feast
Those who are from pure and sacred realms also join the ceremonial feast
They descend into our ceremonial feast in order to examine our merits
Which bring blessings for all families in our region
The three Pure Ones and the Jade Emperor left their palace
The three Ladies left their native Gutian province
The Queen Mother and the Ladies from Mt. Lü all come to our ritual
The sounds of the ceremonial knives and Buffalo's horns of the ritual masters reach the sky

As we know, the three Pure Ones are the essential deities for Taoism and the three Ladies are the founders for the Lüshan school of Taoism. It is clear from these couplets that the rituals must belong to that of the Lüshan (Mt. Lü) School originating in Fujian.[22] The ritual masters, however, did not identify themselves as such. When asked whether they belonged to the Lüshan School, they denied it and indicated that they did not know much of the school notwithstanding their use of some well-known Lüshan ritual implements and the mentioning of the school's name and its founders, the three Ladies, *sannai furen,* in their ritual manuscripts.

The long name of the ritual written in the record book describes the ritual succinctly: a Pure *jiao* (to pray) for the officials and High Worthies in Heaven to Bestow Blessings and Peace for the Region and to Generate Merits by Assembling (Divine) Troops for A Big Worship. Seven villages in Huangpu plus a close-by village in Hunan were united to sponsor this ritual.

The purpose of this ritual was stated in the Record Book. It said that on the twelfth day of the second month of last year, a promise has been made in the form of a memorial which was presented to a local god, the Great King of the Seventh Old Men of the Luoliu (Luoliu Qigong daiwang). This was witnessed by the Buddha and it promised that, should the harvest for the year be good, a *jiao* would be performed to worship him and all the other gods in the temple. To fulfill this promise a *jiao* of three days was performed. The portraits of the (Buddhist) Three Jewels and the (Taoist) Three Pure Ones were hung. Also hanging on the two sides were the portraits of the four commanders. In the middle of the altar, the tablet of the emperor of this period was shown and under the altar there was a set up for the divine troops. It is also stated in the Record Book that by the virtue of the Three Jewels, Buddha, Dharma and Sangha, the disciple, that is, the Ritual Masters, will burn incenses and candles as well as presenting offerings. A handy 'outline' of the ritual that consists of nine steps is given in the Record book.

(1) Invocation of all Buddhas and ten thousands saints. Giving thanks to the heaven and earth for (the supply of) land and water
(2) Presenting memorials, flying flags and posting public notices, burning incense and reciting scriptures
(3) Penance by reciting with incense the names of ten thousand Buddha and by the performing of the ritual of worshipping stars[23]
(4) Offering money and a feast to the upper palace
(5) Walking the stars to get rid of disasters
(6) Almsgiving to wandering ghosts by performing the *mengshan* ritual
(7) Sending wandering ghosts off in boats
(8) Sacrifice to the kitchen god
(9) Recruiting divine troops for gods and rewarding them with a feast

These are performed to give thanks to the gods and pray for prosperity in farming and for their livestock while delivering the villagers from disasters, leaving them in peace and blessings.

In the following, for the sake of simplicity, we will analyse the ritual in accordance with the summary outlined in the nine steps in the Record Book. The dividing line for the military part in this case should be step seven, sending off wandering ghosts, which has an element of exorcism. Our analysis of the ritual aims to show that a substantial part of the ritual consists of Buddhist components.

The Civil Altar

Of the nine steps given in the record book, the first four belong to the civil part. In the Record Book, the civil rites include invocation of gods, sending off memorials by officials who examine merits, flying the sacred flags and posting notices before the altar. It also includes performing the confession of sins and presenting offerings to benefit both the living and the dead. 'The offerings are for repaying the grace of the gods and the memorials are for getting rid of disasters.' This indicates that presenting offerings and memorials[24] are two main components in the civil altar. In the ritual manuscripts, the first set of rituals is known as the 'first civil ritual in the altar'. Instructions begin with four rhymed lines:

The Three Jewels Buddha, Dharma, and Sangha
are good fields to produce merits for the human world
Anyone who is able to take refuge in them
Can greatly increase their blessings and life span

After chanting these lines, the instructions read: ritual masters should proceed to say, 'Today we follow the Way of the Buddha to burn the incense and offer the sacrifice...' It is therefore obvious enough that the civil part of the ritual is basically a Buddhist ritual.

Next in the instruction we have a list of secret formulae *zhenyan* or *mantras*; each begins with praise for that particular *mantra*. The *mantras* are :

Mantra for (inviting deities) to settle in their respective seats
Mantra for purification by water
Mantra for burning incense
Mantra for burning candles

Following the *mantras* is the chanting of four couplets of praise that had been hung over the hall. After chanting these, there is a long invocation of deities by incense and flowers. The section, like other sections of the ritual, ended with a Dedication in which a slightly different pantheon was found. These two pantheons are compared with the one used in the presentation of 24 memorials burnt in the section called *Xiao wenshu* in the following table (Table 1).

From the table, we can see that the ratio of Taoist gods to Buddhist gods is 15:10 and there are 6 local gods. Although we must be cautious about drawing a clear line between these deities,[25] this general classification of the gods invoked in the ritual shows how the ritual masters construct their pantheon by drawing resources from the Buddhist, Taoist and local traditions. A substantial number of deities invoked in the ritual are of clear Buddhist origin. Puxian (Samantabhadra), Wenshu (Mãnjusrii), Prajvalosnisah, Sakyamuni,

Table : 1

Names of gods	Buddhist	Taoist	Local	Invocaton	Dedication	Memorials
Officials who examine merits		✓		✓	✓	✓
The three Pure Ones		✓		✓		✓
The Queen Mother		✓		✓		✓
Lushan Immortals		✓		✓		
The Old Master (Laojun)		✓		✓		
True Warrior (Zhenwu)		✓			✓	
Jade Emperor		✓		✓	✓	✓
City gods and local gods			✓		✓	✓
The three rulers		✓		✓	✓	✓
Right and Left Officials who Guide the way		✓			✓	
Taisui and other star deities		✓		✓	✓	✓
Patrolling gods in space		✓				
Nuozha		✓			✓	✓
Generals of the protector of faith		✓			✓	✓
The god of farming			✓			✓
Deity in Hell			✓			✓
Ocean and Mountain gods			✓		✓	✓
Immortals		✓				
Military and Civil Patriarchs of ritual masters		✓		✓	✓	
Ancestors			✓		✓	
Saints			✓		✓	
Puxian (Samantabhadra)	✓				✓	
Wenshu (Mãnjuśrii)	✓				✓	
Buddhas of the ten directions and of the three periods	✓				✓	
Prajvaloṣṇiṣah	✓			✓	✓	
Sākyamuni	✓			✓	✓	✓
Guanyin (Avalokiteśvara)	✓			✓	✓	
Arhats	✓				✓	
Nāgārjuna	✓				✓	
Nanquan Puan	✓			✓	✓	
Huaguang	✓					✓

Guanyin (Avalokiteśvara) are clear cases. The same applies to the two famous local deities Nanquan Puan[26] and Huaguang.

Noon worship and the Penance Ritual

The ritual of worship was performed twice a day. It is known as the noon worship and the night worship. Both worships are similar and our analysis will follow the ritual of the noon worship. As pointed out previously, presenting offerings is a major component of the whole civil part of ritual. We will try to analyse how this component was performed. The noon worship started with a *gatha*:

> Buddhas and Bodhisattvas of the ten direction
> Who appear everywhere
> Always protected by Dragons in heaven
> Their teachings save every human

Then there was an invocation of deities, mostly Buddhist, including the Prajvaloṣniṣah Buddha, Star Deities, thousand Buddhas and ten thousand Bodhisattavas. After the invocation, there was a chanting of taking refuge in the Three Jewels and paying homage to the Three Jewels and tutelary deities. Next there was a purification of the ritual area by sprinkling water followed by another recitation of taking refuge in different deities and invoking them to empower the ritual masters to transform the food as an offering to gods. The deities invoked this time were also of Buddhist origin. They included the Three Jewels, Sakyamuni Buddha, patriarchs, masters who transmit the teaching orally, Guanyin, the Ten Kings, Mañjuśrii and Puxian (or Samantabhadra), Arhats, Bodhisattvas in Heaven, saints who attended the *jiao*. The transformation of food was carried out by a recitation of a *mantra*. This *mantra* was followed by another *mantra* of invocation of the Three Jewels and other deities to c6me down from their Lotus seats.

The main part of the noon worship is to offer all the invited deities incenses, flowers, lamps, perfumes, fruits, tea, food, treasures (cornelians, corals, amber, pearls) and clothes. A memorial was also presented. Then the ritual masters moved over to the flag to recite the *Heart Sutra*, burnt some paper money, inviting the official who examined the merits and burnt the memorials. Next, the ritual masters went over to the kitchen to worship the guardian of the vegetarian feast by sprinkling purifying water. Going back to the altar, the ritual masters ended the session by dedicating the merits to the Three Jewels Mañjuśrii and Puxian (Samantabhadra), Guanyin, the eighteen Arhats (*lohan*), and the deities in the Heavens. The chanting ended with praise of the Buddha in four couplets, each of which started with the Chinese word for Buddha.

If the noon worship is basically a worship of Buddhist gods, the penance ritual or the redemption of sin by prostration is actually a Buddhist ritual. Two manuscripts were used. One is 'The Penance by Chanting the Names of Thousand Buddhas' (982 according to our count) which is obviously a Buddhist ritual.[27] The other is 'The Penance by Chanting the Names of Star Deities'. In the manuscript, it was said the penance was taught by the Sakyamuni Buddha.[28] Therefore the chanting started by praising the Three Jewels followed by the chanting of names of 130 Star Deities.

Mengshan

This ritual is based on the Ulka-mukha ritual of Buddhism which is to bestow food on a flaming mouth, a hungry ghost or *preta* which appeared to Ānanda (in *Taishō* 1313, vol. 21). An expanded version dated 1693 (Kangxi 32) was collected by the Japanese scholar Kamata Shigeo in his *Chūgoku no bukkyō girei*.

The ritual started with a long chanting of praise to pay homage to the Three Jewels. Before the chanting of the *mantra* to empower the Five-Buddha crown, the Cundi (a form of Guanyin) *mantra* was recited three times. The association of five Buddhas with direction, colour, offerings, and ritual implements is given in a table contained in the ritual manuscripts (see Table 2) :

Table : 2

The Five Buddhas	Position	Colour	Offerings	Implements
Vaicocana	Centre	Yellow	Fruits	Scepter
Akṣobhya	East	Blue	Incense	Mani gem
Ratnasambhava	South	Red	Flower	Lotus
Amitābha	West	White	Lamp	Two crossing wheels
Amoghasiddhi	North	Black	Perfume	Wheel of thousand spokes

This matches exactly the Buddhist manuscript found in Kamata's collection.[29]

Next was the Purification by the nectar of Guanyin. Instructions given in the manuscript are that the ritual master has to visualise two Sanskrit letters '*om*', one on the top of his head and the other in his belly button symbolising blessings and wisdom. Flicking the water with his fingers into the air and rubbing some perfume on his palms, the ritual master has to visualise the nectar passing out from his throat. The instruction reads: 'While looking around both inside and outside the altar, the ritual master visualises that they were purified'. The use of tantric ritual structure, that is, the use of visualisation, *mudra* and *mantra*, is clear throughout the whole ritual of Mengshan. Following this particular purification is intended to empower the rice. The ritual master held some rice in his hand three times while visualising that they became precious treasures covering the sky. Next, to empower the bell and scepter, the ritual master threw some rice over them and visualised that they became seeds of wisdom. Then the ritual master recited the *mantra* of the twelve chains of codependent origination or *paticcasamuppāda*. The rest of the ritual consists of:

Performing *mudra* and reciting *mantra* to send off demons
Performing *mudra* and reciting *mantra* to subdue demons
Presenting five offerings: incense, flowers, lamps, perfume, and fruits and chanting *mantra* of five offerings
Performing *mudra* and reciting *mantra* for breaking into the hells

Next was an invocation of deities mostly in the underworld including:

Dizang wang (Kṣitigarbha)
Bodhisattva who holds a flag to lead living beings the way to the ritual
Heavenly kings, officials in the underworld, immortals in the world of water, City gods and earth gods, tutelary deities (guardian spirit, Sanghāgāra and Dragon gods), and the ten kings.[30]

After the invocaton of deities was the invocation by bells and by the *mantra* of wandering ghosts, the subject of this ritual. Finally *mudra* and *mantra* for invocation of hungry ghosts were once again performed and recited. The main idea of the ritual was to invoke the ghosts and:

(1) To give them joy of the teaching by chanting a famous quotation from the *Avatamsa sūtra;* anyone who wishes for the wisdom of the Buddhas of all ages should contemplate that the physical universe, *dharmadhātu,* are all creation of the mind
(2) To chant three times the *mantra* to break (out from) the hell
(3) To chant three times the *mantra* of invocation and exoneration
(4) To pay homage to the *Avatamsa sutra*, the Three Jewels, Śākyamuni Buddha, Ānanda Bodhisattva and to take refuge in the Three Jewels
(5) To confess sins (all *karma* are created by one's body, words, and consciousness because of greed, hate and ignorance)
(6) To recite the four universal vows of a Buddha or bodhisattva (that is, to save all living beings without limit, to put an end to all passions and delusions however numerous, to study and learn all methods and means without end, to become perfect in the supreme Buddha-law)
(7) To recite three times the *mantras* to destroy *karma* and obstruction, opening up the thin throat (of hungry ghosts), precepts, transformation of food, nectar
(8) To pay homage to the seven Tathāgata Buddhas:
    i) Ratnaketu Tathāgata
    ii) Prabhūtaratna, the Ancient Buddha of abundant treasures who appears in his stūpa to hear the Buddha preach the Lotus doctrine, by his presence revealing that nirvāṇa is not annihilation and that the Lotus doctrine is the Buddha-gospel.
    iii) Amṛta Tathāgata, the Buddha of Nectar
    iv) Abhayamkara Tathāgata, Buddha who gives security from fear,
    v) Surūpakāya Tathagata, the Buddha of the wonderful form (Akṣobhya, the Buddha of the East) addressed when offerings are made to the hungry spirits
    vi) Vairocanan, the one whose body fills space,
    vii) Amitābha Buddha.

The ritual ended with a dedication and with the performing of the *mudra* and reciting the *mantra* to dismiss gods and spirits . The similarity of the structure as well as the identity of many of the *mantras* in the manuscripts we collected in the field with those collected by Kamata Shigeo leads us to believe that the Mengshan ritual manuscript used by the ritual masters in Huangpu is based on a version of the ritual commonly practiced by Buddhist monks during the Qing period.

Military Altar

According to the record book, the military altar consists of walking the stars[31] and fending off the altar in order to build a golden bridge to invite the gods to come down to command their troops. Then the ritual master will present a memorial to the Three Pure Ones and the Jade emperor for a permit to recruit divine soldiers. The divine soldiers are to support the local god in defending the region. According to this description, there are two main points involved in the military part of the *jiao* ritual. One is to purify the altar area and the other is to recruit divine soldiers.

The main part of the military ritual was for the ritual master to transform himself into the female patriarchs, the Three Ladies, who would do the 'star walking' in a ritual called Reporting to Gods, arrayed in ceremonial dresses. This shows clearly the legacy of the Lüshan School. The ritual master recited the following:

> Borrowing the silk turban, dresses, skirt, girdle to subdue the hundred (kinds) of ghosts and perverted spirits. Invoking the three masters who get rid of the filth of the Lüshan School. Invoking the three masters and three infants of the Lüshan School who empower the clothing. This clothing is not ordinary clothing but transformed as the Yellow spotted black tiger which hurts the ghosts but not humans. As urgent as an order, ordering Wanglao, the fairy maiden, together with immortal soldiers, to come down to the altar to help the disciple. Giving me your seven yang souls and help me to be arrayed in ceremonial robe and say the championing spells. Your younger brother will pace the stars and remove the perverted. This clothing is not ordinary clothing but is transformed into those of the three ladies.

When the ritual master finished transforming into the Three Ladies, he not only dressed in female clothing but would behave as if he were actually one of the Three Ladies. He would therefore comb his turban as if it were his long hair. He would wash his face and put on makeup just as all ladies would do. Many villagers, therefore, found this part of the ritual quite amusing. Besides walking the star, there was a section called Purification of the altars in which the ritual master chanted:

> Invoking the four heavenly kings in the four directions to guard our altar by the virtue of the old Master of the Supreme High, as urgent as a legal writ. Invoking the three masters and infant of the five directions who get rid of filth by the virtue of the Old Master of the Supreme High, as urgent as a legal writ. Invoking the heavenly generals of the five directions to guard us by the virtue of the Old Master of the Supreme High, as urgent as a legal writ.
> *Heavenly Worthy of the Primordial Beginning*
> *Heavenly Worthy of the Numinous Treasure*
> *Heavenly Worthy of the Way and Its Power*

Therefore it is clear enough that the military altar is basically Taoist in nature. A Buddhist component, however, can be found among the deities invoked during the performance of the ritual on the military altar. They are 'The middle altar Huiji, Liji, Huaguang and the masters of six divisions in the Assembly of Yujia, Nagarjuna on the left altar, Zhenwu, True Warrior, on the right altar....The Chan master who lost in the fire Bodhisattva Guanyin, Patriarch Puan, and the ancient Buddha Dingguang....'[32]

Conclusion

In this paper, we have attempted to describe Chinese religion in the context of villages in China. Instead of finding three religions as such, we find that local village gods dominate the scene. We have also challenged the assumed Taoist nature of one of the most important local religious rituals in Chinese villages, namely, the *jiao* ritual, or the communal sacrifice, by analysing closely the Buddhist component of a *jiao* ritual we observed from 11-15 November 2000. This is an example of how the traditional framework of 'three religions' breaks down when we take a local approach to studying Chinese religion involving textual analysis and anthropological fieldwork. It shows the existence of a realm of beliefs and behaviours quite separate from elite religion but not isolated from it. This broadens the range of our understanding and appreciation of the Chinese religious traditions. There can be meaningful cooperative interactions between Indian and Chinese scholars in their deconstruction of Western-inspired labels such as Hinduism or the three religions in China and in the re-discovering of their cultural legacy from a local perspective. Through this interaction and collaboration we may establish contexts and revitalise our links, and also promote peace and cross-cultural understanding that can contribute to the harmonious co-existence of these two great cultures. It is for these goals that this paper is written.

NOTES AND REFERENCES

1. Thierry Verhelst, 'Cultures, Religions and Development in India: Interviews conducted and recorded by Thierry Verhelst', 14 to 23 January 1985, Mimeo, p. 9, quoted in S.N. Balagangadhara, *The Heathen in His Blindness: Asia, the West and the Dyanmic of Religion*, Leiden, E.J. Brill, 1994, p. 16; also quoted by Richard King in his *Orientalism and Religion: Postcolonial Theory, India and the 'Mystic East'*, London and New York: Routledge, 1999, p.99.
2. Wifred Cantwell Smith, *The Meaning and End of Religion* (Minneapolis: Fortress Press [1974] 1991), p. 61. Similarly, Stietencron calls Hinduism a deceptive term, see H. von Stietencron, 'Hinduism on the proper use of a deceptive term' in Gunter D. Sontheimer and Hermann Kulke, eds. *Hinduism Reconsidered*, New Delhi, Manohar Publications, 1991.
3. Richard King, *Orientalism and Religion: Postcolonical Theory, India and the 'Mytic East'* (London and New York: Routledge, 1999), pp. 98-99.
4. Romila Thapar, 'Syndicated Moksha', *Seminar* 313, September 1985.
5. G. Eichinger Ferro-Luzzi. 'The polythetic-prototype approach to Hinduism' in Sontheimer and Kulke, op. cit., p. 192.
6. Examples of Indian reformist movements are the movements led by Sri Ramakrishna, Swami Vivekananda, Sri Ramana Maharshi, and Sri Aurobindo. For a brief discussion see Karan Singh, *Essays on Hinduism* (Delhi, Ratna Sagar P. Ltd., 1990), pp. 28-39.
7. Valerie Hansen, *Changing Gods in Medieval China, 1127-1276* (Princeton, N.J., Princeton University Press, 1990), p. ix.
8. *Beishi*, Li Yanshu (seventh century), Bona, ed. (Beijing P Zhouhua shuju, 1974), p. 1234; quoted by Stephen F. Teiser, 'The Spirits of Chinese Religion' in Donald S. Lopez Kr., ed., *Religions of China in Practice*, Princeton: Princeton University Press, 1996, p. 3.
9. Jordan Paper, *The Spirits are Drunk: Comparative Approaches to Chinese Religion* (State University of New York Press: New York 1995), p. 3.
10. The three provinces are Fujian, Jiangxi, and Guangdong. Some of our research results are published in a series called the Traditional Hakka Society Series (Hong Kong, International Hakka Studies Association, Overseas Chinese Archives, Ecole Francaise D'Extreme-orient) planned for 20 volumes. So far eleven volumes have been published.

11. This section and the two sections that follow are based on the description of my research partner John Lagerwey's 'imaginary village' in his unpublished paper, 'The Rational Character of Chinese Religion' pp. 2-3, and pp.7-10. This paper is a public lecture on Chinese Religion, organised by the Centre for the Study of Religion and Chinese Society, Chung Chi College, The Chinese University of Hong Kong, on 19 September 1997. His model of an imaginary village in China represents a summary account of his fieldwork data in South China. I participated in his fieldwork on Northern Guangdong.
12. See for instance, J. J. M. Degroot, *The Religion of the Chinese* (New York: Macmillan, 1910); Emily M. Ahern, *The Cult of the Dead in a Chinese Village* (Stanford, Calif., Stanford University Press, 1973); and Francis Hsu, L.K., *Under the Ancestors'Shadow: Chinese Culture and Personality* (London: Routledge & Kegan Paul, 1949).
13. An important work that challenges all preconceptions about Chinese divinities is Meir Shahar and Robert P. Weller, *Unruly Gods : Divinity and Society in China* (Honolulu: University of Hawaii Press, 1996.
14. John Lagervey, 'The Rational Character of Chinese Religion', Public lecture on Chinese Religion, organised by the Centre for the Study of Religion and Chinese Society, Chung Chi College, The Chinese University of Hong Kong, 19 September, 1997, p. 7.
15. Yu Kuang-hong, 'Making a Malefactor a Benefactor: Ghost Worship in Taiwan' *Bulletin of the Institute of Ethnology* Academia Sinica, No. 70 (Autumn 1990), 39-65. See also Arthur Wolf, 'God, Ghosts and Ancestors' in Arthur P. Wolf, ed., *Religion and Ritual in Chinese Society* (Stanford: Stanford University Press, 1974), pp. 131-82.
16. Poul Andersen, 'The Transformation of the Body in Taoist Ritual' in Jane Marie Law, ed. *Religious Reflections on the Human Body* (Bloomington and Indianapolis: Indiana University Press, 1995), p. 187.
17. On Taoist ritual see John Lagerwey, *Taoist Ritual in Chinese Society and History* (New York: Macmillan Publishing Company, 1987). See also Kristofer M. Schipper, 'An Outline of Taoist Ritual' in Anne-Marie Blondeau and Kristofer Schipper, eds. *Essais Sur Le Rituel III* (Lovvain-Paris: Peeters, 1995), pp. 97-126.
18. The data presented in this paper are some of the results of the project 'Religious Festivals in Northern Guangdong' funded by the Research Grant Council of the Hong Kong Special Administrative Region (CUHK4457/99H).
19. The ritual manuscript contains hagiographies of many prominent local gods of the region including the Qigong daiwang. The short hagiography states that the temple of Qigong daiwang was in (Hu) chang Shan (a place near Huangpu). He was accomplished in the Way and was canonized as god by an imperial decree in the Tang dynasty. He was an official in Kangzhou and when he returned home from office he predicted fortune in the human world during daytime and ordered divine soldiers in the underworld during the night. Now he is constantly protecting the teaching of the Tao and drawing away evil spirits without prejudice.

20. David Faure, 'The changes of Chinese village society in the Ming and Qing dynasties as seen from the fieldwork in Hong Kong New Territories villages' in (*Qingdai quyu shehui jingii yanjiu*—Studies on the Economy of Regional Societies in the Qing Dynasties), pp. 484-45.
21. John Lagerwey, 'Question of Vocabulary, or How Shall We Talk About Chinese Religion?' in Lai Chi Tim, ed. *Daojiao yu minjian zongjiao yanjiu lunji* (Anthology of Taoism and Popular Religion) (Hong Kong, Xuefeng wenhua, 1999), p. 175.
22. For a discussion on the Lüshan school, see Brigitte Baptandier,'The Lady Linshui: How a woman became a goddess' in Meir Shahar and Robert P. Weller, eds. *Unruly Gods: Divinity and Society in China* (Honolulu: University of Hawaii Press, 1996) pp. 105-183.
23. Based on *Taisho shinshu dairokyo* (here and after quoted as Taisho) 14:65, no. 426 *Qianfo yinyuanjin* translated by Kumārajīva.
24. The ritual of presenting memorials to the deity comes from the Taoist tradition, see Kristofer M. Schipper, 'The Written Memorial in Taoist Ceremonies' in Arthur P. Wolf, ed. *Religion and Ritual in Chinese Society* (Stanford: Stanford University Press, 1974), pp. 309-324.
25. A good example would be the official who examines the merits. In the ritual manuscript, it is stated the officials belong to the Buddhist section. The dividing line between Taoist and popular deities is very difficult to draw. The purpose of the table is to show that a substantial number of deities invoked in the ritual are of clear Buddhist origin.
26. For a discussion on Puan, see 'The Chan Master Puan and Popular Faith' in International Conference on Buddhism and Chinese Culture, 1995, 485-97.
27. Based on the texts in *Taishō* 446-448. For a study see Kuo Li-ying 'The Scripture of Buddha's Names—the Precursor of Recitative Literature and Novels' in International Conference on Buddhism and Chinese Culture, 1995, pp. 529-45.
28. The text is not to be found in the *Taishō shinshū daizōkyo*; however the idea of star worship is not absent. See for instance, *Taisho* 1304 and *Taishō* 1305
29. Kamata Shigeo in his *Chūgoku no bukkyō girei* (Tokyor: Tokyo Daigaku Toyo Bunka Kenkyujo, 61), pp. 830-31.
30. On the ten kings, see Neal Donnelly, *A Journey Through Chinese Hell: Hell Scrolls of Taiwan* (Taipei: Artist Publishing Co., 1990). The ten kings are : Qin guang (1st court), Chu jiang (2nd court), Song di (3rd court), Wu guan (4th court), Yan lo (5th court), Bian cheng (6th court), Taishan (7th court), Pingdeng (8th court), Dushi (9th court), Zhuanlun (10th court).
31. For a study on the Taoist ritual dance, see the article by Poul Andersen, 'The Practice of Bugang' *Cahiers d 'Extreme-Asie* 5 (1989-1990), pp. 15-53.
32. For a study on this local saint, see John Lagerwey, 'Dingguang Gufo: Oral and written sources in the study of a saint', in *Cahiers d'Extreme-Asie* 10 (1988), pp. 77-129.

Legacies of Liberation in India and China

MANORANJAN MOHANTY

This initiative of the IIC comes at a time when a lot of effort in that direction is taking place in different parts of Asia. An Asian forum has just been set up with 26 countries participating through scholars and unofficial representatives. We have been meeting for the last five years in the Indian Congress of Asian and Pacific Studies. It is time to understand what Asia is all about, particularly as most discussions have been too economy oriented and people have so many dimensions, which are interconnected. I am a student of 20th century China and India. I have done research on the Chinese revolution and for the last 10-15 years I have been studying China's rural development, its political changes, and so on. Some ten years ago I wrote a paper on the freedom discourse in India and China.

It focused on the freedom discourse during the revolution period in China and the freedom struggle in India. What I have done today is to apply the same idea to the history of the two countries as a whole and the last fifty years' history of the two countries again. I wanted to see if we have a vantage point on the idea of liberation. I wanted to look at history, to make some sense out of human history as a whole from the Asian perspective and see how to cope with globalisation and the kind of challenges we face today. I have felt extremely constrained by the fact that we have hardly any communication among the ancient history experts, the early 20th century experts and the contemporary studies experts.

What I would like to do here is to take up the idea of liberation, which is *mukti* in most of the Sanskrit related languages of India and *jiefang* in Chinese. The idea of liberation links up some of the important legacies of ancient history and the modern history of Asia, i.e. the colonial period. It links up those with contemporary history and the challenges that we face today. Liberation from social shackles as well as liberation to attain higher consciousness characterise the ancient history of India and China. I would like to take that as well as the historical experience of the liberation struggle.

Liberation from political domination especially colonial rule brought the idea of liberation into a concrete agenda of self-determination. In the recent decades as individuals, groups, nations and societies became more and more conscious of their creative potentialities they became determined to liberate themselves from structures and practices which stood in their way as obstacles. Thus the idea of liberation is a running theme in the march of human civilisation. I think the chairperson referred to the notion of the Asian perspective and quoted some Japanese writing to say that the individual and collective, the individual and the group are not dichotomous in the Asian tradition. But I would like to expand that and say that in the Asian context, and if we look at world history more deeply perhaps we can see other parallels. There are various identities of individuals, groups, nations and societies, which interact with each other. It's not even a binary individual and group dichotomy. Then I take whatever little I know of ancient history and try to show that liberation is not a negative concept, it is a positive concept and something more which cannot be reduced either to negative or positive. It's not only a moral concept; it's also a material concept.

Liberation like freedom has both negative and positive dimensions and indeed dimensions which cannot be described as either positive or negative. The negative meaning refers to release from bondage. This is a crucial aspect of the concept of liberation both in the Chinese and in the Indian traditions. The liberation of slaves in one form or the other has been one of the earliest reference points to understand the meaning of liberation. The religious reform movements not only sought to free vast masses of the lower castes in India from upper caste domination, they also put forward visions of liberated society. I think this is extremely important. I think the religious reform movements from Buddhism till today illustrates what I'm talking about—both moral and material, negative and positive and more. The abolition of feudal kingdoms in China illustrated similar processes of breaking up of the limiting structures and opening up of possibilities of more just societies. Buddhism's role in this process was most significant. It reoriented Confucianism in China and Brahmanism in India from harmony and order towards struggle ethics. Harmony through struggle, order through struggle—that kind of formulation. The idea of liberation was thus part of a social and ideological struggle throughout history. It was both a social as well as an ideological and thought process struggle.

The peasant uprising in Chinese history challenged the prevailing social structure. At the same time the dominant Confucian ideology continued to evolve in response to new challenges. The great upsurges of the new religious movements in India—Buddhism, Vaishnavism, Sufism and Sikhism heralded both social changes as well as fresh ideologies of liberation. The formation of many cults such as (I think cult is a wrong word but I've no substitute right now) Adi Dharm, Radhasoami, Mahima Dharm, Guru Narayan Swamy and many others represented a clear assertion of the lower castes and the other oppressed groups. The adoption of Islam and Christianity by many groups in some parts of China and India were also a part of similar processes. On the one hand they broke away from the existing social-cultural or social-religious orders. To that extent their movements were negative. But clearly they were movements of affirmation of alternative visions of social and moral order. They were positive and more and more in terms of lived experiences of liberation in organisations, in religious institutions and society at large, and values and behaviour, and so on. Thus the understanding of the concept of liberation in history should be located in social processes, cultural movements as well as the religious discourses on liberation. The idea of liberation, which is essentially a political idea (political because it is in pursuit of freedom, it is to reduce domination and subjugation, and that is politics, politics is about freedom) must always be historicised so that the struggle through which the idea has evolved is understood better. That is why the philosopher and the historian have to work together.

Liberation and Swaraj

I will make a big jump here to the modern period particularly to the colonial period and struggle for liberation from colonialism. In modern history the struggle against colonial rule gave a concrete meaning to the concept of liberation. But how this concept has widened in the course of the anti-colonial struggle, that is the point I want to make. In India this discourse started with a positive assertion of *swaraj,* literally meaning self-rule or self-determination, when Tilak gave the clarion call in 1892 (one historian traces this to 1892 but there is a problem about this date) saying, 'Swaraj is my birthright and I shall have it.' The liberation discourse in India entered a new phase with this. The earlier discussion of this idea in *Hind Swaraj* (1908) spelt out the philosophy of liberation in some detail. Driving out the English rulers from India was not adequate for *swaraj.* Every village according to Gandhi must achieve self-rule and every oppressed group should attain *swaraj. Swaraj* for women, *swaraj* for various oppressed groups became a theme later on for Gandhi. This line of thought originated in Hind Swaraj by which Gandhi stood throughout his life. That *swaraj* was the other name for *mukti* in the Indian freedom discourse or the Indian liberation discourse.

In China after the emancipation of the slaves (*jiefang nuli*) most references to *jiefang* were made in the context of liberating the women from foot binding (*jiefang jiao*). During the Chinese revolution *the liberated* areas meant those areas which were liberated from Japanese occupation. The anti-Japanese war was described as a Liberation War. Incidentally, in Europe too whenever an area was recovered from the Fascists or Nazi occupation it was described as liberated. The re-naming of the armed forces under the control of the Communist Party of China (CPC) as Peoples' Liberation Army in 1946 gave an added meaning to the term. From the Nanchang Uprising of 1 August 1927 till 1936 the CPC-led forces were called Workers and Peasants Red Army.

During the second United Front they were regrouped as the Eighth Route Army in the South and the New Fourth Army in the North to fight the Japanese. After the victory over Japan the newly formed PLA (Peoples' Liberation Army) was engaged in the Civil War against the Kuomintang. Thus the prevailing connotation of liberation meaning national liberation during the Anti-Japanese and the Anti-Fascist War now acquired a wider meaning. In the final phase of the Chinese Revolution it meant liberation from imperialism, feudalism and compradore capitalism. The New Democratic Revolution as theorised by MaoTse Tung and the CPC provided the content and meaning to this concept. The proclamation of the Peoples' Republic of China on the 1 October 1949 was described by the Chinese historians as Liberation—the day of the Chinese peoples liberation.

Liberation at the Dawn of the 21st Century

The second half of the 20th century witnessed a steady rise of social movements. Oppressed groups articulated their aspirations in the language of liberation. In India innumerable forms of *'mukti morchas'* (liberation fronts) appeared. For example, backward regions seeking autonomy or self-determination formed liberation fronts to pursue their struggle, viz., Chhattisgarh Mukti Morcha, Jharhkhand Mukti Morcha, and so on. The scheduled castes, called 'Harijans' in the Gandhian framework and 'Dalits' in the Ambedkar framework, asserted their right to equality and dignity in a framework of Dalit liberation that challenged the caste order. The Women's Liberation Movement is a worldwide phenomenon exposing patriarchy everywhere in structures, cultures and behaviour. Movements of tribal and indigenous peoples affirm their right to culture, identity and local resources through liberation struggles. Thus, with the emergence of a creative society (this is the term I have been using for the last ten years) in which individuals and groups consciously seek fulfillment of their human self, of their creative potentiality, liberation has become an even more relevant idea. It is not only about the liberation of the human self from all forms of constraints, not only about a nation's right to self governance, not only liberation of an exploited class from the domination by the ruling classes but also liberation from caste, race, ethnic, gender and every form of bondage so that humans can achieve their creative potential.

Liberation and Civilisational Dialogue

When India celebrated the Golden Jubilee of her independence there was hardly any reference to the idea of *swaraj* or liberation. In 1999 China observed the 50th anniversary of the founding of the Peoples Republic of China rather than the golden jubilee of liberation. In other words, in both the countries liberation consciousness has receded to the background. In China the only major usage of the term was visible when the post-reforms regime launched a campaign to Emancipate Thought (*Jiefang sixiang*), that is, to get rid of the old ideas of socialism of the era of Mao Zedong and vigorously adopt a market perspective. As globalisation and liberalisation push ahead the building of an acquisitive society with increasing alienation, criminalisation and corruption, the value of the idea of liberation will continue to challenge us. It has a central place in any civilisational dialogue. After all, struggles for liberation have a glorious history spanning thousands of years. Their legacies will continue to haunt generations—present and future.

REVISITING CIVILISATIONAL DIALOGUE BETWEEN INDIA AND CHINA

TAN CHUNG

Revisiting civilisational dialogue between India and Chian brings back to memory what an active initiator of this dialogue wrote in 1944: 'From times immemorial these two ancient nations [India and China] approached each other with love, affection and respect. They exchanged their greetings and gifts just as noble friends would do. They had "treaded in ideas, in art, in culture, and grown rich in their own inheritance by the other's offerings"' (Pandit Jawaharlal Nehru's words). There never happened such things as diplomatic quarrels, political conflicts, military invasions, economic exploitations, commercial struggles, and so on between these two great countries, India and China. Who would dare say that such amicable contact and noble relationship between China and India is not a rare thing and wonder at the history of human society and international relations?[1] Perhaps, nowhere else has the India-China relationship been described as succinctly as in these words.

Scholars now talk of 'Eastern Civilisation' without the suffix 's'. This is a holistic view that befits the true origin and nature of human activities in the Eastern hemisphere. One cannot discuss 'Eastern Civilisation' without going to the root and tracing the genesis. The story will go back 200 million years ago when there were only two continents on earth, one called Laurasia (somewhat corresponding to the present Eurasia) and another called Gandwana which later split into South America, Antarctica and Africa. The continental plate of India that formed a part of Africa then, quit its home and travelled towards the continental plate of China at the eastern end of Laurasia. About 65 million years ago, the continental plates of India and China hugged each other like a couple of ardent lovers. The front part of India went under that of China and lifted a mass of land to unprecedented heights around 40 million years ago. Then, around 10 million years ago, there was another major lift, and the 'Roof of the World', i.e. the Qinghai-Tibetan Plateau and the earth's 'Third Pole', i.e. the Himalaya, came firmly in place. But the forward dynamism of the Indian continental plate never ceases. After advancing 150 kilometres northwards it is still pushing, and the youngest mountain range on earth, Himalaya, is still growing by a few centimetres every year. Geologists have coined the term of 'mountain-making movements' for the creation of the Himalaya. It is, indeed, the greatest architectural feat on earth.

The Himalayan region is the best life environment on earth for living beings. In the first place, the Himalaya has provided a great variety of meteorological and geographical dynamism. There is an abundance of sun, rain, snow, wind, eddy, cumulus, storm, seasonal changes on the same day or within the same horizon; wet in one corner and dry in another, or cold at one spot and chill at another. In addition, not only are there positioned with the massif, peak, ravine, glacier, waterfall, stream, lake, river, cold, heat, water, ice, etc., but earthquakes, avalanches, erosion, freeze and thaw, solidification and evaporation are taking place everywhere and all the time. All these have created a paradise for the multiplication of life. In the second place, the high rise of the Himalaya and the wind and rain created by it have caused a drastic reduction of carbon dioxide in the atmosphere, sending back the sun's radiant heat to outer space. This place, the Himalaya has environmentally quarantined the Indian subcontinent from the vagaries of Eurasia, especially the trans-Siberian chill that tortures the Chinese mainland every winter. The Himalayan heights also prevent the monsoon winds from travelling beyond the Indian peninsula, giving Indians a monopoly of growth-sustaining rain in the summer months. The adjacent areas of India too, share its ideal environment for the multiplication of lives. A trans-Himalayan nursery has, thus, been created and about one-third of the total flora and fauna species on earth have thrived here.

As if the Himalaya and its extension, the Qinghai-Tibetan Plateau, wished to redeem their gratitude to their creators—the continental plates of India and China—they sent down for civilisation-giving rivers: Indus and Ganga southwards, creating the Indian civilisation; Huanghe (Yellow River) and Yangtse northwards, creating the Chinese civilisation. The Indian subcontinent, to which we have just alluded, is the made-to-order nursery and paradise on earth for living beings, ideal for a great civilisation. China, however, especially the middle and low reach of the Huanghe, is rather far away from the Himalayan region. But, as botanists observe, there is the 'phytogeographical affinity' created by the Himalayan flora species migrating to Southeast Asia and East Asia. All told, we see a two-fold engineering feat that has first created the Himalaya, and then the world's two important civilisations—India and China.

Enjoying the favourable Himalayan living environment are the apes and monkeys—the direct ancestors of humans. No wonder the particular ape that metamorphosed into man belonged to the Himalayan region. It was named 'Ramapithecus' because a fossil from it was first discovered at Rama on the Indian subcontinent (now in Pakistan territory). But, many more of its fossils have been discovered in the Yunnan province in southwest China. The Chuxiong county of Yunnan has the reputation of being the 'homeland of Ramapithecus' for this reason.[2] Yunnan also features one of the earliest man-apes on earth, called the 'Yuanmou Man' (whose fossils are found in Yuanmou county not far from Chuxiong) who lived about 1.7 million years ago. There was an even earlier human species living around 1.8 million years ago whose fossilized skullcaps were discovered near the Hathnora village at Hoshangabad district in Madhya Pradesh in Central India.[3] It is certain that more such archaeological discoveries are in the offing, but 'Rama' and 'Chusiong', 'Hoshangabad' and 'Yuanmou' have already mapped out a zone of the genesis of human civilisation. That is to say, from western Punjab to Madhya Pradesh to Yunnan, there lay a vast stretch of earth where apes metamorphosed into humans. This stretch was the unmistakable cradle of mankind and human civilisation. Since all the fossils now discovered on earth (disregard their being discovered at Rama, or Chuxiong, or Africa, or any other place) are uniformly called Ramapithecus , we can also give a uniform title to the Yuanmou Man and Hoshangabad Man who are the descendants of the same Ramapithecus . We can call them the 'Himalayan man-apes' or 'Himalayan Man'. Indians and Chinese are the descendants of this Himalayan Man . The 'Himalayan nursery' creating the Himalayan Man is all the more logical than conceiving two separate origins for Indians and Chinese. In conclusion, the Indian and Chinese civilisations were born from the same Himalayan cradle, and were the offspring of the same Himalayan course of evolution.

From the Himalayan nursery the offspring of the Himalayan man engineered mankind's first revolution—agriculture. Both India and China are the motherlands of agriculture. Rice culture, like civilisation, blurs its place of origin. It is a Sino-Indian joint invention and joint venture to begin with. While cotton is an exclusive Indian invention, silk carries a story of intimate India-China intercourse. Silkworm and mulberry tree are trans-Himalayan species. The Chinese in Sichuan, Shaanxi and Henan were the earliest people to develop a highly lucrative silk industry. Indians were most probably the earliest foreigners to know this Chinese trade secret and take keen interest in its industry. By the time of Kautilya in the 4th century B.C., India had set up her silk industry. This was testified to by a sentence in Arthasastra as below:

'*Kayseyam cinapattasca cinabhumijah*'
(Stacks of) Chinese silk cocoons and bundles of Chinese silk these are all originated from China.[4]

Beyond doubt, this is a vivid description of a silk workshop, and sounds like someone explaining to a visitor where the cocoons and silk came from. Records left behind by Indians and Graeco-Romans are the earliest among foreign writings describing the wonder fibre that was Chinese silk. The only difference lies in the fact that while the ancient Greeks and Romans never stopped believing that silk was gathered from the trees, the Indians had already started producing it in their workshops. M.C. Joshi, a Sanskritist and Indian archaeological expert, told me that in ancient Sanskrit literature there were references to ancient Indians depicting the predilection of Hindu gods for *kauseyam* — the Chinese invented silk cocoons— and particularly Lord Siva for the yellow variety. Beyond doubt, from the time idol worship became a vogue till today, Indian deities have been clothed in silk thanks to the Chinese invention and the Himalayan affinity.

Those who lived away from India and China have a clear vision of the oneness of the two civilisations. They called Central Asia 'Serindia' with the first syllable representing 'Serica' or 'Sares', meaning 'the silk country' — China. 'Serindia', i.e. 'China-India' made the Indian and Chinese civilisations merge into one identity in the geographical strip that formed the vital linkage of Europe and Asia. Then, peninsular Southeast Asia begot the name 'Indochina' for the same reason. 'Serindia' and 'Indochina', in this way, have presented a new dimension to India-China relations. If we put anything in the centre of a flame it does not burn because the burning temperature is reached only at the top of the flame — its oxidizing zone. Civilisation has a similar phenomenon. 'Serindia' and 'Indochina' are just two stray symbols indicating that Indian and Chinese civilisations have their oxidizing zones extending far away from the heartland of India and China. The two oxidizing zones have actually met in many other places, e.g. Korea, Japan and the entire Southeast Asia. Thinking of the relationship of Indian and Chinese civilisations makes us envision two flames on the southern and northern sides of the Himalaya shining upon a vast geographical area covering the entire eastern part of Eurasia as well as many Pacific islands such as Japan and Indonesia.

Today, we see a dark innuendo in international studies to displace India from the centre of Asia by creating the 'East Asian' syndrome. 'East Asia' has been usurped as an identity that encompasses Southeast Asia ending at the western boundary of Myanmar. We also see another syndrome of 'Asia-Pacific', a blatantly American-dominated identity in which India becomes irrelevant. These attempts to remove India from the mainstream of Asia have overlooked the historical fact that the identities of 'Asia', 'Orient', and 'East' were first conceived by the European minds out of a European obsession with India and China. For the Europeans, these three identities actually connote 'India, China and their neighbours'. In other words,'As' the first two syllables of 'Asia', should read: 'Ind' to mean 'Asia is India', and 'India is Asia'. Of course, the same is also true for China, i.e. 'Asia is China' and 'China is Asia'. No one should erase 'India' from the 'Asian' identity, and no one should forget the symbiotic relationship between the two identities of 'Sino-India' and 'Asia'. In sum, the concept of Asia has bound India and China together in the course of civilisational development.

Why were the historical Europeans obsessed with India and China? It was because they wanted to get to these legendary 'wonderlands' (legends created by Marco Polo and others) to see, to trade ... and also to conquer. The Danish and British 'East India Companies' and the famous 'East Indiamen' (erstwhile British ocean-liners sailing to the 'Far East') pronounced 'East India' in the same breath as the modern experts on strategy, security and development speak of 'East Asia'. The British East India Company's East Indiamen always had two destinations on their way out: first to reach India to unload persons and things for the 'British Raj', and then, anchoring in Chinese territorial waters to load tea and other China goods for Britain. All such historical memories would permit no obliteration of India from the concept of 'East Asia', let alone that of 'Asia'.

From a historical perspective, India and China are not merely two developing countries, let alone two miserable examples of overpopulation, malnutrition, backwardness and poverty. In the development of human civilisation, India and China have travelled a long course of 5,000 years. Only in the last 200 years have they become less developed than a few parts of the world. In the other 4,800 years, India and China exemplified development, prosperity and advancement. In other words, from a historical perspective, India and China are shining examples of human progress and economic dynamism. They are the pioneers of the First Human Revolution—Agriculture. They are the inventors of rice culture, wheat culture, cotton and silk industries, spice industries, tea industries, porcelain industries, etc. Had the Indians not invented pepper to spice meat and export it, the slaughtered cattle in Europe would not have been properly preserved, and there would have been perennial starvation and famine from Manchester to Istanbul.

It was also the quest for Indian pepper that led to the discovery of America. Had the Chinese not gifted the mariner's compass to Columbus, he would not have sailed, and the Americas not discovered. And thanks to the China-invented gunpowder Columbus and his companions, as well as their descendants in later years, could save themselves from being vanquished by the sharp arrows of the Red Indians and eventualy become the vanquishers of.the latter. Columbus' mistaken identity of America for 'Cathay' (China) when he first sighted the new continent, and his crew's mistaken identity of native Americans for 'Indians' speak volumes for the importance of China and India in the Era of Exploration. There was also the Chinese invention of printing to induce the birth pangs of Renaissance without which the Industrial Revolution would not have been conceived.

What we have discussed above constitutes an important chapter in the history of international relations. To borrow the words of professor Donald Lach of Chicago University, this chapter may assume the title of 'Asia in the Making of Europe' with a sub-title 'India and China as the Midwives of the Birth of Modern Europe'.

From a Eurocentric perspective, Modern Europe means the 'modern world'. One plus one is equal to two: India and China are simply the midwives of modern civilisation. All this enables us to claim credit for India and China in the modernisation of Europe and the world. We are, thus, putting India and China in the seat of architects of modernisation.

I may have sounded a little chauvinistic here although I do not intend to revisit the cemetery where rest many German and other European cross-bearing Christian civilisational crusaders of the vintage of the 19th century, and also of the First World War (reiterating Europe's civilising mission all over the world). *Revanche* is never the best way to win. Indians and Chinese always think of Europe kindly instead of the unforgettable bitter memories. While no Indian or Chinese (Mongols apart) ever tried to conquer Europe, their civilisational influence merely played the role of passive giver in the game of demand and supply between Europe and Asia. It was almost always so in the transmission of silk, pepper, tea, cotton textiles and other commodities, proto-modern technology, and philosopical ideas, etc., from Asia to Europe. Indians and Chinese have the reputation of being inventors but not of Patent and Intellectual Property Rights. These are the chains of the strong to bind the weak. Today, while being willingly bound by such chains, India and China might as well lay claim on their Intellectual Property Rights for what the Europeans had indebted to them in history — rather a 'demand to be heard' than a claim for material compensation.

This proposition may be vindicated by quoting a passage from an important address. Honourable K.R. Narayanan, President of the Republic of India, whose state visit to China last year symbolised the revival of civilisational dialogue between India and China, said in his address to Peking University on 30 May 2000:

> China and India have made immortal contributions to human civilization. Where would be the scientific-technological civilization of today without paper, the printing, the compass and the gun powder invented by China, besides, the ethical values and the way of life contributed to the world by the Chinese civilization. Likewise, what human advance could have been possible without the concept of 'the zero' and the decimal system invented by ancient India apart from its great philosophical ideas?[5]

Even when European powers were dominating the entire world, India and China's strategic importance was by no means diminishing. Among those who had an insight in this was Dr Sun Yat-sen, 'Father of Modern China'. In his essay entitled '*Zhongguo cunwang wenti*' ('The Issue of China's Survival') written in the summer of 1917, Sun wrote:

> Britain minus India is but a third class country. . . Being three islands northwest to Europe, her territory was all over the globe, and she brags that the sun never sets on her land. . . How does she manage? It is not due to the power of her parliamentary politics, nor due to the power of her navy of second-class standard, nor due to the Teutonic gentlemen spirit, but to the possession of the Indian colony. Only by possessing India can she control her colonies around the world. Only by possessing India can the London market occupy the central position of the world. Only by possessing India has Britain become the leader and hegemony on earth.... What has made Britain an empire is not the British islands, but India.[6]

Sun Yat-sen further reiterated: 'The total population of Britain is about 400 million, of which 350 million are Indians . . . a proof that without India there is no [British] Empire.' He continued: 'It is India that maintains the colonies on which the Union Jack never sees sunset.'

> Minus India a greater part of British commerce is gone, and its foundation injured. It [Britain] loses attraction and, hence, she would have no qualification for dominating the world market. The survival of India is the survival of Britain. Without India means without the [British] colonies, commerce, navigation, and [Britain] will not be self-sufficient internally and not be able to take advantage of others externally. Even if [Britain] wants to survive it will not be possible.

Sun concluded: 'Being an imperialist power Britain has to depend upon India as its foundation. Thus, Britain would sacrifice everything and leave no stone unturned to protect its Indian possession.'[7]

Interestingly, Sun Yat-sen, in the same essay, propounded a theory not only refreshing, but also quite convincing. The essay was actually focusing on the international situation during the First World War and on the intentions of the big powers' scrambling for world hegemony. Sun was convinced that the occupation of India and China was foremost in the expansionist designs of not only Britain, but also Russia, Germany and Japan. He thought if Russia 'wanted to occupy China it would be helped by Britain and opposed by Japan'. If it 'wanted to occupy India it would be helped by Japan and opposed by Britain'. But, he was sure that after occupying China, Russia would still want to occupy India. Similarly, Germany's plans were to build railways to connect Turkey, Persia and India in order to occupy India. And it would want to expand further eastwards to occupy China after possessing India. While discussing all this, Sun Yat-sen felt that the powers had arrived at a consensus that 'after occupying India they can enjoy the benefit of China, while after occupying China they cannot enjoy the benefit of India at the same time'. He then propounded:

> China is today a market enjoyed by all world powers, not prejudicial to any particular power. Hence, from the economic consideration one can enjoy the benefit of China even without occupying it . . . viewing from this point China is still independent. The power that occupies India is able to control a greater part of the Chinese interest. But, on the contrary, occupying China would not gain any benefit from India. This is the reason why China has so far survived as an independent country.[8]

Few, if any, analysts have seen the interdependence of India and China during the height of the colonial era with such an incisive and intricate insight.

The strategic importance of India and China in modern times is also reflected in the fact that both the countries have produced headline news for the world. India was the leader of the demolishing squad of the 'the sun never set's' Empire. Not only did India inspire all former European colonies in Asia, Africa and Latin America to fight for independence, but the independent Indian Republic also stood at the forefront in demanding attention for the voices of the Third World. The Non-Alignment Movement led by India made a large part of the world safe havens from the hurricane of the Cold War. On the other hand, China succeeded in resurrecting the Napoleonic fear of the awakening of the world-shaking giant. Whether in defiance or in universal acknowledgement, China was already inside the ring of the heavyweight bout during the larger part of the 20th century. In short, both India and China have joined hands to bury the Eurocentric hegemony, and demoted all European powers, save Russia, to the second and third classes. India and China are a couple of Goliath-humbling Davids, reversing their positions from colonial twin-sufferers to anti-colonial twin-heroes in the second half of the 20th century.

All this indicates the strength and vibrancy of the two great civilisations. India and China have ranked as the most ancient civilisations on earth; they still rank as the foremost civilisations in the modern world. Only the Indian and Chinese civilisations can claim a vigorous and energetic continuum through the vicissitudes of human history. Today, when one looks at India and China, at their society and culture, one feels that they are youthful and growing, robust with life, activity, courage and dynamism.

I may venture to liken this wonderful historical India-China relationship to the ideal Oriental marriage, exemplifying a 'back-to-back' equation. It is 'back-to-back' like the husband and wife fighting shy to glare at each other, and even hesitating to use the word 'you' towards each other. It is 'back-to-back' because they always support each other, sticking to each other through thick and thin. In contrast, a 'face-to-face' relationship reminds us of those cases of quarrelsome couples of modern times, constantly asserting one individual's right over that of one's life partner, unmindful of one's obligations to the other, constantly living in mutual suspicion, jealousy, and even malice and hatred. Before 1962, India and China had not, for a single day, lived together in the conditions of the latter. But, the assertion of 'nationalism' (a mundane Western cultural heritage to usurp the rightful place of Oriental internationalism) has poisoned the traditional 'back-to-back' relationship between India and China.

Obviously, this 'back-to-back' relationship has a close connection with the geographical and environmental background, i.e. the Himalayan context I have spelled out earlier. It was this factor that provided a safety valve to prevent the two civilisations of India and China from falling into the 'face-to-face' relationship. The same Himalayan factor does not exist between Egypt and Babylon, or Egypt and Greece and Rome, depriving them of the chance of mutual support and sustenance. Paradoxically, this Himalayan protection was destroyed by British colonialism that gave birth to the specter of territorial disputes between India and China, ultimately positioning the Indian and Chinese civilisations in a face-to-face equation.

Returning to present times, both India and China in the new era are poised at the threshold of the Superpowers' Club. Population-wise, they are already superpowers of the first order. The Information Technology of the new era is reshuffling the cards of the international order, with human resources becoming the most important resources of development, advancement, and competition. Knowledge-based economy has stolen the charm of capital-intensive economy, while knowledge is human-based—without human brains computers cannot create knowledge. In other words, more humans means greater resources and potentials, and there is only one bridge to cross from their present 'population superpower' status on to the next—obtaining a capital 'S' by dropping the qualifier of 'population' Already, the Silicon Valley in California is called the 'I C Valley' with 'I' for Indians, and 'C' for Chinese. This is convincing proof that Indians and Chinese are second to none in wisdom programming, knowledge-creation and all other prerequisites of information-technology and 'new economic' development.

Much water has flowed in the Thames, Ganga, and Yangtse since Adams Smith launched the human quest for wealth. Today, a whole industrial age is being put aside. The best minds of the world are dedicating themselves to the pursuit of a sustainable development that is friendly to both the earth and to mankind living on it. Manufacturing need no longer be injurious to the environment, nor is it desirable to go for mass production of monotonous and durable consumer goods. Living standards are oriented towards variety, individuality, health, aesthetics, and spiritual values. Industry is dissolved into agriculture and services. Agriculture will no longer be backbreaking labour, but sophisticated application of life science and bioengineering. Coarse foodgrain will be processed into health care nutrition. Horticulture will beautify green economy. Organic food and medicine will be raised by organic farming and fertilising methodology. Herbal values will conquer the obsession for chemical ingredients.

After the European domination in the last couple of centuries had destroyed the Himalayan context of the world civilisation, it is now the joint responsibility of India and China to revive it, giving full play to what the Creator has invested in the Himalayan eco-human environment. India and China will not only continue to be mankind's important farmhouses and food suppliers in future, but will re-fashion the human way of life toward moderation in intake (eliminating wastefulness), entrails' caring (avoiding injury to one's inner organs), compassionate treatment to animal life (giving up predatory habits), mental and physical endurance and adaptability, mind cultivation and temperament control, etc. There are bright prospects in future collaboration and synergy between the Indian and Chinese civilisations. We must not forget that we are the offspring of the Himalayan Man, preservers of the Himalayan tradition, and proponents of the Himalayan lifestyle for the entire world.

NOTES AND REFERENCES

1. Tan Yun-shan, 'Introduction' to 'Sino-Indian Cultural Society', see Tan Chung (ed.), *In the Footsteps of Xuanzang : Tan Yun-shan and India*, New Delhi: Indira Gandhi National Centre for the Arts & Gyan Publishing House, 1998, p. 237.
2. I visited the Museum of Chuxiong inside which there is a large exhibition room staging the finds and the claim.
3. M.C. Joshi, 'Archaeology: Filling the Blanks', in Hiranmay Karlekar (ed.), *Independent India: The Fifty Years*, Delhi: Oxford University Press, 1998, p. 454.
4. This sentence was first noticed by Prof. Ji Xianlin who had some doubts about the exact meaning of 'kauseyam'. I discussed it with Mr. M.C. Joshi when both of us were working in the Indira Gandhi National Centre for the Arts. He is an authority on both Sanskrit and archeaology, and affirms that 'Kayseyam' was the ancient Indian word for Chinese silk cocoons.
5. Text supplied by the Indian Embassy, Beijing.
6. *Guofu Quanshu* (Collected Works of the Father of the Nation), Taipei: National Defence Academy, 3rd print, 1966, p. 732.
7. Ibid., p. 733.
8. Ibid., p. 742.

Cultural Globalisation and Localisation in Taiwan

HSIN-HUANG MICHAEL HSIAO

Introduction

Globalisation is a multidimensional process which unfolds in multiple realms of existence simultaneously, going beyond economy, finance, market, technology, communication, politics, and even extending to the realm of culture and identity. The essential character of globalisation is actually the rise and expansion of the individual consciousness of the global situation, that is, the world is an arena in which we all participate. But it does not suggest that globalisation involves massive forces of homogenisation or global sameness under which local and national identities, cultures and traditions are inevitably being profoundly threatened or even obliterated. Far from it, globalisation actually also involves the promotion or facilitation of local difference and diversity, that is, the rise of local heterogeneity.

To acknowledge the globality of locality as a possible outcome of globalisation may sound ironic, but it is true that discourse and ideas concerning the local, and the indigenous, are promoted and advocated by global and transnational movements. It is possible to discover that the result of a negotiation between globality and locality is the creation or invention of cultural authenticity. In this sense, local cultural responses really matter for the way globalisation finally ends up and globalisation also matters for the manner in which local culture eventually transforms.

Berger (p. 24) has formulated four such distinctive processes and phenomena of cultural globalisation that are going on simultaneously, relating to each other and interacting with many indigenous cultures on which they have impinged. The four cultural globalisation processes that many parts of the world have been experiencing are: 1) the business culture, 2) the popular culture, 3) the intellectual culture, and 4) the popular religious culture. What follows is a synopsis of the Taiwanese case study of cultural globalisation and the local responses since the 1980s.

The Business Culture

Without doubt, Taiwan's capitalist outward looking industrial development with significant international trade and foreign investment since the 1960s has already integrated Taiwan's economy into the world market. Among the different sectors of Taiwan's business enterprises, a very high percentage have had in one way or the other connections with the global business community. Their contact with the international business companies and their CEOs and managers over the last three decades certainly has been very intense.

At the individual behavioural level, it is no surprise to observe an almost universalised trend for Taiwanese businessmen and managerial classes in many modern industrial and service sectors to dress, talk, and act like their counterparts in the world. Business English is the common language among them; for them to have English first names is almost a required practice. They have also developed a globalised pattern of life with similar tastes. In Taipei, Kaoshiung, and other high cities, it is easy to find such a globalised business class working in many larger, modern high-tech corporations, financial firms, and international trade-related sectors. It is also interesting to note that many local Taiwanese managers employed in the international firms have in fact developed a dual behavioural pattern. At the workplace, they usually behave exactly like any other globalised managerial class around the world, while in the local community where the foreign firms locate, they conduct themseves differently.

They not only shift from English to the local Minnanese or Hakka in the locality, they also somehow change their mindset. To many of them, doing business or managing enterprises is one thing, other aspects of it are another, and business is not everything. To act like an international businessman or manager is a learned behaviour at the workplace, and the newly adopted code of conduct is an 'addition', rather than a 'replacement', of what a Taiwanese manager has learned from the local culture to his life.

Those local small business owners or self-made entrepreneurs in most of the traditional businesses or even in the export manufacturing sectors, who have run their business all along rather successfully without having dressed, talked, or acted like the 'world business class', might not even know how such businessmen should behave, but they know well enough how to deal with the trade agent and know exactly when to deliver their order. Obviously, these Taiwanese small businessmen who have made the 'Taiwan miracle' known to the world have separated their learned business know-how in dealing with the world market from the pattern of everyday life learned from the indigenous culture. To them, the two cultures that guide their two different life domains have been in a state of co-existence without much conflict.

At the business organisation level, many multinational corporation managers have acknowledged the local way of doing business and they have indeed made efforts to adapt to them by either decentralising the decision making to the local managers or indigenising the high rank personnel. Over the past decades of globalising of Taiwan's economy and business, it is quite clear that neither American nor Japanese managerial ideologies or management models have been completely transplanted into the Taiwanese business world or replaced the indigenous business practices. A significant degree of mix or fusion has been detected in their management styles in many multinational corporations orperating in Taiwan and many local world market-oriented larger business companies. No pure American, European, Japanese or Taiwanese-Chinese management model can best characterise the actual business culture in today's Taiwanese business world.

In addition to the above characterisation of the organisational adaptation of globalisation and localisation in the management practice it is important to note that even under the economic globalisation, the traditional practice of doing business and management has been prevailing in Taiwan's business world. To a great extent, Taiwanese businessmen still conduct their business through the 'guanxi' (personal relationships, connection, and the networks) and 'xinyong' (personal reliability or trustworthiness). The personalised 'guanxi' and 'xinyong' - oriented business culture does not limit itself to developing business connections and partnerships, it also contributes to Taiwanese managerial style and entrepreneurship.

Since family is still the prevalent feature of Taiwanese business, there is a close overlap of ownership, control, and family. The familial hierarchical status, authority pattern, and obligatory relationships are taken as models of business organisational roles. There is a strong paternalistic organisational climate inside the business, especially in the mode of decision making and personnel management.

Globalisation has certainly helped in accelerating the transformation of some aspects of Taiwanese family business. The above characterisation of today's Taiwanese business culture is not static and it should not be regarded as the evidence of local business resistance to managerial globalisation. Though such resilient Taiwanese business culture is still not fully comprehended and appreciated by many foreign business executives, most of them do take it as a challenge for them to do business here in Taiwan. These foreign businesses have already formulated indigenisation strategies to deal with the Taiwanese family business culture. Therfore, the analysis so far clearly demonstrates that the 'co-existence' of such Taiwanese family business models with globalised fordism and Taylorism from America or Toyotism from Japan does not necessarily cause much tension or conflict.

The Popular Culture

Besides the efficient presence of an internationalised business environment, today's Taiwan is also a society coloured with globalised popular cultures and life styles. Here in Taiwan, popular culture is commonly defined as the cultural pattern of life produced for the people, to be exact, a body of consumers. International business has indeed created global consumer needs and then fulfilled those needs by its cultural products by the powerful tool of the mass media. In essence, the global popular culture is pretty much media-based, and it is managed by the producers of advertising, television, cinema, pop music, and other branches of the mass communication industry.

The multinational media and communication industry has played a very crucial role in shaping and forming Taiwan's popular culture and public tastes. Today, in many big cities, the residents can watch more than 40 channels of cable television in their living rooms. In Taiwan, more than 68 per cent of the households have subscribed to cable television in 1998. Also, by 1999, more than 3 million Taiwanese were using the internet, forming what is called the 'internet tribe'.

In a survey in 1999, it was found that the Taiwanese have open and diverse tastes in media-driven popular culture such as pop music, soap opera, TV drama, and films in all languages: local Minnanese, Mandarin, English, Korean or Japanese. An average of 50 per cent to 63 per cent of the interviewed respondents showed their fondness for the different local and foreign dramas and films. Significantly, the popularity of Japanese and Korean popular cultures among Taiwanese has been increasing in the recent past especially in Japanese TV drama s and films. In 1994, about 36 per cent of the Taiwanese expressed that they like Japanese drama and films; it increased to 51.3 per cent in 1999.

The infrastructures of the cross-national television industry, such as the media and communication companies, multinational capital, and internationalised languages have all made the globalised culture of Taiwan possible since the 1990s. Indeed, Coca Cola, McDonald's, Disney, Levis, Calvin Clein, Nike, CNN, Poly Gram, EMI, Toyota, Microsoft, Starbucks, and Marlboro all have contributed to the making of a globalised taste, fashion, language, ideas, dreams, and value judgments in contemporary Taiwanese society. But, such global and seemingly homogeneous lifestyles and tastes are still more or less an urban middle class phenomenon.

The Japanese pop culture has been increasingly dominant in the Taiwanese cultural scene in the last decade. The 'tribe of Japanese infatuation' is a young generation who might not know anything about the history, politics, or economy of Japan, nor have they any profound nostalgic feelings toward Japan, as do some of the old Taiwanese generation which grew up during Japanese rule. This new generation of Japanese infatuation is exactly the social product of the Japanese pop culture and media manipulation.

The Japanese melodramas have quite successfully 'localized' and 'indigenised' the American and European modern culture and lifestyles into the Japanese mode which the Taiwanese found more familiar and easier to be associated with. In other words, the Japanese have localised the American dreams and transmitted these to the Taiwanese through pop media programs. The Japanised modern life experience shown in those dramas has provided the young Taiwanese generation with a perfect reference model of modernisation and globalisation. Such identification with the modern global culture via the Japanese pop culture can also be observed in many other societies in Northeast and Southeast Asia.

Side by side with the Americanisation, Europeanisation, and Japanisation of Taiwanese popular culture and lifestyles in the past decades, there has arisen a 'repackaged' cultural localisation and indigenisation. Many local cultures and elements of traditional life-styles were revitaliseld and reinvented, such as traditional Taiwanese cuisine, antique collection and appreciation of tea drinking and tea house, Taiwanese Opera and puppet show, Taiwan rock, and Taiwanese modern art. Several renowned cultural performing arts groups were established with great public enthusiasm and the state's support.

Since the 1980s, Taiwan has entered the world's third wave political democratisation and along with it, the new Taiwanese national identity has also been constructed and developed. The changing political landscapes have also greatly helped facilitate and inspire Taiwans' cultural reconstruction and revitalisation, a move to establish the cultural foundation for the new nation-building process. One such important and typical example is the rewriting and reinterpretation of Taiwanese history by political and academic circles in the past decade.

In an island-wide survey conducted in 1999 by Academia Sinica, 57 per cent of the interviewed repondents felt that all nations' cultures in the world would be more and more similar, a clear sign of the consciousness of the global homogeneity and sameness. But in the same survey, it is also found that 65 per cent felt that even under the world cultural convergence, Taiwan still needs to keep its own cultural characteristics, a call for cultural authenticity.

In short, under the impact of cultural globalisation, Taiwan society has witnessed both the rise of the indigenised commercial consumer culture and a conscious effort towards the reconstruction of Taiwanese cultural identity. The globalisation of popular culture in Taiwan has once again facilitated the growth of cultural diversity and the search for cultural authenticity. Even the globalisation forces in popular culture have been powerful and their presence in contemporary Taiwan's cultural life is prevailing over the localisation responses, as manifested in the above two fronts which appear to have co-existed with globalisation.

The Intellectual Culture

It is the intellectuals who have actually served as 'carriers' of the emerging ideas, values, and thoughts from abroad. The 'reverse brain drain' in Taiwan took place in the late 1970s and early 1980s when more and more Taiwanese young talent with advanced academic degrees from American universities returned to Taiwan and began to take on different jobs. The returned intellectuals have since become the 'carriers' and 'localizers' of many Western/global values.

They have even formed a 'new knowledge class' in Taiwan. This 'new knowledge class' in academic, social service, media, and other cultural institutions has 'diffused' what they learned overseas in their workplace and in the public sphere. They have been teaching or writing about those new ideas and thinking in university classrooms, newspapers, and journals. Many have also translated important works into Chinese. It is thus no surprise that since the 1980s, Taiwan's publishing industry has been growing very fast with a large amount of newly translated books on almost all subject matters filling the shelves.

There has been another 'institutionalization' of important foreign Western thinking and discourses. Such institutionalisation involves both the globalisation and localisation of foreign ideas, values, and ideologies. Quite a few forms of Western thinking have been adopted and practiced in many new social movements in Taiwan since the 1980s.

These new Western/global values and discourses were taken up by the respective social movement organisations and activists as guiding principles and frames of reference to legitimate their causes. Activists for human rights, and environmental and womens movements have learned fast in drawing on Western respective discourses to persuade Taiwan's general public to support the new social movements. The intellectuals in Taiwan have always been the most influential social class in leading new social thinking and reform, and have done so in awakening environmental consciousness, human rights conception and gender equality awareness.

Among the activists, many of them are in fact returnee intellectuals with experiences abroad as students. During the course of mobilisation of social support on the discourses of the environment, human rights, and gender equality, sympathetic journalists in the media have also played a role by initiating and facilitating public concern over the issues. In other words, the local social movements have indeed 'globalized' Taiwan with new discourses originating in the West side by side with 'localisation' efforts to shape the Western/global values to make these acceptable to local society through indigenous cultural language and grassroots mobilisation. The relationship between Western discourse and local civil society and social movements has witnessed the dynamic interplay of cultural globalisation and localisation.

In conclusion, the import and acceptance of the West's new thinking since the 1980s can be seen as a process of cultural globalisation through which Taiwanese culture has been brought closer to the 'imagined' world intellectual culture. Such cultural globalisation also has brought about cultural localisation, and the interplay of globalisation and indigenisation has futher facilitated Taiwan's cultural heterogenisation since the 1990s.

Popular Religious Culture

Though Taiwan may not be called a 'religious supermarket', by the end of 1999, Taiwan's religious scene can be described as a 'winow of world religions'. Though the Ministry of Interior recognises only 11 'conventional' 'legitimate' religions in Taiwan, there are in fact about 250 religious sects of all sorts existing in today's Taiwanese society. Terms like 'new religions', 'new religious phenomena', or 'new religious movements' all refer to either the rise of many newly emerging religious sects from abroad or the revitalisation of local traditional Buddhism.

Many of the new religious groups in the first category are transplanted and imported from foreign cultures such as India, Japan, Vietnam and France. Among the imported new religious sects, the noticeable ones include New Age, Osho, Krishnamurti, Transcendental Meditation (from India), Nichiren Shoshu, Soka Gakkai, Aum Shinrikyo (from Japan), the Supreme Chign Hai (from Vietnam), and Raelian Religion (from France). Taiwan also has new religious sects transplanted from America such as Scientology and ISKCON, but they seem to operate with a much lower profile. These religious groups originated abroad and were introduced into Taiwan in the new political climate of democratisation under which the government no longer had absolute control over social associations and religious groupings.

The second category of new religious movements came as a result of the rejuvenation of traditional Buddhism. In comparison with the stagnation in development of Western Catholic and Protestant religions in Taiwan since 1965, local Buddhism has entered a new developmental era known as 'new religious renaissance'. The most striking difference between the newly revitalised Buddhism and traditional Buddhism lies in its philosophical strand. It has adopted a hands-on approach in reaching out to society by promoting charity work and social causes. The new Buddhist groups have been involved in social welfare and medical service, education, publication culture, and environmentalism. This worldly approach has dramatically changed the way Buddhism has been practiced in Taiwan for centuries.

The comparison between the two camps of the emerging new religious movements in Taiwan has further revealed that both have been taking different views and approaches to modernity, i.e. the sacred way to search for self-identity and the secular path to develop a collective conscience. Both popular religious cultures have expanded Taiwan's religious territories and made Taiwan's religious landscapes more heterogeneous rather that homogeneous. Their co-existence since the 1990s has separately fulfilled the diverse needs of the different classes which pursue them. No significant and obvious synthesis has ever been observed.

Conclusion

From the above analysis, one can say that the Taiwanese experience of the interplay of globalisation and localisation has clearly demonstrated a form of 'multiple coexistence' in all of the four cultural domains. In the globalisation of business culture and intellectual culture, the Taiwanese case has even revealed various degrees of 'synthesis' between cultural globalising forces and organised local reponses. Overall, there is no evidence that the encounter between globalisation and localisation has ever resulted in serious cultural conflict or clash. The global culture has neither taken over Taiwanese local culture, nor has it faced severe rejection from the local. In this connection, Taiwan's experience has further illustrated the possible non-conflictual character of the cause and effect of cultural globalisation.

The role of the state in all these has been varying. On the one hand, the state has played a key role as 'facilitator' and 'promoter' in globalising Taiwan's local business and local popular cultures. One the other the state has held rather ambivalent attitudes toward the import of the world intellectual culture and foreign new religious sects in Taiwan. In contrast to the state, the sectors in civil society such as intellectuals, cultural industry, and religious entrepreneurs have played much more active roles in both promoting cultural globalisation and even responding to it by means of localisation. In the localisation process of the four cultural globalisation forces under study, the state has not taken any domineering position either. Rather, the state has pretty much gone along with the demands from various localising forces in civil society.

Finally, Taiwan's case of cultural globalisation and localisation may well again point to the very nature ofTaiwan as an open, plural, ever-changing and self-adapting modern society.

REFERENCES

Peter Berger, 'Four Faces of Global Culture', *The National Internet*, no. 49, 1997, pp.23-29.

Ying-Hwa Chang, *Taiwan Social Change Basic Survey, 2000*, Institute of Sociology, Academia Sinica, 2000.

Mike Featherstone, Lash Scott and Roland Robertson (eds.), *Global Modernities*, London: Sage Publications, 1995.

H.H. Michael Hsiao et al., 'Culture and Asian Styles of Environmental Movements', in Y.S. Lee and Alvin So (eds.), *Asia's Environmental Movements*, pp. 210-229. London: M.E. Sharpe, 1999.

H.H. Michael Hsiao and Hwa-pi Tseng, 'The Formation of Environmental Consciousness in Taiwan: Intellectuals, Media, and the Public Mind', *Asian Geographer*, 18(1-2), 1999, pp. 99-109.

Koichi Iwabuchi,'Japanese Culture in Taiwan' (in Chinese), *Contemporary*, 125, 1998, pp. 14-22.

Roland Robertson and Habib Haque Khondker, 'Discourses of Globalization: Preliminary Considerations', *International Sociology*, vol. 13 (1), 1998, pp. 25-40.

Malcolm Waters, *Globalization*, London: Poutledge, 1995.

The Worlds of Japanese Culture

BRIJ TANKHA

Culture is a contested terrain. To talk of culture is to take a position in an ideological debate that is of crucial importance to the way we define our lives and mould our future. The Taliban's destruction of the Bamiyan Buddhas and other Buddhist artefacts or the destruction of Babri Masjid here in our own country are dramatic, if very sad, examples of the way cultural boundaries are being re-drawn but these are not the only ones. Boundaries are being re-drawn in subtler and less obvious ways as well. So discussions of culture are also interventions in the current debate.

First, there is the question of what culture we are going to talk about. There is a dominant image of Japan in which perhaps an aesthetic vision is the core of a unique Japanese cultural system. This is manifested in various art forms as well as in the daily lives of the people: *No* and *kabuki* theatre, the tea ceremony, flower arrangement (*ikebana*), viewing cherry blossoms, and the enigmatic Haiku poetry. The list can be lengthened to include a language that is considered stronger in expressing emotions than analytic rigour. These views of Japanese culture are not the product of just a Western view but have worked together with Japanese conceptions and redefinitions of their own culture over a period of time to identify what I would call the official culture. That these cultural forms and practices play a role is not in doubt but what needs to be underlined is that there are other elements that make up the living culture of the Japanese. There are many co-existing worlds that form and shape the cultural practices of the people of Japan.

Before turning to Japan let me first touch on some of the larger issues that can help to locate what I would like to say about Japan, the way Japanese culture has been formed and the principles that serve to define its shape and trajectory. First, there are the historical processes that need to be understood. If we talk of modern Japanese culture then we need to understand the way the modern nation-state system was introduced and the way it built upon and re-moulded existing ideas and institutions. The transformation of subjects (*tami*) into citizens (*kokumin*) followed a trajectory similar to Europe, from where the idea of the nation-state was brought, but it was carried out during a period of intense colonisation. The boundaries of being Japanese were created under this all-pervasive threat. The example of China was all too clear, as was that of other Asian countries. Modernity meant a hardening of geographical boundaries but also of internal differentiation. The Ainu, for instance, and other groups, such as the Ryukyuan islanders who had earlier enjoyed a degree of autonomy where their differences were respected, were now seen as 'peripheral people' that needed to be developed. Just as the Western powers were the most advanced so these were people lower down on the developmental scale.

Japanese definitions of modernity were articulated within a Western framework but developed arguments and ideas advanced from the 18th century. To understand this we need to break out of colonial categories that would see the main impetus for progress flowing from the Western impact. We need to broaden and locate our inquiry within a larger regional framework but at the same time we need to go below the national level to see developments at the level of the locality/province. The colonial period distorted or altered relationships within the region. The idea of national cultures is part and parcel of the idea of the nation-state and to understand the larger patterns of cultural formation we need to go beyond the boundaries of the nation-state and dissect the history that it writes about its past.

Consider the case of Japan. The homogenisation of Japan and Japanese traditions was the creation of Meiji government policies. It helped to create a Japan that saw itself as 'one country, one language, one people'. At the core of this identity was the Imperial House, direct descendants of the Sun Goddess. This myth of divine origin helped to differentiate the Japanese from others. Japanese culture, too, was then a matter of birth rather than acquisition. Its core values could not be expressed but only intuitively understood. This conception grew out of the philological researches in the Tokugawa period of Kamo no Mabuchi and was later developed by his disciple Motoori Norinaga, famous for his commentaries on the *Tale of the Genji*. These philosophers and others, like Hirata Atsutane, sought to remove the encrustations of Chinese culture and reveal the true beauty of Japan's real identity. The language, they argued, of this pure past was intuitive, emotional and not deformed as it later became by dry Chinese rationalism. They traced the true heart of Japan back to the myth of divine origin and its expression to the classical literature of the Heian. What set Japan apart from China was the Imperial House, directly descended from the Sun Goddess, and to whom the people were bound in a unique relationship that could be neither severed nor extended.

In the modern period, building on this philosophical foundation the Meiji government consciously set about elevating the Emperor and the Imperial House to a position above the clouds. He was elevated to a position of remote authority, taken on carefully stage-managed processions in different parts of the country and the legal framework was designed to keep the people in check and suppress dissent. Censorship laws were stringent when it came to criticism of the Imperial House. That is why even in the 1930s heterodox cults that seemed to threaten Imperial authority were dealt with far more severely than left wing movements.

Similarly, religion was used to strengthen Japanese national identity. After an initial period of experimentation the government carried out a policy to excise Buddhism and make Shinto what they called the rite of state. In other words Shinto was seen not as a religion. This policy meant that Shinto shrines that had often been part of Buddhist temples were separated and the priests brought under state control. The shrines were categorised in a hierarchy and many small shrines were amalgamated for easier administrative control. The priests sought this patronage as it increased their influence. Scholars such as Kuroda Toshio have long argued that in classical literature there is hardly any reference to Shinto and today scholars distinguish between *kami* worship as practised by the people and state Shinto or the system under the control of the government in pre-war Japan. Western observers also contributed their view on this when they saw Shinto as the true religion of Japan that for them defined and set Japan apart.

In the modern period the Japanese language was also standardised with the Tokyo dialect becoming the national standard. The Japanese ideograph and the distinction between written language and spoken language was a great barrier to the spread of education and the domination of the educated elite in China and so also in Japan. However, Japan had two phonetic scripts or *kana* and these played a pivotal role in the diffusion of ideas and the creation of a common culture. In medieval Japan Buddhist texts were often written in *katakana* and these helped in the diffusion and popularisation of ideas. These tracts were often carried by travelling priests who had renounced the wealth and prestige of the great monastic orders.

Similarly, through interaction at the popular level of Shamans, dancers, singers, entertainers and prostitutes the Japanese islands were bound by a common culture that grew out of shared social rituals that differed from the elite culture typified by *yugen* and *sabi*. Here among the people, in the words of Barbara Ruch, 'tonsure, pilgrimage and travel, wine and song, rites to activate good and nullify evil forces, communication with the spirits of the dead, and rituals to ensure an afterlife in paradise' were the key elements. This dynamic and vibrant aspect of Japanese culture that seems so far removed from the reticent ideal of the elite has been excised from the national heritage because this was the culture of the marginal and powerless. Historians who have sought to recover these lost histories point us to a more complex past that forms an integral part of Japan's many cultures and it is by understanding the inter-relationships between these that we can approach the whole. Otherwise the 'search for larger synthetic patterns in cultural history will fail if half the lights are out'.

It is this inter-relationship that is also of great importance in defining the boundaries of Japanese-ness. Japan is part of a globalising world and has been open, and even actively sought to become a part of the Western world. Whether it was the *moga* (modern girl) in the early 20th century or the *ganguro* (black face), today Japanese popular fashions have followed their counterparts in the developed world and changed with equal, if not greater, rapidity. Fashions in Japan are even more ephemeral than the cherry blossoms. Foreign films attract twice the number of viewers than Japanese films. *No* and *kabuki* have a small audience. Sumo on the other hand has developed with TV and become more of a national sport than it probably ever was. But that also brings problems. The entry of foreign players has raised controversies about discrimination and racism. The real national sport is baseball and now football has become the next major attraction. The favoured destination for Japanese travellers is the United States and when eating out Italian food is the cuisine of choice. This is no different from other countries but in our discussion of culture we need to locate cultural practices and their relationship with the long-term characteristics and patterns of the past otherwise our understanding would be impoverished.

Let me touch on the question of Asia. Is it just a figment of the colonial imagination? I would suggest that a regional history that examines the inter-relationships before colonialism would show that this is a more complex issue. Looked at within a regional context Japan's history takes on a slightly different dynamism. The classical worldview of the Japanese divided the world into three countries: Japan (*honcho*), the continent including China and Korea (*shintan* or *kara*), and India (*tenjiku*). When the Portuguese first appeared in the middle of the 15th century they were thought to be Indians but soon the Japanese realised the difference. As the real picture began to emerge, and Japanese ideas of world geography began to take shape, *tenjiku* began to fall from its favoured place. Hideyoshi thought that if the Portuguese can come here to Japan then surely he could, after conquering Korea and China, take *tenjiku* as well. Japanese writers like Nishikawa Joken now began to divide the world into China (*chugoku*), foreign countries (*gaikoku*) and barbarians in the outer world (*gaii*). Along with the decline of *tenjiku* the emphasis on Japan as a divine country helped to underline the importance of Japan within a China-dominated world. It provided the foundation for trying to create a Japan-centric order in East Asia.

Similarly, the impetus for economic growth was in part provided not by the need to catch up with the West in the mid-19th century but by the need to stem the outflow of silver in the 17th century. This led the Tokugawa rulers to carry out a policy of import substitution, encouraging through subsidies the silk industry in Nishijin, Kyoto and in other ways. This combined with the development of the economy and skills that enabled Japan to successfully manage the transition in the middle of the 19th century.

The Meiji transformation was built on this basis and in a context where Asian nations were seen as examples of defeated cultures. Early Meiji intellectuals sought to ally with China and Korea because they felt that Japan was too small to resist the Western nations alone. Even then there was a strong expansionist impulse that grew out of the experience of the early 19th century and the opening of Japan within a climate of Western expansion. The desire to create an eastern alliance soon changed as the Japanese defeated China and then Russia and then went on to colonise Taiwan, Korea and then gain control over large parts of China. The initial liberationist ideas behind the rallying cry of an Eastern civilisation was soon lost as it became the ideological cover for an expansionist policy.

In today's Japan then the burden of this expansionist past continues to play an important role and the question of Asian values is inextricably linked to this past. For instance, Mishima Yukio is an example of a writer who sought to counter the Americanisation of Japan and reassert the core values that centred on the Emperor. On the other hand the writer Oe Kenzaburo represents a diametrically opposite position. Oe, a trenchant critic of Emperor-centred nationalism, crafted his fiction within a post-modernist tradition. He championed the cause of the Korean minority and other marginalised groups and to underline his distance from a Tokyo-centric Japan refers to himself as a man from Iyo, the old name of the prefecture that he comes from.

While Japan has developed economically and is an integral part of the developed world in the matter of culture it is still operating within a Western framework. It has made inroads as Japanese TV serials and music spread within the East and Southeast Asian region but it is its graphical productions that have truly achieved a global status. The popularity of Nintendo and Super Mario has been followed by Pokemon and other characters and now animated or anime films have acquired a global audience. In East Asia, Japanese fashions have come to play a dominant role, as witnessed by the developments in Shanghai, Manila or Hong Kong. This movement of culture at the popular level is a process by which Japanese culture feeds on and develops within a global cultural framework.

These interactions have become greater in scale and intensity but they have been going on since the early period; the spread of Buddhism and its shaping of Japanese life is the most striking example but there were others. The export of Japanese and Chinese pottery to Europe played an important role in the production of certain designs that came to be identified as particularly Japanese. Professor Yuko Tanaka of Hosei University studies the design and production of a small accessory worn by the smart Samurai in the 17th and 18th centuries to show the flow of influences from Holland and Italy to Japan and Indonesia. This linking of worlds considered far apart is also visible in the influence of Madras textiles imported into Japan on *kimono* designs in the same period. This was happening when Japan was supposedly a closed country.

Japanese society is now dealing with immigrant populations, though on a smaller scale than Europe or the United States, and this also puts pressure to change and adapt. There are of course complaints and fears that Japan is being ruined but there are also greater signs of cultural activity from foreign groups resident in Japan, particularly those of Korean origin. It is still the Asians who are the workers and who are seen as the problem, and the Americans-Europeans who come in at high level jobs are seen as an example of the internationalisation of Japan. The increase in foreign students is also helping to alter perceptions and attitudes and in cities like Kyoto you now see signs in Korean as well as Japanese.

In conclusion I would like to suggest that Japan cannot be reduced to a certain essence. Such reductions do not actually help in allowing us to grasp a civilisation with greater clarity but rather end up distorting a far more complex and interesting reality. History as practised today is not divided between one that is event-centred and one that looks at flows and processes but it is about looking at both. The one without the other is at best an impoverished effort.

India in Japanese Literature

SATYA BHUSHAN VERMA

Buddhism was introduced to Japan in A.D. 552 by the king of Korea. Twenty years later, Prince Umayado, known as Shotoku Taishi in Japan, accepted Buddhism, studied it himself and dispatched a number of Japanese students to China for the study of Buddhism. In China, Buddhism found its way during the reign of Emperor Ming of the Han dynasty (A.D. 25 - 200). Translations of Buddhist scriptures soon became popular activities with scholars usually working under imperial patronage. Most of the translations were cooperative efforts between Indian and Chinese monks. In this process, many Chinese monks mastered Sanskrit. Foremost among them were Yun Ts'ung (A.D.557 - 611) and Hsuan Tsang (645 - 664) known as Genso and Genjo in Japan respectively.

The first Chinese manuscripts reached Japan in A.D. 607. By A.D. 624, there were 46 Budhist temples, 800 monks and 569 nuns in Japan. The first temple of Horyuji was built in 607. Prince Shotoku, a devotee of Buddhism himself, used to come to give commentaries on the Buddhist Sutras. These commentaries are still preserved in Horyuji temple in Japan. With many Japanese students visiting China for the study of Buddhism, at least some of them learnt Sanskrit also. In 715, we find a Japanese Doji studying Sanskrit from Shubhakar. During the 8th and 9th centuries, when Japan had established direct ambassadorial relations with China, many scholars and Buddhist monks were also sent to China with Japanese ambassadors. Among the Japanese scholars who contributed to Buddhist studies in Japan, names of Saicho (766 - 822), Kukai (773 - 835) and Annen (841-) cannot be forgotten. During this period, a large number of works dealing with various aspects of the Sanskrit language and the Shittan (Siddham) script appeared. A large number of Indian works available in Chinese script were brought to Japan from China and were translated into Japanese. The tradition of studying Sanskrit in the institutes of Buddhist learning is alive in Japan. In the words of Professor Hajime Nakamura, the well-known

Japanese Indologist, the number of students learning Sanskrit in universities and other institutes of learning anywhere outside India is highest in Japan. We find mention of two Indian monks who went to Japan in those centuries. The first was Dharmbodhi, known as Daruma Sama in Japanese, who reached Japan travelling through China and Korea. He lived in China, spending a number of years in meditation and is said to have died in China. Whether he actually went to Japan or not is a mystery but he has become a myth in Japan. The other was a south Indian Brahmin, Bodhisen, who was given the title of Baramon Sozo by the Emperor of Japan. Baramon went to China through the sea route via Indonesia. In China, he met the Japanese Ambassador Hironari who invited him to Japan. Accompanied by some Japanese monks, he reached Japan in 736 and was given a warm welcome. It is said that the consecration ceremony of the huge statue of Buddha, known as Daibutsu, in Todaiji temple in Nara, the then capital of Japan, was performed by him. After the ceremony, he seems to have been appointed by the emperor to teach Sanskrit *mantra* and *dharini* to Buddhist monks.

India, known as *Tenjiku,* remained for many centuries the country of dreams for the Japanese. Prince Takaoka, son of emperor Heizei, born in the year 800 took an arduous trip to India. He became crown prince at the age of 10, a monk at the age of 22 and studied at Todaiji. In 835, he gave all his land and possessions to the temple and left for China in search of the Truth. He studied for more than 10 years in China and then decided to visit India. He could undertake this trip to India only when he had already crossed eighty. He took a route which crossed the Indo-China peninsula but was killed by a tiger somewhere in Vietnam or Laos. An accompanying monk reported his death to the imperial court. Ichikawa Jukai staged his adventures in 1910 in Japan.

By the end of the 19th century Japan found itself enriched with a huge collection of Buddhist literature. According to Japanese scholars, some of the manuscripts of Indian works are older than the Indian manuscripts as, while the climatic conditions in India could destroy the manuscripts, they are still preserved in Japan. Medieval Japanese literature shows the deep influence of Buddhism. The first Monogatari (tale) of Japan, the *Taketori Monogatari,* is said to have been taken from some Buddhist story. Jataka tales had been translated into Japanese and many of them have found a place in Japanese folk literature, in Japanese adaptation. The *Konjaku*

Monogatari (a 12th century collection of tales of the past and present) has one section of stories from India, the other two being from China and Japan. The Haiku poetry of Japan had its inspiration in Zen Buddhism and many of the Haiku poets of the medieval period had themselves been Zen practitioners and philosophers. The word 'zen' itself is the Japanese phonetic translation of the Sanskrit word *dhyana*. A number of gods and goddesses of Indian origin were adapted in Japan as the protector deities of the Buddha, called the *bodhisattvas*. These gods and goddesses became the objects of painting and sculpture in Japan. A large number of Sanskrit words found their way into the Japanese language through Buddhism. These words were absorbed into the Japanese language in three ways: (1) through translation into Chinese ideographic characters and adapted to the Japanese readings of those characters—such words have completely lost their original identity and have become Japanese words; (2) phonetically adapted into ideographic characters in China and translated into their Japanese readings; (3) directly borrowed from Sanskrit and changed into Japanese pronunciation.

The systematised learning of Indian literature and philosophy started only at the end of the 19th century when Japan came in contact with the West. Among many ancient Indian works translated into Japanese, the most important work of the present century is perhaps the Japanese translation of the Tripitakas in 70 volumes during the period 1935 - 41. Dr Takakusu translated some hymns from the Rigveda which were published in 1921. Some portions of the Atharvaveda were also published in Japanese translation around the same period. Dr Takakusu also translated 126 chapters from the Upanishads which were published in 9 volumes during 1922 - 24. The translation of the *Gita* was also done by Dr Takakusu, and published in 1918. The other important work on the *Gita* was the commentary on it by Tsuji Naoshiro, published in 1955. Today, a number of translations of the *Gita* are available in the Japanese language. Dr Hajime Nakamura's *History of Vedanta Philosophy* was published during the period 1950-56 in four volumes. Dr Heiji Nakamura published a collection of Indian tales in two volumes titled *Indo no Minwa* and *Indo no Setsuwa.*

Indian philosophy rather than literature had been of more interest to scholars. But the study of Sanskrit in universities encouraged interest in literature also. The translations of Sanskrit works in Japanese include *Abhijnana Shakuntalam*, *Ritusamhar*, and

Meghaduta of Kalidas, the *Mricchkatika* of Shudrak, and the *Naganandam* of Shri Harsh. All the three *Shatakas* of Bhartrihari, *Chaur Panchashika* of Bilhan and *Gita Govindam* of Jaydeva have also appeared in Japanese translation. Interestingly, the story of the *Ramayana* was known to the Japanese through *Dasharatha Jataka* and from other sources, and some stories from the *Mahabharata* like 'Savitri Upakhyana' have been translated into Japanese but it seems the two great epics of India, the *Ramayana* and the *Mahabharata,* did not evoke much interest in Japan. During the last decade, some attempts have been made to translate the epics into Japanese. Professor Iwamoto Yutaka, a well-known Sanskrit scholar, started translating Valmiki's *Ramayana* but he could not complete the work during his lifetime. Un Ikeda has translated *Ramacharit Manasa* of Tulsidas from the original Awadhi into prose form but it has still not been published.

The *Panchatantra* and *Hitopadesh* are popular in Japan. Dr Iwamoto Yutaka translated some parts of *Katha Saritsagar*. Among other Sanskrit works available in Japanese are Dr Ojihara's *Madan Sanjivan*, Professor Nakano Gishi's *Arthshastra* of Kautilya, the *Manu Smriti* and Dr Iwamoto's *Kamasutra*. Dr Iwamoto wrote a book *Indo no Setsuwa* in which he analysed the influence of Indian fiction on Japanese, Chinese and European literature. Dr Hajime Nakamura, in his work *The Way of Thinking of Eastern People,* enumerated the ways of thinking of the Indians as follows:

1. Preponderance of abstract notions.
2. The bestowal of substantiality to the abstract conception.
3. Fondness for the negative expression, such as non-victory in place of defeat (*jayaajaya*), non-idleness (*Ap'maad*), non-violence (*AihMsaa*), non-theft (*Astoya*), non-property (*Apirga'h*), etc.
4. Negative grasping of the absolute.
5. Attraction to the unknown.
6. Disregard for the individual and the particular.
7. Concept of unity of all things.
8. Subjective comprehension of personality.
9. Supremacy of universal self over the individual self.
10. Alienation from the objective natural world.
11. Spirit of tolerance and conciliation.

The list is long. He comments:

> Love of peace by Indians is already recognized by the western scholars. The word 'Peace' signifies in itself to recognize others or other views besides one. So the peace-loving attitude in Indian people must have come from the unique way of thinking that the different philosophies and different conceptions of the world are nothing but the manifestation of absolute one.

During the present century, many important works on Indological studies have appeared in Japanese but these are mainly for scholars. Among the modern writers, Rabindranath Tagore ranks the highest. According to a Japanese journal *Aporon,89*, 89 books (translations and books on Tagore) and 267 items on Tagore in newspapers and journals were published in Japan by 1959. The whole Tagore literature in Japanese translation appeared in 1993 in 12 volumes as the *Collected Works of Tagore*. The other modern writers translated in Japanese were Prem Chand, Sumitranandan Pant, Iqbal, and Sharatchandra. Hindi novels like *Girati Divaren* of Upendranath Ash and *Tamasa* of Bhishma Sahni appeared in Japanese translations in 1991. Professor Tomio Mizukami of the Osaka University of Foreign Studies brought out the complete text of the Doordarshan serial *Ramayana* in Devanagari script in two volumes in 1992. The list is not complete. But a large number of writings on India today are journalistic writings or books of tourist interest. In comparison, hardly any Japanese literature is available in Indian languages. The very small number of translations of Japanese literature available in Indian languages are mostly from their English translations.

In October 1964, the International Amity Club of Sophia University, Japan, published an English translation of a survey report on the occasion of the Tokyo Olympics. The report has two sections: (i) How is Japan understood in the world; and (ii) the national character of countries in the world. Talking about India, the report says:

> The Indian is generally a very talkative person who with a receptive audience, tends to forget the passage of time while giving somewhat a religious sermon or telling of his personal life. Part of the Indian nationality is his spiritual life and idealization of the next world. The Indians are proud people and think of themselves and their country as the best...

The report concludes: 'In India, when people say a successful man, they point to a bureaucrat. It is a suitable word to show modern India "the paradise of bureaucrats".' The image of India presented in this survey report reflects the journalistic writings of Japan. During the sixties, any television report on India would symbolise India with scenes of cows sitting on streets or on railway tracks obstructing the traffic or trains. Moriaki Ishida was a teacher of Japanese language in the School of Foreign Languages in the Ministry of Defence in India. After his return to Japan he wrote a book *Indo de Kurashi* (My life in India) published in 1963. The opening pages of the book relate his experiences in the following words:

> Train reached Allahabad station at 9.30. I was taking my breakfast, which came from the dining car. An old woman appeared on the window. And in a singing tone, she started crying 'Babuji . . .' She was begging for food. I could not eat. This shabbily dressed poor old woman was only the beginning of my agony, which I experienced during my whole stay of three years in India. On hearing her pathetic voice of 'Babuji', whether I felt disgusted with the woman, or with the food or whether I felt bitter about India itself, it is difficult to say.

Later, he talks of red-tapism in administration, complains of a clerk who was out for buying his Japanese wrist-watch which was for his personal use, grumbles against the low quality of chalks and the blackboard in the class-room, and expresses his annoyance with the behaviour of the students. In short, the whole book reflects the dislike of the author for anything Indian.

Yoshio Hotta's approach to India is different. Hotta came to India to participate in the First Asian Writers Conference in 1956 as a Japanese delegate. He writes in his book *Indo de Kangaeta Koto*:

> Is the land of India something unknown to we Japanese? I don't think. More than a thousand years ago, our ancestors accepted, for internal necessities, the thoughts conceived and developed in this land and made these thoughts the foundation stone of our culture and civilization...During my stay in India, I had always been thinking that the prototype of our thoughts is here in this land and I was faced with the question whether we really possess a scale or compass, whatever we may call it, which we use to judge or look at this prototype! Any scale or

compass which I have as a writer has, in fact, been granted to me originally by this very source.

But Hotta also relates some interesting experiences in his book. The author is crossing the rural land travelling in a bus and is conversing with his co-passenger. A young boy says:

'We are a poor nation. But after 50 years ...'

'After 50 years — ? I never thought what Japan will be after 50 years.'

In a Japanese legend, a tortoise takes a fisher-boy, Urashima taro, to the Sea-god's palace where he lives for long forgetting the passage of time. Finally, he decides to return and is given a small box by the princess with instructions not to open it under any circumstances. The boy reaches back to his village, finds everything changed and in bewilderment, opens the box. Shockingly, the boy changes into a white-haired old man. The legendary box is called Tamatebako in Japanese.

Hotta compares the language problem of India with Tamatebako. He was the sectional chairman in the conference in 1956. He decided to invite the delegates in alphabetical order of the respective countries. As the delegate from Afghanistan was not present, he called the delegate from Burma. An Indian delegate stood up and objected that according to the alphabetical order Assam comes after Afghanistan. Hotta writes:

> 'Is Assam not in India?' I asked in mute amazement.
>
> 'It is, of course. But there is nothing like an Indian language. The delegates of 17 different languages of India are present here.'
>
> 'In that case, will each of the 17 delegates of India be qualified to represent as a separate country?'
>
> 'Yes', the Indian delegate answered so coolly as if nothing had happened. This will mean that the number of participant countries is to be increased by an addition of 17 to the already participating 16 countries. This will be too much, I thought.
>
> In the meantime, the Burmese delegate lost his patience. He said, 'We have to think over this problem. The UNO is situated in New York in America. There are 48 states in America. What will happen if all the 48 states claim separate seats in the UNO. No doubt, India has 17 languages but India is India. Let us take one or two delegates from India. Chairman may declare a short break and try to solve this matter.'

'No. . . No. . ., this is impossible', the Indian side spoke in one voice.

India fascinated Yukio Mishima, one of the leading novelists of today, who committed *harakiri* at the age of 45 in November 1970. Before his death, he completed his masterpiece work, a tetralogy entitled *Hogyo no Umi,* a series of four novels, *Spring Snow, Runaway Horses, The Temple of Dawn,* and *The Decay of the Angel.* The whole cycle of novels is based on the main character Honda's faith in the theory of reincarnation. In the first novel, *Spring Snow* (*Haru no Yuki*), Honda gets hold of a book on Buddhist thought. In the words of the author, here for the first time he was treated to a fascinating account of the varied origins of the doctrine of Karma, and he was reminded of the Law of Manu, which had so absorbed him at the beginning of the winter.

In the *Temple of Dawn* (*Akatsuki no Tera*), Honda reaches Bangkok in connection with a lawsuit. The client firm offers him a bonus in the form of a pleasure trip. Honda decides to visit the Ajanta caves and Benaras. Here three chapters of the novel deal with his visit to the three places, Calcutta, Benaras and the Ajanta caves. Mishima presents a vivid and very lively description of the places visited and the rites performed there, particularly in the Kali temple in Calcutta and cremation at Dashashvamedh Ghat in Benaras, embedded with explanations of connected mythology and legends. On the sacrifice of goats in the Kali temple, he comments:

> The young man's skill with the sword was remarkable; he was following faithfully and unemotionally the practice [of] this holy, yet abominable profession. Holiness dripped in the most ordinary way, like perspiration, from the blood spotting his soiled shirt, from the depths of his deep, clear eyes, and from his large, peasant like hands. The festival goers, accustomed to the sight, did not even turn around, and the holiness with its dirty hands and feet sat confidently in their midst.

Quoting Vedic hymns on sacred waters of the Ganges, Mishima describes the scene at Benaras in the following words:

> Yet, Benaras was a city of extreme filth as well as of extreme holiness. On both sides of the narrow, sunless alleys stalls for fried food and cakes, astrologers, grain and flour vendors were all crowded together; and the area was filled with stench,

dampness, and disease. As one passed through and emerged on the Flagstone Square by the river, clusters of crouching leprous mendicants had gathered; they had come from all parts of the country as pilgrims, and now they begged for alms while waiting death. Flocks of pigeons. Sultry late afternoon sky. A leper was sitting in front of a tin can containing a few coppers; his one eye was red and festered and his fingerless hands like the stumps of felled mulberry trees were raised to the evening sky.

Mishima's description of Benaras continues:

> Benaras, A piece of carpet, hideous to the point of brilliance. A riotous carpet joyously hoisted day and night by temples and people and children—fifteen hundred temples, temples of love with red pillars and black ebony relief's illustrating all the possible positions of sexual intercourse, the House of Widows whose inmates earnestly await death, loudly chanting Sutras night and day, inhabitants, visitors, the quick, the dead, children covered with pox, dying children clinging to their mother's breast...

About cremation, he writes,

> The slow progress of purification of the human body, returning in parts to its four elemental constituents...The resistant human flesh and its useless odour lingers after death...something red opening in the flames, something shiny writhing, black powdery particles dancing up with the fiery sparks. There was a flashing animation in the flames, as though something were being created. From time to time, when suddenly the firewood noisily collapsed and part of the fire disappeared, the cremator would pile on more wood; and from time to time unexpectedly lofty flames would leap upward, almost licking at the temple balcony.
>
> There was no sadness. What seemed heartless was actually pure joy. Not only were *Samsara* and *reincarnation* basic belief, but they were actually accepted as a part of nature, constantly renewing itself before one's eyes, the rice paddy and its growing plants, the trees bringing forth their fruit. Some assistance from human hands was necessary, just as harvest and cultivation required human intervention; people were born to take their turns in this natural progression.

From the Ajanta cave temples, Honda writes in his letter to his wife, 'I am here to see the cave temples at Ajanta. The tour's about to start. I can't drink the orange drink in front of me, because I see the edge of the glass is all dotted with fly spots ... India is really astonishing.' India is always in Honda's mind. In *The Decay of the Angel*, the fourth and the last novel in the cycle of *Sea of Fertility*, Honda is awake at midnight:

> The mists would seem to have cleared and the moon to have come out. The window, a little too tall for the curtain, was shining at the bottom a faint silver-blue, like a shadow of the giant reclining peninsula beyond the waters. So India would look, thought Honda, to a ship approaching from the Indian Ocean at night. He went back to sleep.

Honda is above seventy-six now. Near the closing pages of the novel, we read:

> Perhaps somewhere, sometime, Honda would meet the hundredth, the ten thousandth, the hundred millionth reincarnation. There was no hurry. Why hurry? He did not know even where his own rut was taking. So concluded Honda, a man who had not been in a hurry to die. What he had seen at Benaras was human indestructibility as the fundamental essence of the universe.

A brief but thorough study of India is presented in a book *Nihon to Indo* (Japan and India) published in 1978. The book is a collected work of nine scholars of Indian Studies in Japan. We may quote Professor Heiji Nakamura from this book. He says:

> Free India developed great appreciation by the Japanese people for its non-alignment and policy of peace in international affairs. In those days, Nehru was the most respected politician of the world [and] in Japan India was ranking first among the countries of the world liked by [the] Japanese. Every university registered a large number of students offering subjects related to India for dissertations. Though studies on Indian philosophy and Buddhism, which were quite advanced in pre-war Japan, continued as before but more interest was now shown in modern India and studies on varied aspects like history, politics, economic system and society became popular among Japanese

researchers. But after [the] fifties, the image of India in Japan started changing. Indo - China conflict of 1962 and India's decreasing role in world politics lowered the image of India in Japan. Added to that, Japan's high economic growth and India being a poor and underdeveloped country were perhaps the contributory factors.

THE RAMAYANA IN JAPAN

SATYA BHUSHAN VERMA

Buddhism was introduced to Japan in the year A.D. 552 by the king of Korea. Twenty years later, Prince Umayado, later known as Shotoku Taishi, accepted Buddhism. He constructed Buddhist temples, *viharas*, hospitals, and homes for the destitute and also dispatched a number of Japanese students to China for the study of Buddhism. The first temple of Horyuji was built in A.D. 607, where Prince Shotoku himself used to give commentaries on Buddhism. Till the end of the 7th century, Japan did not show any interest in India. It is possible that Japan did not even know that China was not the origin of Buddhism.

During the 8th and 9th centuries, when Japan had established direct ambassadorial relations with China, many scholars and monks also were dispatched to China and there some of them came in contact with some Indian monks. Some of them learnt Sanskrit also, and a large number of Sanskrit works available in Chinese script were brought to Japan from China and were translated into Japanese. India in Japanese came to be known as *Tenjiku*. China was a reality for Japan. India was a dream, a land of imagination where Hotokesama or Buddha was born. We find mention of two Indians who reached Japan. One was Dharmbodhi, known in Japan as 'Daruma' or 'Darumasama' who is believed to have reached Japan travelling through China and Korea and crossing the sea riding on a reed. The other was a south Indian Brahmin who was given the title of 'Baramon Sozo' in Japan. Baramon is the Japanese way of pronouncing Brahmin. Daruma is a myth whereas Baramon is a reality in Japan. Both of them made significant contribution to Japan.

Studying Bongo (Sanskrit) in the institutions of Buddhist learning became a tradition in Japan. Even today, in the words of Professor Hajime Nakamura, the well-known Japanese Indologist, the number of students learning Sanskrit in universities and other centres of learning anywhere outside India is highest in Japan. Indian philosophy rather than literature has been of more interest to Japanese scholars. The two Indian epics, the *Ramayana* and *Mahabharata* did not evoke much interest in Japan. However, the *Panchtantra*, *Katha-Saritsagar*, and the *Jataka* tales, translated into Chinese, reached Japan also and found place in Japanese folk tales and in works like *Konjaku Monogatari*. Although the *Ramayana* had not been translated into Japanese till recently, but its story reached Japan in various forms.

The story of *Ramayana* is available in a Japanese collection of popular tales named *Hobutsushu* by Taira-no-Yasuyori as a Buddhist tale taken from the Chinese version of *Dasaratha Jataka*. The outline of the story given in *Hobutsushu* is as follows:

'Once upon a time, Tathagata Sakyamuni was king of a great kingdom. At that time the people of another kingdom Kyushi were starving to death because of famine and were jealous of the peace and prosperity of the kingdom of Sakyamuni. They decided to invade the country of Sakyamuni. When Sakyamuni heard of this, he decided to leave the country and go to mountains and practice dharma to avoid unnecessary killing and death of innocent people. The queen did not agree to stay back and accompanied him. The king Sakyamuni started living a simple life in mountains alongwith his wife. One day, a Brahmin ascetic came to live with them and when Sakyamuni was away to mountains for gathering fruits, he took away his wife and disappeared. Sakyamuni set forth in search of his wife. He met a huge bird with both its wings broken. The bird told Sakyamuni that an ascetic was carrying Sakyamuni's wife and when the bird gave a fight to him, he changed into dragon king and cut its wings. After narrating this happening the bird died and was burried by Sakyamuni.

'As advised by the bird before its death, Sakyamuni travelled to South in search of the dragon king. On his way, he met thousands of monkeys who had lost their kingdom to a neighbouring king. Sakyamuni won their kingdom back for them showing excellent skill of archery. The monkeys, in gratitude, accompanied Sakyamuni in search of the dragon king and thousands of monkeys reached the south end of the earth facing the sea.

'Indra, touched by the practice of Ahimsa by Sakyamuni and by the sense of gratitude of the monkeys, transformed himself into a small monkey and joined them. A bridge was built on the sea.

Shakyamuni and all the monkeys reached the mansion of the dragon king. The dragon king roared and released fire from his eyes. The monkeys became unconscious. The small monkey went to Himalayas and brought a branch of a herb tree. All the monkeys were brought to life with more strength and energy with the treatment of that herbal tree. The dragon king was killed by an arrow of Sakyamuni and the queen was rescued. On the other hand, the king of Kyushi had died. The people of Kyushi and the people of the country of Sakyamuni invited Sakyamuni and made him king of both the countries.'

The variation of this story from Valmiki's *Ramayana* is obvious. In the Japanese tale, Sakyamuni leaves his kingdom because of the evil designs of the neighbouring king. Ravana, the demon king of the island of Lanka becomes the dragon king in this story. *Hobutsushu* is a work of the 12th century. The conclusion of the story mentions the Chinese work *Lie-tu-tsi-ching* as the source of this story. As the Japanese story differs from Valmiki's *Ramayana*, it differs from its Chinese source as well at various points. In the Chinese version, Jatayu, the bird, loses one wing; in the Japanese version, it loses both its wings. In the Chinese version, Hanuman is related to Ravana; in the Japanese version, there is no mention of that. In the Chinese version, the abduction of Sita and the death of Jatayu take place after the battle of Bali and Sugriva whereas in the Japanese version, the events take their own course according to Valmiki's *Ramayana*.

It seems the story of *Ramayana* was known to the Japanese even before it was taken in *Hobutsushu*. Along with Buddhist culture, Japan had imported some forms of music and dance also which have been preserved for the last over one thousand years, known as 'Bugaku' or 'Gagaku', as the music and dance of the imperial household of Japan. This includes much that has its origin in Southeast Asia, India and China. One such dance form is 'Doragaku' which is believed to have developed during the 8th to the 12th centuries at the Imperial court in Nara and Heian periods of Japanese history. *Doragaku* means music and dance of Dora. According to a Japanese Sanskrit scholar, Professor Junjiro Takakusu, 'Dora' is derived from the word *dwaravati* which is the old name of the ancient city Ayudhiya in Thailand. According to the ancient manuscript, *Doragaku* consisted of four dances, the themes of which have a close resemblance to various episodes of the *Ramayana*. The four dance forms were: (1) Bari-mai, which presents the scene of the fight between monkey kings Bali and Sugriva. In the Japanese language, the sound of 'l' changes to 'r' and *mai* means dance. As such, *Bari-mai* will mean Bali-dance; (2) *Sita-mai*, which is Sita-dance; (3) *Ja-kin-jo-no-mai*, which presents the confinement of Sita at Lanka; and (4) *Kan-to-soto-mo-onna-wo-ubau-mai* which presents the scene of battle between Rama and Ravana. The details about the number of performers, distinguished features and descriptions of each dance given in the old manuscripts support the belief that these dances refer to the *Ramayana* scenes. It can be presumed that these dance forms and stories might have travelled to Japan from Southeast Asia.

Masakazu Tamori, in his paper 'Ramayana kara Mita Momotaro' ('Momotaro seen from *Ramayana*') presented at the 20th Congress of Japanese Folklore at Kokugakuin University in May 1996, suggests that the popular Japanese tale of Momotaro has its roots in the story of *Ramayana*. In *Ramayana*, Rama and his brothers are born after eating a fruit given to the queens by a *rishi*. Momotaro, the peachboy, is born out of a peach. Rama takes the army of monkeys to invade Lanka, the kingdom of demon king Ravana. Momotaro takes a dog, a monkey, and a pheasant with him, travels to Oni-no-shima (island of demons), conquers the demon king and comes back home with his three companions.

In another collection of tales named *Samboekotoba* by Minamoto-no-tamenori belonging to the 10th century, we come across the story of Dasaratha unwittingly killing the young son in the service of his old and blind parents. This story is again from the *Ramayana,* representing the Japanese version of the 'Sravana-vadh' episode which seems to have travelled to Japan through China as a Buddhist tale. The summary of the story is as follows:

'A rich merchant couple lived in the country of Kaira with their only son Semu who believed in the ten virtues of dharma and served his parents faithfully. With advancement of age, both the parents lost their eyesight. To fulfill the desire of the parents, Semu took them to the depths of the mountains and settled there. One day, when he was out with a coat made of deer skin, he came across a herd of deer drinking water. Just at that time, King of Kaira, who had come for hunting, shot an arrow aiming at the deer which pierced the heart of Semu. The king, after realizing his mistake, went to his parents, told them about the incident and on their request, brought them to the site where Semu was lying dead. The old couple cried in prayer that if their son had followed Buddha, Dharma and Sangha in his life and if he had been truly devoted to his parents, he should come to life. The gods touched by their prayer gathered together. Indra came in human form and poured Amrit (nectar) into the mouth of Semu. Semu came back to life and his parents got their eyesight back. Semu preached the king to keep self-control, desist from hunting and practice dharma.'

The Japanese story differs from the original *Ramayana* story in its conclusion which ends with a happy note.

During the last decades, attempts to translate the epic into Japanese have been made by Japanese scholars. Professor Iwamoto Yutaka, a well-known Sanskrit scholar, translated the Valmiki's *Ramayana* from Sanskrit into Japanese. Un Ikeda has translated *Ramacharit Manas* of Tulsidas from Avadhi into Japanese in prose form although it is still unpublished. The story of *Ramayana* has been made into an animated film also.

GROWING INDO-MONGOLIAN RELATIONS IN RECENT YEARS

D. DASHPUREV

Mongolia cherishes the age-old, warm and friendly relationship with India. The message of spirituality that their contacts, spanning over 1,500 years, have produced constitute a strong foundation for friendship and understanding among the two countries which share religious and cultural affinities. Indian cultural and religious influence found its way to Mongolia via Tibet, primarily through the efforts of Buddhist missionaries. Mongolia was the first country to which the Holy Relics of the Buddha were brought from India. As we stand on the threshold of a new millennium, our joint endeavour must be to protect and enrich our spiritual values even as we seek to provide material prosperity to our people in our quest for globalisation.

Last year we celebrated the 45th anniversary of the establishment of diplomatic relations between Mongolia and India, which were first established between the two countries on 24 December 1955.

Economic Cooperation

Bilateral trade between Mongolia and India has not developed much due to the problems of distance requiring trans-shipment through Chinese ports, high freight rates and delayed delivery schedules. Despite this, in recent years several Indian companies have shown their interest in trade with Mongolia. Many Indian companies have been participating in international tenders floated by Mongolia. A New Delhi-based construction company, has established a long-term presence in Mongolia working as consultants for two important road projects. Another Indian company from New Delhi has a representative office in Mongolia and is engaged in trade and supply of materials. An Indian company supplied accounting software to the Central Bank of Mongolia. The Mongolian Chamber of Commerce signed an agreement of cooperation with FICCI

(Federation of Indian Chambers of Commerce) in 1991. The Mumbai-based Indo-Mongolian Chamber of Commerce and Industry has visited Mongolia for discussions twice, the last visit having taken place in September 1997.

India is a regular participant in the Donors meet. The seventh round was held in Ulaanbaatar from 21-22 June 1999. It was announced that Indian assistance to Mongolia stands increased by 117 per cent, that is, Rs. 13.9 million (approx. US $ 3 million).

Technological and Cultural Cooperation

The technological and information revolutions have brought about unprecedented social and economic transformations, the benefits of which must be harvested for the advancement of our peoples. In its relations with India, the Mongolian effort is now directed towards benefiting from the Indian experience through increased cooperation in the economic, scientific, technical, educational and cultural fields. In February 1994, the Treaty of Friendly Relations and Co-operation was signed during the visit of President Ochirbat to India. This treaty is valid for ten years with a provision for automatic five-year renewals.

Indian Technical and Economic Co-operation (ITEC) Training: In the last five years, Mongolia has emerged as one of the major beneficiaries under ITEC (civilian) Training Programme conducted by the Government of India which provides 35 training slots every year for Mongolia under the ITEC programme. A vocational training centre, named after late Prime Minister Rajiv Gandhi, was established in Ulaanbaatar in 1996. The centre earlier had five faculties, namely, machine shop, plumbing workshop, electrical repair shop, radio and TV workshop, and automobile repair workshop. India added two more faculties of gemstone cutting and polishing and computer centre, and the Vice President of India, inaugurated them on 29 August 1999 at RGVTC (Rajiv Gandhi Vocational Training Centre) in Ulaanbaatar during his official visit to Mongolia in August 1999.

In view of the tremendous goodwill Mongolians have for India and their enthusiasm and interest to know more about India, the Indian Culture Centre (ICC) was established in Ulaanbaatar in January 1992. The centre is presently located in the premises of the RGVTC. Two to three students are sent to India every year for studying Hindi at the Kendriya Hindi Sansthan, Agra.

In addition, India also provides 20 scholarship slots per annum to Mongolian students under the Indo-Mongolian Cultural Exchange Programme and the General Cultural Scholarship Scheme, for pursuing undergraduate and postgraduate courses in India.

The Rajiv Gandhi Vocational Training Centre in Ulaanbaatar is an enduring landmark of Mongolia-India cooperation and of India's commitment to assisting Mongolia's social and economic development through human resource development. It is an investment in Mongolia for Mongolia's future. Hundreds of Mongolian students have already trained here. Several of them would already be contributing to Mongolia's economy by successfully using the skills they have acquired here. The late Indian Prime Minister, Rajiv Gandhi maintained that a strong nation requires educated and well-trained youth who would lead the way into the future. It is a tribute to his memory that this centre is fashioning precisely such men and women.

Agricultural Cooperation

The Indo-Mongolian Friendship Farm in Darkhan is a significant symbol of our co-operation in sharing the experience of India's Green Revolution programme. It was conceived so that India would share the fruits of the research conducted in agriculture in India with Mongolia, especially with regard to the development of cold resistant and early maturing varieties of wheat and potatoes. This is aimed at assisting Mongolia in attaining self-sufficiency in seed production and eventually in food production. To implement this, the Indo-Mongolian Friendship Farm was formally inaugurated on 19 May 1997 at Darkhan.

International Cooperation

While we work together at the bilateral level, there is also immense scope for continuing cooperation at the global level. The world is changing rapidly. Both countries cooperate closely in the international fora. Mongolia has traditionally valued India's role in international affairs. It recalls with gratitude the contribution of Pandit Jawaharlal Nehru in obtaining international recognition for Mongolia. It has expressed appreciation for India's support for its admission to the Non-Aligned Movement (NAM) as a full member in 1991 as also to other international agencies, including international financial institutions.

Apart from these common views, we must find some other facts which have taken an important place in political relations between the two countries.

India is one of the greatest countries in the world, having a large population with trained manpower, whereas Mongolia is a land-locked country having a sizeable territory with a comparatively smaller population. As Mongolia has deep-rooted historical, cultural and spiritual ties with the countries of Asia and, in particular, with India, it explains the establishment of wide human relations and demographical exchange ties between them.

Strategically, Mongolia is situated between the two giants of Asia, that is Russia in the northwest and the People's Republic of China in the southeast. That is why, due to its geopolitical situation, it is only natural that Mongolia attaches primary importance to the continued relationship and cooperation with other powerful nation-states. In my opinion India and China have different interests regarding several problems. So if India cordially increases its influence in Mongolia then it is possible to find some plus aspects for Indian policy regarding China.

Today we stand at the threshold of a new millennium. In assessing the evolution of the world during this century, we must ensure that the emerging world order is conducive to and compatible with the realisation of the people of the developing world. We must learn from the experience of the century that has just ended. The coming century must be one of partnership between the developed and developing world. Our peoples must be able to look to a future of peace, stability and human freedom. Let us work with hope for that noble cause.

LITERARY EXCHANGES BEWEEN MONGOLIA AND INDIA

YU. MUNKH-AMGALAN

Mongolia and India are spiritual neighbours with deep-rooted and age-old historical and cultural relations. One facet of these ancient traditional relations between the countries is the literary links. Mongols have a long and rich tradition of translating literary works from other languages and this tradition is a component part of the nation's intellect. As mentioned by the well-known scholar, Professor L. Khurelbaatar:

> It is safe to maintain that the Mongolian tradition of translating literary works from foreign languages has originated since ancient time, if you study the script which was used in the 5th century, and the historical fact that the Tripitaka, India's famous collection of writings, were translated into Mongolian under the stewardship of Uigar and Sogdian teachers. We can see from the historical facts and sources that Mongolians have translated various scholarly writings and literary works from Uigar, Perchian [i.e. Persian], Arabic, Chinese, Tibetan and Sanskrit languages (Khurelbaatar, pp. 2,154).

It will be hard and time-consuming work trying to determine exactly when Mongolians began to translate books and writings relating to different spheres of human knowledge and wisdom from foreign languages, especially from the multi-faceted Indian languages. I will be discussing Indian literature and literary works which were translated and published in Mongolia from 1921 to 2000, some of the most dramatic years in the history of Mongolian society and politics. During these years 10 series of books, including other foreign literatures translated into Mongolian, were published. These included works by M. Bayanzul, D. Burendalai, G. Purevdorj and Sh. Bazar. We studied the Indian literature series and compared them with the very first originals.

India's ancient writings have been translated and published since 1921. Ts. Damdinsuren, an academician, published '*Bigermijid king's story*', 'Bodhicarya-vatara' and 'History of Ushaandar King' in his book *Hundred Wisdoms of Mongolian literature* in 1959. *The Panchatantra* (five teachings) by V. Sharma was translated from the Hindi by J. Gendendaram. In 1305 the Mongolian philologist, Chos-Kyi'Od-zer pandita, translated *The Bodhicaryavatara* of Shantideva (*ca* 7th century) from Tibetan to Mongolian and in 1312 he wrote an extensive commentary on it in Mongolian. Some parts of the *Mahabharata* were translated into Mongolian and published in Mongolia. A Mongolian resume of the *Mahabharata* is included in the commentary of the *Subhasita-yintayilburi Cindamani-yintulkigur kemegdeku* (see Mukden, p. 220ff). This work was translated in 1778 - 79 by Blo-bzan-tshul-khrims, the doctor from the *Cajanajala-yin sume* or White Mountain Monastery in the Chagar province, from the Tibetan original by Sa-skya pandita. The Mongolian commentary, which contains the epic, is a revised version of the Tibetan commentary of *Rin-chen-dpal-bzan-po*. 'It has remained a very popular work among the Mongols as a model of literary composition and didactic writing for centuries. It has been a powerful vehicle for transmitting the classical stories and epics of India to the remote regions of Northern Asia inhabited by Mongolian-speaking people.' The 'Araji Booji', Stories of King Vikramaditya', and 'Tales of King Vikramaditya and the Thirty-two Wooden Men' have also been translated into the Mongolian language.

Paramount importance was attached to the publication of source materials on the history of Indian and Mongolian literary relations. In the 1920s the Mongolian versions of Vikramaditya's tales, the stories of King Raja Bhoja and *Vetalapancavincatica* were published separately. In the series of *Corpus Scriptorum Mongolorum* (CSM) the fairy tales of '*Vitala*' and the '*Stories from Panchatantra*', '*Damamukona-masutra*', '*Kavyadarsa*' by Dandin, 'Bodhicary-avatara' and others were published.

The *Ramayana* collection by Jagarvadi Rajgobalatarya was translated from Hindi by D. Nyamsuren in 1969. Academician Ts.Damdinsuren wrote a monograph, '*Ramayana in Mongolia*', which was published in Mongolian in the Mongolian People's Republic (MPR), and in Russian in the USSR in 1976. In Mongolia several institutions are engaged in oriental studies, including Indology. The Institute of Language and Literature of the Academy of Science of the MPR is the biggest centre undertaking tremendous research work and publication of literary masterpieces. Scholars and scientific workers of the institute had written many articles and monographs on traditional links with Indian culture. Among the recent publications there are *The Ramayana's Spreading in Mongolia* by Ts.Damdinsuren (new translation), *Collection of Four Versions of Kalidasa's Meghuduta* by B. Rinchin, a short version of the *Ramayana* translated from Hindi by D. Nyamsuren, and the *Panchatantra* by Bishnu Sharma, translated from Hindi by J. Gendendaram, noted translator.

The renowned Mongolist Lama Chimpa wrote, 'The tradition of interest in Indian literature is still very well maintained in modern Mongolia. It seems that a number of scholars are engaging themselves in Indian studies. Articles and translations of Indian literature including modern literature are constantly being published in Mongolia. Two such books done by very recent scholars were a short version of the *Ramayana,* translated by D. Nyamsuren and a beautiful translation of the *Panchatantra* by G. Gendendaram. These two works indicate the higher standard of education in Mongolia. Unless one reads both the original and the translations, of course, one cannot really judge the quality of the translation. I read the *Panchatantra* both in Sanskrit and Hindi and I read that of Gendendaram, which was superb.

Poems. One of the most widely translated forms of Indian literature into Mongolian is poetry. From the prior survey of our studies we can see that 332 poems written by 53 Indian poets were translated into Mongolian from Hindi and Russian. For instance, there are 145 verses and poems by Rabindranath Tagore translated into Mongolian, but 128 of the verses, for example, 'Gitanjali' (Songs of Offering) were translated into Mongolian directly from Hindi by J. Badraa. The rest were translated from Russian by M. Tsedendorj, D. Tsedev, N. Jambalsuren and others. In 1987, O. Sukhbaatar translated 149 verses, which were written by 33 Indian poets, from Hindi and published a book called *Rhythm of Ganga River* dedicating it to the fortieth anniversary of Indian independence.

The following Indian poets were translated into the Mongolian languages: Kedarnath Agarwal (16 poems); Rajesh Joshi (13 poems); Harivanshrai Bachhan (11 poems); Ramdayaari Sinha Dinkar, Sarweshwar Dayal Saxena, Srikaant Varma (9 poems each); Bharat Bhushan Agarwal (8 poems); Shamsher Bahadur Sinha (7 poems);

Uday Prakash and Raguvir Saha (6 poems each); Aruna Kamal, Nagarjun, Subhash Mukerjee (5 poems each); Balathal, Ganga Prasad Vimal, Kumar Vikas (4 poems each); Divek Ramesh, Kedarnath Sinha, Liladhar Jaguri, Munnulal, Narendar Jain, Narendar Sharma, Naresh Mehta, Sumitranand Panth, Suryakant Tripathi, Trilochan Shastri (3 poems each); Baldev Bansi, Bhaghvat Ravat, Bhaivir Singh, Kunmar Anupam, Kunvar Narayan, Parvej Shaheed, Sudheer Saxena, Shyam Kishan (2 poems each); Ashok Chakradhar, Bari Rahmat Holida, S. Bhattarcharya, Vishnudev, Vimal Chandra Ghosh, Gurajat Aprao, P. Dhawan, A. S. Jafri, Jugmandir Dayal, Mannulal Sharma, Mohammed Iqbal, Nirala, Meham Singh, B. Shankar, Shankar Sheilandra, P. Sharma, Sukanta Bhot Tacharjo, Teg Allah Abadi (1 poem each).

These 184 poems were translated by more than 20 translators but the main translators were J. Badraa, M. Tsedendorj, S. Adiihuu, O. Sukhbaatar, S. Enebish and Sh. Tsendgombo. One of the Indian poems was published in newspapers, books and magazines four times. One poem has been translated by three different translators. A poem by Balathal was translated several times and each time it was given a different name by its translators. D. Burendalai translated the poem in 1955 and called it 'Lenin's tomb', S. Sandagdorj translated it in 1958 and called it 'Lenin's graveyard'. Sh. Tsendgombo translated it in 1968 and called it 'Lenin's mausoleum'.

It may be very fruitful for the theory and practice of translation if we compare the original translations from Hindi to English and Russian with the three different Mongolian versions.

Narratives. The works of contemporary Indian writers have been translated from Hindi and published in Mongolia. *Gitanjali* and *Gora* by Rabindranath Tagore were translated by J. Batra and D. Nyamsuren; *Goudan* by Prem Chand and *Abha* by Acharaya Chatursen Shastri were translated by J. Gendendaram as well as works by Mulk Raj and K. Chandra. Six Indian narratives were translated into Mongolian. 'A Tree Growing Upside Down' by K. Chandra was translated from Russian by M. Tsedendorj and this story was serialised in 14 instalments in the newspaper called *Pioneers' Truth* in 1957 and later published as a book. 'Abha' by A. Shastri was translated from Hindi by J. Gendendaram and in 1963 it was brought out as a book. In addition to the above mentioned S. Purevjav translated 'Sundari' by J. Singh from the Russian language in 1977. O. Sukhbaatar translated two narratives and 14 stories by

Mohan Rakesh from Hindi. In 1999 J. Gendendaram translated and published from Hindi the narrative 'The Sin and Goodness' by Sh. N. Gulshin.

Proverbs. Since 1968 Indian proverbs and parables have been translated into Mongolian and published in literature textbooks used by eighth grade schoolchildren of the secondary schools. J. Badraa translated Indian proverbs from Sanskrit and prefaced them with a commentary before publishing it in a magazine called *Tsog*.

Humorous. In 1977, O. Sukhbaatar translated Indian humorous writings and stories entitled 'Thief was Exposed' into Mongolian and published it.

Novels. Mongolian translators translated 8 novels into their language during 1921-2000. J. Gendendaram translated *Sufferings from Poverty* by Prem Chand from Hindi but another novel, *Hirmala* by the same author was translated by Ts. Shuger from Russian. The following novels were translated from Russian into Mongolian: K. Chander's *A Woman who had Won Thousand Mens' Heart* (trans. S. Purevjav), Khwaja Ahmed Abbas's *Happy Time Comes* (trans. Ts. Shuger), Niranjan's *Fallacy* (trans. G. Khadbaatar), P. Sandrityan's *In Forgotten Country* (trans. S. Tsedev), and Bhishma Sahni's *Vasanti* (trans. D. Purevdorj).

Short Stories. In the period mentioned above 106 short stories written by 31 Indian authors were translated from Hindi, English and Russian into Mongolian as follows: 22 stories by Rabindranath Tagore, 16 stories by Prem Chand, 15 stories by Krishan Chander, 14 stories by Mohan Rakesh, 7 stories by Khwaja Ahmed Abbas, and one story each by Yashpal, Mulk Raj Anand, Bhishma Sahni. The remaining translated short stories were of various writers like Mitro Premendro, Ahilyan Buchhibabu, Shuboth Ghosh, Dandanany Jiyakantan, Kartar Singh Duggal, Shokhot Osman, Amrita Pritam, Mohan Rakesh, Annabhay Sahte, Peddibhotla Subbaramaya, Bhabany Bhattachary, Upendra Ashk, Bhagvakcharana Varma, Maheshvary Jakori, Vishvambharanath Koushik, Narayan Gongopadhaya, Mukhra Sharma, N. Dalal, M. Banerji, S. R. Tottekkatt, Umeshchandra Sharma.

In 1959 P. Choijil, who translated one of the short stories by Mitro Premendro, wrote 'Robinzon Kruzo was a woman', but in 1998 D. Bold translated it as 'Robinzon Kruzo was an Attractive Woman' from Russian, to make it sound interesting.

An interesting collection of short stories translated from Hindi is the set of humorous stories about wise Birbal who was King Akbar's best friend and advisor. Akbar was the Great Moghul king of the 16th century. The renowned linguist and translator O. Sukhbaatar studied many humorous books on Birbal and gathered some material from the books by Rama Anand Dvivedi (Varanasi 1947) and Bal Krishna Malvi (Varanasi 1959). But his main source was the handbook compiled by Vishvanath and published in New Delhi in 1972. He translated the book *Birbal's Mind* and published it in 1989. One hundred and forty-one humorous stories about Birbal were included in this book.

O. Sukhbaatar translated 'Melody of Six Seasons' by Kalidasa. D. Bold translated 'Taj Mahal' by Paghunat Verma Dighe from the Russian. The famous poem 'Cloud Messenger' (Meghdoot) was translated from English, Hindi, Tibetan and Sanskrit into Mongolian and it was published many times. Kalidasa's play *Shakuntala* was translated by J. Badraa in 1959.

Folk Tales. The version of Indian folklore which was translated into Mongolian in large quantities was the tale. Between 1921-2000 nearly 253 tales were translated from the Russian, Hindi, English and Sanskrit. These translated tales appeared partly in text-books, newspapers and magazines and sometimes they were also published as a book. For instance, *Indian Folk Tales,* translated from Russian by D. Purev-Oidov, was published in 1957 and 18 tales were included in it. Later in 1965, *Indian Tales* comprising 37 tales was published after being translated from Russian by D. Sundev. U. Nyamdorj translated 39 tales from Russian for the book *Well-taught Doctrine* in 1965. The collection *Indian, Nepal and Fiji Folk Tales* included 34 tales translated from Hindi and Sanskrit by O. Sukhbaatar and were published in 1980. Kh. Suvd and Yu.Munkh-Amgalan translated *Folk Tales from India* from English containing 23 tales, and published it in 1995. Besides these, *Tales in the Different Countries* and *Oriental Tales* were also translated and published. *Monkey's Heart* by Shiva Kumar containing 25 tales was translated from Hindi and Sanskrit by O. Sukhbaatar.

I have attempted to give a survey of Indian literature that has been translated in Mongolia between 1921-2000. Mongolian and Indian scholars have been doing research on the literary links between the two countries. We can see from the research that there are sufficient research materials and writings on traditional interactions between ancient Indian, Tibetan and Mongolian literatures. But there are few factual records and material on their modern or up-to-date literature.

REFERENCES

Chimpa Lama, *Mongolia-Indian Literary Links-I. Perspectives on Mongolia.* Ed., R. C. Sharma, Seema Publications, New.Delhi, 1988. Pp. 85-90.

D. Yondon, 'Mongolia and India', *Indological Studies in Mongolia,* Ed., Sh. Bira. Ulaanbaatar, 1989. Pp. 312-24.

J. Gendendaram, *Mongolia-Indian Literary Links-II. Perspectives on Mongolia.* Ed., R. C. Sharma, Seema Publications, New Delhi, 1988. Pp. 90-93.

L. Khurelbaatar, *History of Mongolian Translation Works* (in Mongolian). Ulaanbaatar, 1995.

Lokesh Chandra, *Mahabharata in Asian Literatures and Arts. Cultural Horizons of India.* Vol. III. Sata–pitaka Series. Vol. 370. IAIC and Aditya Prakashan, New Delhi, 1993. Pp.148-155

The Heritage of Folk Painting in India and Korea

MAN-YOUNG HWANG

All civilised nations have formed their own peculiar cultures. Folk painting especially has played a role as one of the most important mediums, as it shows the ethnic characteristics and traditions of a nation. Folk painting did not simply develop in a natural way, and its content depends on the ability and intellect of each nation. It would not be too much to say that India and Korea have the most developed folk painting in the world from the point of view of standard and variety.

In the process of making the instruments required for everyday survival, human beings developed their aesthetic sense and created wall paintings as a means of expression of primitive beliefs, survival and beauty. Of course, paintings expressed their life itself, and were not created for aesthetic purposes in the beginning. But through the process of history, they acquired a collective characteristic and developed into what we today know as folk painting. These had their value in that they revealed the pure emotions of the nation. In the paintings we can catch the way of thinking, aesthetic expression and reality of the times.

India and Korea have both suffered from foreign aggression, but both have in common the respect for ethnic tradition in the cultural arts. Also, the aesthetic sense of both nations is highly developed and pure aesthetic expression is a unique national characteristic.

Folk painting, before we discuss its aesthetic value, was a product of emotions resulting from the nation's mental, cultural and historical background. A folk artist was not required to study orthodox drawing, arts and artistic expressions. A painting was a subjective and symbolic creation of ordinary people with some artistic talent. It had the value of a popular culture. It was the result of people's beliefs and life itself and a symbol of special ceremonies.

Folk paintings had various subjects: they expressed human desires. They were employed as a protective medium against objects of fear. They expressed the adoration of beauty, humor in life, religious fervour and devotion. They were used to interpret dreams about the past, present and the future, etc.

Korea, unlike India and China, has a small mass of land and hence a regional classification of folk painting makes no sense. But the content of folk painting shows a vast variety.

Korean Folk Painting

At a time when human beliefs were grounded in animism, the Korean people believed that there was a god in each and every thing that had any relation to everyday life. This meant that people regarded the identification with Nature as an existential consciousness and as a motif for folk art.

Among the gods that humans have worshipped since ancient times are the solar gods (the sun, fire, the moon, stars, horses and birds), the earth gods (snakes, cattle, lions, tigers), the water gods (water plants like the lotus, fish, buffaloes, bears and frogs) the mountain gods (trees, antelopes and deer), the sea gods (turtles, dragons, shellfish and whales), and the gods of birth (pigs, and sex symbols), and so on. These have their own symbolic meanings. One interesting fact is that in Korea, abstract shapes, such as phantoms, are human shapes with only one leg or half-human and half-animal. Also, most animals seem to have human and good-humoured looks, and do not show fear and aversion. Animals are regarded as familiar objects.

In Sasindo ('the picture for four gods'), a wall painting which was related to directions and colours, the East (Chungryong or 'blue dragon'), the West (Bakho or 'white tiger'), the South (Jujak or 'red peacock'), and the North (Hyunmu or 'black turtle') were pictured through animals. Though these animals were realistically expressed, their shapes were transformed. As a mountain or earth god mountain animals appeared in the paintings. There are many pictures of tigers in Korea, expressed singly as well as with figures regarded as mountain gods in the pictures. Tigers in Korean folk painting are presented humorously and sometimes appear with other animals in a picture. Magpies are one of the most frequent animals represented with tigers. We can see in many pictures in which a magpie sits on the tree and stares at a tiger, that the tiger, the magpie and the pine tree are in a fatal relationship. When we see the picture in which a tiger, as a beast, is faced with a small and weak rabbit, we can find out its meaning in our folk tales or legends. The tiger is symbolised as a tolerant being, not as a beast.

The most frequently used colour in Korean painting was red. Red as a colour was used to keep away spirits, while in China red was used to call in good luck. Generally a widespread subject matter of folk tales is the fowl. There are legends that relate how spirits were afraid of red and when wandering around on hazy days and dark nights would disappear on hearing the cry of the fowl at dawn. The fowl frequently appeared in Korean painting as a being which kept spirits away.

Flowers and birds had their own beauty, but they were dealt with as symbols of good luck. A peony and a lotus, especially, symbolised higher nature. Birds, including the mandarin duck, etc., were pictured in twos, as were fish. These symbolised the pursuit of peaceful happiness and the love between husband and wife. There are some paintings showing hundreds of children and many fruits, symbolising the hope of bearing many children.

Another one of the subjects in Korean folk painting is *Sipjangseng* ('Ten long-living things, the sun, clouds, water, stone, turtles, deer, cranes, pine trees, bamboos, and herbs of age-less youth). All the things in *Sipjangseng* could be used in a picture to make folding screens; some or one of them could be used in a picture. *Sipjangseng*, which was widely used by all, from the royal family to ordinary families who wished to live long, had its own attraction. Like all Korean folk painting styles, *Sipjangsengs* are various and unconventional.

Indian Folk Painting

Though India is a large land and its folk paintings vary in their regional characteristics, India's own unique characteristics emerge in all its folk paintings. At first, in view of artistic values Indian folk paintings are much more remarkable. Whether the size is large or small, they include many stories. Also, there are many cases beyond the specified subjects that are included in a picture. So the pictures lure us into a world of fantasy as if we are travelling in a small universe, and we feel it natural to adapt ourselves to that world.

In their technical aspects, Indian folk paintings have varying frames. Some of them show a series of regular patterns, some show irregular arrangements of the subjects, regardless of the top and bottom or the left and right orientation of the subject. Others show various forms without considering the composition of the whole frame. In these paintings the appearances of things are constantly being redefined in live picturesque expressions, with images of the animals and plants in relation to beliefs and in scenes that naturally harmonise with humans.

Subjects that are mainly dealt with are decorative flowers and animals as well as many gods and goddesses. Also, pleasure, music and dance, folk illustrations, legends of Hinduism, etc., and wings of butterflies and patterns of snakes, ripples of surfaces of streams, alternation of leaves and branches looking up to the sky, the colours of the rainbow, etc., and even a horoscope of astrology are shown in them. Delicate expressions are shown through the miniature technique, and the use of natural dyes and brilliant colours.

Colours are made from various plants, minerals, animals, etc. Cattle excrement, thought to be divine, was used in many ways. It is known that this material is used as a fuel, but what is very surprising is not only that it has been scientifically used in paving roads but also that it has been used as a medium in folk painting. This means that the experiences of the folk artists, arrived at through experimental processes, have soaked into their very lives, from where the brilliant colour culture has developed. The colours in Indian folk painting are brilliant but never gaudy and show a supreme aesthetic sense even when used in excess.

Although Korea and India are in the same cultural area, India, unlike China and Japan, has not had a frequent cultural exchange with Korea. India and Korea are related through Buddhism via a third country, and not directly. But the two nations have many similarities in their historical backgrounds and in their ways of thinking. Korean folk paintings were inspired on Korean folk beliefs which were associated with Buddhism and Confucianism. Like Korea, India is rich in both its folk painting and its religious beliefs, like Buddhism, Hinduism, Jainism and Islam.

Though their contents and expressive methods are different, the mythical materials in West Bengal and Orissa are similar to the divine images of animals which originate in Korea's primitive beliefs. Dragon pictures of the *Monpa* and *Unyongdo* ('Cloud-Dragon pictures') of Korea are very similar. Symbols of deified animals are different depending on geographic conditions, ideas and beliefs. Elephants, which inhabit tropical climates, do not appear in Korean folk painting. Humans adapt themselves to representing those objects that are observed in their daily lives, and even if these beings and objects arouse fear, they are deified for self-protection. This explains why Korean folk painting deals with tigers and Indian folk paintings use many elephants.

One strange fact is that cattle, one of the most revered of all animals in India, has hardly appeared in folk painting, probably because cattle are deified. Ordinary people's mythical representation/ nature was used as the subject matter of folk paintings, with the intention of condemning social injustice. Artists sometimes pictured hell and portrayed expressions that were meant to chastise vice. This had a great influence on the mask cultures of Korea and India and gave them a curious similarity despite the different expressive methods.

The vivacious colours used in Korean and Indian costumes are consistent with the colours in folk paintings. Both nations also have a common tendency to wear white and black clothes. Since each colour reflects its own emotional expression and has its own characteristic symbols, every nation has a colour that the people frequently use, a folk colour. The folk colour that Chinese and Koreans frequently use is the red colour. Koreans use the colour to keep away the spirits, but the Chinese use it to wish good luck.

Indian traditional folk art, unlike Korean traditional folk art, shows a convergence in the different art forms, such as sculpture, painting and architecture. This is evident from the rock carvings, grottoes, tombs, palaces, forts, pagodas, pavilions, gates, temples or houses. In all such forms, attempts have been made to establish bridges between ethical conduct and theology, physical beauty and the radiance of spiritual fervour, masculine and feminine principles of life, ideas of visualisation and performance, functional utility and decorative fitness.

Ritual and religious masks, objects of household or ceremonial use, have formed the corpus of Indian and Korean art for centuries. Korean folk painting, which was associated with everyday philosophy and beliefs, simply seems to pursue symbolism, while Indian folk painting pursues the fantastic and mysterious as its theme. Again, Korean folk painting hardly uses human figures as its subject. There are no more than a few examples, if any, of such portraits, as for example the portrait of Dangun, the founder of the nation, and some mountain gods and supernatural beings. But in India almost all folk painting includes human figures. These are similar to the painted human figures of Egypt, in which the eyes take up a large percentage of the face and to the portraits in profile, where the subject is often shown immersed in some secret thought. Whether the subject of a painting is in costume or nude, many accessories accompany the central figure. There is a sharp difference between Korea and India in this. Korea, which had a closed system, had no nude paintings, while India often had nude subjects in its folk painting which also emphasized voluptuous beauty. Korean folk painting mainly shows animals which either symbolise good luck, help in avoiding bad luck or help in warding away phantoms. Animals in Indian folk painting instead seem to be simply the functional detail that embellishes the main subject of the picture.

Materials used in India and Korea show different characteristics according to the climates. Korean painting employed the fine paper and fabric that was produced in East Asia, but India used specific materials to get special effects. Indian painters seem to have enjoyed making wall paintings. In Uttar Pradesh human figures are painted on smooth white walls. In Orissa they are portrayed on mud walls with special materials. But in Assam, which has a lot of annual precipitation, there are no wall paintings because walls are made of rattans and bamboos to protect them from the rainfall. In India we can see large wall paintings in temples or sanctuaries and traces have survived of paintings that had been done on common boundary walls or in various spots in the villages. In Korea, we can find wall paintings in temples or ancient tombs.

Although Korea has shown outstanding aesthetic sense in its historic and traditional art, it has not realised its potential and has ignored its value. Likewise, India has lauded the creative mind since independence, but its artistic output as regards folk painting has not kept pace with the other arts. Undoubtedly the reason is that this fine art has been ignored and has not been given the support needed. But it is important to note that the heritage of folk painting has received much recognition from the standpoint of new values. We need to scientifically re-illustrate many theories about folk painting and classify them systematically.

Korean and Indian folk painting has developed most naturally. Through their folk paintings we can understand their ethnic natures and evaluate their creative abilities. A nation's way of thinking and its cultural output is established and changes according to the lifestyle and historical processes which determine its national characteristics. The aesthetic sense of human beings develops into a molding ability, that is, a creative ability according to some particular forms and methods. Some ethnic characteristics accordingly may sometimes show a coincidence with other nations, or may be interpreted independently.

It is interesting that there is a similarity between the two countries, because it means that they have equal consciousness and thought. Though Korea and India are separated by distance, the fact that despite each one's unique ethnic characteristics, there is a similarity in the content of their folk painting shows that the substantial ideals humans pursue are the same and their aesthetic senses have developed on the same lines. I believe that, as in Korea so in India, art and life, form and function have been blended to make life artistic and art alive. Today, new techniques for creativity are developing very rapidly. It seems that we have reached the limits of human endeavour and there is nothing to discover any more. But as times change, there is no doubt that new forms of creativity will develop.

The rapid changes taking place today in human civilisation have brought mankind face to face with critical crises and even a loss of human nature itself. What are the values we should pursue in such moments? Positive values will disappear if material civilisation outdoes mental culture.

Tagore's Quatrain on Korea
Context and Beyond

R.R. KRISHNAN

In the golden age of Asia
Korea was one of the lamp bearers
That lamp waits to be lighted once again
For the illumination of the East

Rabindranath Tagore

Gurudev Tagore handed over his poem to Korean students who called on him during his third and last visit to Japan in 1929.[1] He graciously responded to the request for a message to commemorate the tenth anniversary of the March First 1919 movement,[2] a mass upsurge against Japanese colonialism.[3] It was a remarkable quatrain, succinct, profound, timely and powerful. It touched the hearts of the Koreans and stirred their historical national consciousness and sensitivity during the dark era of colonial subjugation. It gave them pride in their distinct national identity and reinforced their hope and optimism for a bright future. No literary luminary, creative artist, humanist, internationalist of Tagore's stature or any notable international figure has said anything more eloquently about Korea or has had a greater appeal for the Koreans than the simple four-line poem by the first Asian Noble prize winner.

The emotive appeal of Tagore's poem was due to a number of reasons. It recalled the distinct and historical role of Korea as a 'lamp bearer' in the 'golden age of Asia'. It was obviously an allusion to Korea's transmission of Buddhism with its spiritual, philosophical, aesthetic and temporal features to Japan. The fascinating process began in A.D. 552, about two centuries after Buddhism was introduced in Korea, 'when Japan received the first Buddhist statue from Korea along with teachers, artists, scriptures, objects for rituals and technicians'. In the following decades, 'Korean Buddhists and men of learning in divination, calendar-making, astronomy, medicine and architects, painters, sculptors, weavers and craftsmen and so forth came to Japan bringing with them arts and knowledge.'[4] True to Buddhist principles and traditions, no force or coercion was used by the Koreans while transmitting and propagating Buddhism. Korea, based on its own experience and on the experiences of Buddhism in other parts of Asia, left it to the Japanese to develop and modify their forms of Buddhism that could accommodate and assimilate certain historically inherited pre-Buddhist traditions and direct influences from India and China.[5]

Although we have not come across Tagore locating any particular period as 'the golden age of Asia', he had spoken passionately and forcefully about Asia, Asian unity, etc., in a spiritual and civilisational framework. For example, addressing a gathering of students from all private universities at Keio University on 'the spirit of Japan' on 2 July 1916, Tagore said:

> I cannot but bring to your mind those days when the whole of Eastern Asia from Burma to Japan was united with India in the closest of friendship, the only natural tie which can exist between nations. There was a living communication of hearts, a nervous system evolved through which messages ran between us about the deepest needs of humanity. We did not stand in fear of each other, we had not to arm ourselves to keep each other in check; our relations was not of self-interest, of exploration and spoliation of each other's pockets; ideas and ideals were exchanged, gifts of the highest love were offered and taken; no difference of languages and customs hindered us in approaching each other heart to heart; no pride of race or insolent consciousness of superiority, physical or mental, marred our relation; our arts and literatures put forth new leaves and flowers under the influence of the sunlight of united hearts; and races belonging to different lands and languages and histories acknowledged the highest unity of man and the deepest bond of love.[6]

There is probably no direct reference to Korea or Indo-Korean relations in Tagore's writings. However, it may suffice to mention here that Mahayana Buddhism or 'Sino-Indian Mahayanism' was introduced to Korea in A.D. 372 and further developed by the Koreans and transmitted to Japan. The 'heavy load of ancient Indian cultural treasures' included 'ideas, logic, fantasies, cosmology, astrology and astronomy, alchemy, sculptures, carve art, music, dance, boxing, breath control, etc.'[7] The visit of innumerable Korean monks to sacred Buddhist sites and to the renowned centre of learning at Nalanda, the great Hyejo's decade long travel through the Indian subcontinent and his fascinating travelogue *Wango Ch'onch'uk Kukchon* (Account of Visits to the Five Lands) throwing light on various aspects of 8th century A.D. Indian society, etc., have been extensively researched and commented upon.[8] However, what is necessary to emphasize is that the almost total absence of any movement of scholars to and from India after the 8th century, the hegemony of neo-Confucianism during the Yi-dynasty, the emergence and enrichment of 'whole Buddhism' or other cultural and social developments following interactions with the West, did not undermine the distinct cultural space and proximity between Korea and India. This is because the Koreans assigned a special space, a niche, in their national consciousness and tradition to 'Indo' as a land of Amitabha Sakyamuni Buddha, as one of the five original centres of world civilisation and as a repository of higher human values and ideals.

There were clear differences in the manner in which the modern state of Japan in the Meiji era was perceived by intellectuals and social leaders of India and Korea. This was particularly true from about the last quarter of the 19th century to the first decade of the 20th century. A number of prominent leaders like Swami Vivekananda, Dadabhoi Naoroji, B.G. Tilak, G.K. Gokhale and M. Visveswarayya seemed to have uncritically accepted Japan's transformation or the way Japan sought to construct its alliance with England or its relations with the United States during Theodore Roosevelt's presidency. In short, they tended to overlook the way Japan sought to undermine the independence and sovereignty of Korea from the Treaty of Kanghwa in 1876 to colonisation in 1910. The euphoric reaction to Japan's defeat of Russia after Japan had concluded an alliance with Britain was indicative of the understanding of some of the outstanding leaders of India. Tagore 'found in the history an occasion to praise the Japanese warriors in three verses which he composed in Haiku style'.[9]

There was a perceptible shift in Tagore's understanding of the nature of changes in Japan as he gained greater insight into the complexities of Japan's emergence as a modern state and its assertive military power in the region. He along with his close associates, C.F. Andrews, William Pearson and Mukul Dey, visited Japan in

1916. Although he admired several features of Japan, he was 'shocked to see the numerous war memorials which had been raised in the country side to commemorate Japan's victory over China (1894-95) and described them as an "evidence of barbarism".'[10] He was similarly shocked when 'he saw the display of trophies from the Russo-Japanese war in a Tokyo school which he visited'.[11] He said, 'To perpetuate humiliation of defeated nations by exhibiting trophies won from war and using these in schools in order to breed in children's minds contempt for others, is imitating the west where she has a festering sore, whose swelling is the swelling of disease eating into its vitality'.[12] According to C.F. Andrews, the criticism by some Japanese that Tagore was the poet of the defeated country inspired him to write the poem 'The Song of the Defeated'.[13]

The Koreans began to appreciate India's struggle for freedom and held its political leaders and intellectual luminaries in high esteem as the anti-colonial movements in the two countries gained in strength. Tagore and Gandhi were respected for their commitment to human dignity, freedom and equality of nations. Tagore came to be admired after he won the Noble prize in 1913. Although *Gitanjali's* complete translation into Korean by Kim Ok first appeared in 1923, earlier introductions to Tagore's works were in the form of newspaper reporting. It is not surprising that *Gitanjali's* 'where the mind is without fear and head is held high' appealed to the colonised Koreans and that too, under an Asian power. Tagore's poems were not only popular among the Koreans, the translation of his poems into Korean in the 1920s 'far exceeded any other foreign poet'.[14] According to Kim Yang Shik, the well-known authority on Tagore, 'as long as it was written by Tagore for Korean people, the nature of work did not matter. The underlying reason is that from Tagore more can be felt than from the works of Western writers or philosophers'.[15]

When viewed against the backdrop of the Koreans' keen interest in Tagore, it is not surprising that his visit to Japan in 1916 evoked keen interest in Korea. They had every reason to welcome Tagore's disapproval of the Japanese form of militant nationalism. Noting that the Japanese were not as enthused about Tagore after he had spoken against the militant form of Japanese nationalism, C.F Andrews remarked :

> But when he spoke out stronger against the militant imperialism which he saw on every side in Japan and set forward

in contrast his ideal picture of the true meaning of the East and West, with its vista of a world brotherhood, the hint went abroad that such 'pacifist' teaching was a danger in war time and that the Indian poet represented a defeated nation. Therefore, almost as rapidly as the enthusiasm had arisen, it subsided.[16]

According to Andrews, the accusation that Tagore was the poet of the defeated country inspired him to write the poem 'The Song of the Defeated'. Tagore gave his poem to Chi Hakmin, a Korean student in Japan, on 11 July 1916. Choe Nam Son, the editor of *Ch'ongchun* (The Youth) had asked Chi Kakmin to meet the poet and send a report on the meeting. His meeting as well as a translation of the poem with the title, 'T'a Sonsaeng Ui Songyonggi' was published a year later. The poem forcefully put across the poet's belief that it is 'the conquest by swords that calls for shame'.[17]

The impact and enormous significance of Gandhi's concept of *swadeshi* was not only well understood but it also provided an inspiration to launch a similar movement in Korea. The *Dong-A Ilbao*, the nationalist paper wrote in its editorial of 13 November 1922:

> It is well known that the Indian revolutionary leader Gandhi preached national unity and encouragement of cotton spinning, the greatest industry in India, as the only way to attain complete independence for India. . . . Although Gandhi's advocating the revival of primitive industry may seem unmodern, we admire him for his sagacity in pointing out the way towards the eternal welfare and happiness of the Indian people. When we reflect upon ourselves and think about the future, we desperately feel the necessity of devising means for self-protection... It is the unsympathetic who ridicule the Koreans as lacking earnestness. Our only means of survival is to restrict foreign commodities and encourage national (native) products.[18]

The CHAJAKHOE (Self-production Society) set up in December 1922, and the MULSAN CHANGNYOHOE (Society for the Encouragement of Native Products) set up in February 1923, propagated the ideology of *swadeshi* in Korea, taking the cue from Gandhi.[19]

Tagore visited Japan twice in 1929, first on his way to Canada in March and then on his return in May 1929. It was evident that a

into these may facilitate an understanding of not only the art but also the psyche of the creators of this art. Extended beyond the domain of art into life, it may help us to identify what constitutes Asian Civilisation and Cultures, ever in dialogue, but never uniform.

Dr Lokesh Chandra: Dr Kapila Vatsyayan and distinguished colleagues. The distinction between Asia and Europe goes back to the Akkadians, who were a West Asian people. This came to the Greeks from the Akkadians through the Phoenicians. In Akkadia the word Asia or *aasu* meant the rising sun and the word *ereb* meant the setting sun. From *ereb* we have the word Europe or the West. The Greeks used the word for all the Hellenic states and in the 9th century, particularly during the Crusades, the term Europe came to be applied to what are now the European nations. These concepts go back to great Asian antiquity, and through the Phoenicians, via the Greeks they passed on to the Romans and from the Romans into contemporary European usage.

The part of the world which we are going to discuss today—East Asia—has been deeply conditioned by a commonality of cultural perceptions. These have reigned, as Kapilaji has rightly pointed out, from the deepest moorings of the human mind, to the most external expressions, even including the martial arts.

The first contact of Buddhism was with China and Indian teachers of Buddhism went there on white horses. The white horse in the Asian concept of sovereignty represents a *chakravartin* king, and the first monastery in China was the White Horse Monastery. The trading of horses was an important component in the transmission of Buddhism. There was a synchronicity of several interests, which guided the transmission of culture, polity, trade and all other formulations. China is one of the earliest countries to establish multipronged relations with various parts of Central Asia as far as India. The vast deserts of Central Asia gave to China the concept of *shunyata* or emptiness. This emptiness extended to inner emptiness. The oases of Central Asia were the *paramitas*. When Chinese pilgrims crossed these deserts they felt that they had traversed the *dukha* of this *Sansara*, the travails of this world, and had reached the yonder shore of *paramita* when they reached the sancta of India. The deserts became poetry in Chinese thought and the horses on which they travelled became part of the Han military might. It is in the appropriateness of things that we start with discussions on the Chinese approach to research on India.

Indian history has been conditioned by three great Chinese travellers, Fa-hsien, Hsuan-tsang and Itsing, besides many others. The Chinese work, *Biography of Eminent Monks* details lives of several hundred monks but unfortunately these remain untranslated even after their having been known to modern research since two centuries. It is a mine of information on the cultural inter-relations between India and China. Chinese colleagues are here, and I wish that they translate into English the whole of this work and its continuation in the Sung Dynasty. These can become part of India's understanding of herself.

The earliest Sanskrit manuscript known at the time of Max Mueller was not from India, but from the Horyuji Monastery in Japan. It is of the 5th century. The presentation by a great Chinese scholar, Professor Wang, is on the Chinese traditions of research on India. The Chinese tradition on understanding India has been active and detailed since ancient times.

On Indian soil we have next to nothing of the interaction between India and China, which was glorious and grand. A large quantum of literature has survived in China in exceptional translations into Chinese. It awaits translation to become available to a global academic community.

Mr. Nobuaki Ito: Thank you Mr. Chairman. First of all I am making this presentation in my personal capacity and therefore it should not in any way be interpreted either as that of the Japanese Embassy or the Japanese Government.

I basically wish to make three main points—one is on Japan's recent expansion in cultural exchange particularly on the kinds of problems and dilemmas which Japanese society is currently facing. The second is on the impact of the end of the Cold War era, which has had very serious and far-reaching consequences for international politics, and particularly on the prospects (and aspects) of cultural relations. The third point relates to cooperation between India and Japan in cultural exchanges.

Well, first of all, as you know, some of the well known cultural exports from Japan are the tea ceremony, Ikebana, calligraphy and poetry, which are considered to be the main features of Japan's cultural heritage. But the fact is that these are merely the so-called lifestyles of culture, something that is slightly different from traditional cultural heritage. In my view, Japan's traditional lifestyle culture is now at the crossroads in the context of international cultural exchange. Ikebana and tea-ceremony are now much less integral to the normal Japanese lifestyle than they are assumed to be worldwide. The number of people who, for example, write haiku poetry, Japanese poetry, is quite high, but they do it merely as a suitable hobby. Many Japanese women still learn Ikebana and the tea-ceremony, but they are doing it not only for the sake of appreciating the deep meaning of that artistic culture, but also as a part of their preparation for marriage, so necessary, with which they would be able to find their future husbands. But in today's Japan these things are not generally integrated that much into the ordinary Japanese lifestyle.

Ikebana, tea ceremony and calligraphy have been used to project Japan's tradition and culture in the international community. However, if such lifestyle cultures do not possess a steady artistic or special depth then they merely become Japanese hobbies. Whether they should now be promoted as traditional Japanese culture through international cultural exchange is a delicate question to which I have not yet found an appropriate answer.

On the other hand, there are Asian-Japanese traditions like Noh and Kabuki; if they have already become too antique and irrelevant in contemporary Japan, then they can no longer be considered a part of Japanese culture, but merely fossils of the past. We therefore have to ask ourselves whether we should continue exporting this culture with the intention of demonstrating the 'Japaneseness' of the traditional culture of our nation, and whether we can expect it to play a role in promoting international understanding and cultural exchange.

Japan in the past had tried to spread the spiritual and philosophical thoughts that reflected the deep cultural currents of Japanese society. Typical examples of these are Okakura Tenshin's *The Book of Tea* and Nitobe Inazo's *The Spirit of Japanese Samurai*. Japan's defeat in the Second World War and the subsequent moral and psychological destruction that followed had a great impact on the minds of the Japanese people. It is important to observe the post-war phenomenon in which the traditional Japanese 'spirit' more or less tended to be identified with the beautification of militarist thought. And this phenomenon affected very much the way of thinking and the mentality of the Japanese people after the war, as they became somewhat negative towards the value of the so-called Japanese spirit. The traditional Japanese spirit had been something pure in the minds of the Japanese people, which had nothing to do with the so-called militarism.

After the Second World War Japan tried to re-enter the world community and expected the international community to understand that Japan had totally changed. This was done by means of a denial of the traditional Japanese spirit.

The traditional Japanese spirit should not and must not be identified with Japan's past militarism. The Japanese spirit and traditional cultural values need to be reconciled with today's modern Japan. This is really a case in point and a dilemma that Japanese culture is facing today.

After the war a deep and strong feeling dominated the Japanese people's mind and this was that the Japanese people wanted to convince themselves that Japan had really changed. They also wanted to convey this message to the world that Japan had been reborn. As a matter of fact Japan has been attempting to erase the pre-war negative image and stereotyped perception, often held by the American and European people, of Japan for example as the land of Fujiyama and the Geisha.

Selling the new image of Japan as an advanced, modern nation was considered to be more important than promoting Japan's traditional culture. Ironically, this kind of excessive promotion of a new Japan has had an adverse impact on Japan's international image, as today Japan is sometimes considered to be a sort of 'faceless super economic animal'.

There is another problem that today's Japan is facing in cultural interaction, that is, the so-called Americanisation of culture, spreading not only in Japan but also worldwide. First of all I have to point out that the so-called Americanisation, as the global standard-setting force, does not necessarily reflect what is actually happening within American society today. Rather, it seems to be a name given to a general trend in the economic and political developments of the 20th century that gradually found their way into the US, Europe and the rest of the world. In this respect it is very important to differentiate the two aspects of the so-called Americanisation.

The first point is whether Americanisation—in other words cultural unification—is a reflection of the cultural progress of mankind. Maybe it is not. Does such a thing as Americanisation really exist today? The second point is whether the expansion of American culture is due to the spread of American political influence.

In today's world which, after the end of the Cold War era, is sometimes considered to be a unipolar world led by the US, we have to ask ourselves whether American influence is going to be accompanied by the expansion of American culture. In any case, the biggest question that faces Japanese society today is, how will Japan respond to this trend of unification of the world's cultures? And in this forum I would like to pose the same question to you all: how should East Asia and India, both abundant in history, culture and civilisation and both much more spiritually affluent than a young country like the United States, react to this trend of unification of world cultures?

Last but not least, Japan is facing today a sort of conflict between the promotion of traditional culture and the role of the state. Did or did not the state or the government play a role in destroying Japan's past tradition, as a consequence of its vigorous modernisation over the past one and a half century? In the modern era Japan has always been obsessed with the desire for a high degree of Westernisation, and Westernisation was considered to be more important than conserving Japan's cultural traditions.

Japan was reborn after the Meiji restoration. Post-war Japan was a complete transformation from pre-war Japan. Should the government and the state continue endlessly in their role of promoting this newly changed Japan? Or should the state and government become the guardians of culture and tradition? This is a dilemma that is felt very strongly in Japan today. Probably the answer lies in seeking a balance between the two, that is, in both promoting the image of a new, changed Japan, as well as protecting its traditional cultural values in a balanced manner. How to implement this balance is a very difficult task.

Now briefly, the second point about the end of the Cold War and its impact on cultural interaction. When we discuss culture and cultural exchange worldwide, we have to think of the very important impact the Cold War had on contemporary international relations. After the collapse of the Berlin Wall, the exchange of human beings and ideas and economic and political movement became liberated between the East and West, thereby contributing to a smooth exchange of ideas, religions, philosophical beliefs and, above all, enhancing mutual understanding between different cultures. Previously those free movements and exchanges had been prevented by the ideological confrontations during the Cold War era. For the

Japanese, after the end of the Cold War, India and China have become closer and more friendly countries. And therefore there has been an increase in exchange of cultural events and in the exchange of scholars and academicians.

The second impact of the end of the Cold War is that such factors as culture, religion, and spiritual values have become more important determinants than ideology in international politics today. As you may remember, Professor Samuel Huntington—I think he is a professor at Harvard University—has a very famous theory called collision amongst different civilisations. He predicts that after the end of the ideological war and after the end of the Cold War, the confrontation between different civilisations based on different cultures, races and religions will become inevitable. I certainly do not subscribe to his analysis and what I found missing, or what is wrong in his theory, is that humankind is capable of continuing to live in peace and harmony; it is capable of deepening mutual understanding between different cultures, thereby nurturing peace. And humankind has its innate, inherent capacity to grasp the meaning and significance of a different culture, because we share the basic human characteristics of perceiving and thinking, and are able to feel and love different peoples and cultures.

In other words, for example, Western civilisation and Islamic civilisation can co-exist and when different civilisations co-exist they may sometimes have a confrontational relation, but more importantly they can engage in dialogue in order to avoid confrontation.

The end of the Cold War drastically changed the nature of international politics by introducing such new factors as culture, history and tradition instead of political ideology. If, for example, India and Pakistan had proceeded with nuclear tests during the Cold War era, their impact and consequences could have been discussed in the much wider context of nuclear equilibrium between the United States and the Soviet Union. But instead the reaction from the international community was to analyse their implications in the context of religious, ethnical and historical backgrounds, and their implications on the future reconciliation between these two countries.

Today, the foreign policy of many countries, including Japan, incorporates cultural exchange as an important pillar. Cultural exchange and mutual understanding of different cultures provide an important basis for the protection of human rights, freedom and democracy, denial of violence, promoting heart to heart contact, and nurturing tolerance and solidarity among peoples. Therefore culture has become an even more important factor in maintaining peace and security in the world.

During the Cold War era it was generally believed that peace still could be maintained by military balance and nuclear deterrence while in terms of the North-South context, economic and social development was the key factor for peace and security. But today, after the end of the Cold War era, culture is a new and important factor, which can contribute to the peace and security of the international community.

The third impact of the end of the Cold War can be demonstrated by the fact that there no longer exists an ideological confrontation between groups of countries. We have no major enemy to confront but are now in the same camp and have to compete with each other. This new type of competition between the international community means that we have to compete through such means as economic power, technology, history or culture. I still remember very clearly the years when I was posted in New York working for the United Nations in the late eighties. At that time a certain section of American public opinion maintained that the real threat to the national interest of the United States came no longer from the military power of the Soviet Union, but from the super economic power of Japan.

What I want to tell you is that after the end of the Cold War, each nation has to compete with other members of the international community without differentiating between them as partners or adversaries. In such a new international community culture, civilisation, religious and philosophical ideas can be more important factors than conventional military strength in interactions with other countries and for the protection of a country's national interests.

Just very briefly, the third point is commonality or wider relationships between Japan and India in the cultural field. Historical ties between Japan and India can be traced back to the 6th century when Buddhism was introduced in Japan. Since then the Japanese have felt a very special affection for India. Japan feels that we have learnt a lot from India's rich cultural heritage, including the value of spirituality and religious and cultural diversity. Indeed many Japanese have been inspired by philosophical and spiritual ideas originating in India. In modern times the famous friendship between the Nobel Laureate Rabindranath Tagore and the well known Japanese cultural ideologue Tenshin Okakura has served as a very good example of fruitful cultural exchange between these two countries.

I strongly believe that Japan and India have enormous potential to strengthen their relationship further on the basis of the rich and common historical and cultural background of each country. Two points I wish to make are, first, that Japan and India are the two largest parliamentary democracies in Asia. We have a common mission to further promote the values of democracy, freedom, cultural tradition and history. The second point I wish to make is that today Japan is a highly industrialised country with traditional values and spirituality, and for such a country India remains one of the most important sources of cultural and spiritual inspiration. Our two countries can be role models of cultural and human development and work together for the protection of cultural heritage. As you may remember, just a few months back there was the destruction of the Buddha statues in Afghanistan. We feel very strongly that Japan and India should be very important partners in working together for preserving cultural heritage and traditions. Thank you very much.

G.P. DESHPANDE: Are Asian values a myth or reality? There was perhaps no Asia before the Europeans came to the landmass that we now call Asia. Europe had been exploring the various landmasses. Christopher Columbus travelled to America thinking he was going to India. Vasco Da Gama reached the Indian coast. Several Frenchmen and later, Englishmen, reached the Islamic world. In 1869, the year Gandhi was born, the Suez Canal was thrown open to the public.

These were the years of what Edward Said has called 'orientalism'. An 'orient' was being fashioned and designed. 'Asia' or rather the creation of Asia was a part of that project. Asia is an ancient continent but Asia is a new, rather young concept. What is this concept like?

It is a concept which has defied definition or even a full interpretation. It has itself no words for itself in classical or native languages. Sanskrit does not recognise Asia. Prakrits do not either. I am not sure if the Ya Zhou, Asia in Chinese, is a very ancient usage. Asia in our languages is a coinage of colonial times. Our personalities, in so far as they are products of our language, are untouched by Asia. Nagarjuna had argued: 'There cannot be an

Abhidheya (Asian continent in this case) without an Abhidhana ('Asia' the term). We use the word Ashiya as if we have known this word for centuries. One can argue that the myth of Asia was invented by European romanticism and was then internalised by us.'

We are then face to face with two Asias. One is Asia which is the invention of European romanticism. The other is the physical landmass that the term Asia refers to. Are there any values associated with a landmass ever? Values are associated with family, with philosophical perspectives, with religious systems, with individual rights, and so on. They are either universal (extending to the whole of *vasundhara*, i.e. the world) or particular to a given society or a religious system. What then do we mean when we use the expression Asian values? Do we mean the values associated with the societies living on the landmass known as Asia? Or do we mean 'oriental' values? Do we mean the values generated by cultural systems predominant in Asia? And indeed what do they share so that one can justifiably speak in terms of Asian values?

Asian values are a reality in as much as there are values typical of the Arabs or of the Chinese or of the Indians which the Euro-Americans do not share. But that feature may not and does not turn them into a set of transnational Asian values. We talk of Asian values most of the time to distinguish them from the Euro-American values. Europe becomes the 'other' (*swetara*) of our own selves. We talk of European or Western values, real or imaginary, in terms of defining a *swa* in terms of the *swetara*, a good Hegelian exercise. Discussion of values, theirs and ours, becomes an exercise aimed at Euro-America. We seem to reiterate the Asian values for the benefit of Euro-Americans. Euro-Americans are also of two kinds. One set is made of those who stand at a distance, as it were, from Asia or Africa. The other set is made of those who look for a shangri la in Asia. Christopher Isherwood and Koestler (the latter before his disillusionment with the *Yogi and the Commissar*) were admirers of India and its philosophies. Admirers of ancient Indian thinking like, for example, Isherwood were responsible for attributing extraordinary importance to concepts like Samadhi. They raised it to a status which the Upanishads did not bestow upon it. A stage in mystical progression became a civilisational value.

We have thus not only two Asias but two Indias, two Chinas, etc. There have been few attempts to look at India and China or India and the Arab world, etc. Very few Indologists have seen, as

Coomaraswamy did, any relationship between the *atman* of Sanskrit the *ruh* of the Arabic, the *ruach* of Hebrew and the *Chi* (*qi*) of the Chinese. The point is that an Asian understanding of Asia has not emerged to enable or entitle us to speak of Asian values.

We can legitimately speak of Indian values or Chinese values. We cannot be certain and at any rate have to be a little skeptical, of 'Asian' values. The nation-state was born in Europe. Yet none of those nations-states can really be understood without reference to European traditions and values. Asia is still miles away from the nation-state consciousness and yet Asia can be understood only in 'civilisational' terms which are not coterminous with Asia but rather with China, India, etc. These civilisations, as in the case of China, are coterminous with an idea of China. The divisions or partitions of Asian states have not denied that reality. Edward Said has lately spoken of the futility of partitions (in Asia). They are futile inasmuch as they do not solve the problems which they were supposed to solve. Instead, they deny them and their people the civilisational unity. China is perhaps the only exception to these developments which have marked South and Southeast Asia.

Modern international political theory uses the term 'failed state'. But that term would fail to capture the real problem which a state like Pakistan or India faces. That problem arises from the denial to their people of a certain wholeness of values. The partition of India has meant to people on both sides of the divide a negation of shared values which were called India; India in this particular case being an abstraction much larger than either the state of India or Pakistan. Independence of Taiwan in the Chinese view would amount to a similar denial of China as a civilisation area. Some Indonesians might take a similar view of the beginning of the disintegration of their state which the secession of East Timor might represent to them. Koreans would and do take a similar view of the continued division of their country. In this sense position or dismemberment of these states is qualitatively different from the Baltic or Central Asian states moving away from Russia. The latter phenomena have no civilisational and therefore valuational significance.

One can now argue that the significant feature of 'Asian values' is that the forces of civilisation or civilisation-state are stronger in Asia than anywhere else. Clearly they have taken many paths and struggled to emerge as viable valuational entities. From pan-Arabism or pan-Islamism to Islamic fundamentalism, from Muslim Indian or

Hindu Indian consciousness to *sara dharma samabhava* of Gandhi they have taken different forms in their emergence and sustained development. Lee kwan yu's emphasis on the 'Confucian' world and the values typical to it are also a good example of the same. The recent views of greater China (PRC, Taiwan, Hong Kong, Macau and Singapore) also point towards a Chinese value-system which will form the basis of a 'loosely Chinese' economic and political system. It is possible to argue that South Asia has no future unless it recognises the force and strength of a shared value system.

If the above analysis is at least partially plausible it would follow that the 19th and 20th century exercises in determining the Indian or the Chinese worlds have to be now politicised. As purely cultural or religious systems, they can be only self-destructive. Coomaraswamy has, in the same essay cited above, provided a semantic basis to that view. He argues that the literal meaning of *Bhedabheda* is distinction without difference.

In one sense this approach would suggest that South Asia has lost the *Bhedabheda* understanding of many streams in its civilisation. All such features are valuational inasmuch as they provide the *raison d'etre* of civilisations.

Deeply religious though Asia and Asians are, their identities are in the last analysis not religious for two reasons. One is that the Chinese or the Arab or the Indian (i.e. South Asian in terms of modern, ephemeral state systems) identities are not religious. We can easily forget that there are Christian Arabs and they are as significant a part of the Arab world as the Muslim Arabs. Their Arabness may and indeed does have a theological aspect. But they share their metaphysics. In fact the indivisibility of that metaphysic between Sanskrit, Chinese, Arabic and Hebrew is what would make us all Asians.

The 19th century European romanticism took us in one direction. It made us conscious of the Indian or the Chinese world in an Orientalist way. It introduced the word Asia to deny its existence except as a landmass. It acknowledged the cultural or valuational reality while simultaneously destroying it by perpetuating an orientalist nationalism which denied the larger civilisational, valuational unities. It turned the realities (of these unities) into myths and myths (of oriental nationalisms) into realities. The people of Asia are still victims of the same.

It might be useful at this stage to ask if the European view of values has been the same as the Asian one. This has something to do with the European view of philosophy and the Indian and the Chinese view of philosophy. It is at least arguable that India and China do not have philosophy as understood in the West. European philosophies seek to understand. As such they are not closed systems. A Western system draws a map of knowledge. Somebody like Pierce might suggest that (the philosophical) truth is the consensus among those who share the relevant world of discourse. It is doubtful if a Vedantin or a Sankhya philosopher would postulate a similarly exclusive world of discourse. This is also probably true of the world of values. A Jain position like *syadavada*, for example, would hardly be accepted as a philosophical category in terms of what Western philosophies seek to do. The situation in the world of values is not very different. Their values are ontologically and epistemologically different.

The only complicating factor is that a modern Indian, for example, would not clearly see the point that Coomaraswamy was making when he commented that in the expression 'six schools of Indian philosophy' only the words six and Indian are right.

A modern Indian (Asian) is face to face with a reality in which his *Adya* realities have become latter-day myths. How does one solve the problem of Asian values? Are they myths or realities? Whose myths or whose realities? A mythical answer to that question would not give us a *darshana* of reality; a realistic answer might ignore the fact that the escape from mythification of reality may not be very simple after all.

Akash K. Ouchi: I am extremely honoured to discuss the direction and scope of the 21st century, in the light of Asia's culture and spirituality. At the beginning of the 21st century, we, the human beings, are standing at the crucial and yet confused crossroads between New Hope in the new century and the serious problems of humanity. The destruction of the environment, repeated local confrontations, the widening gap between the rich and the poor, the deterioration of morals, spreading of corruption, destruction of social bondages are only some of the limitless list of problems.

In spite of the rich tradition of values and spirituality of India and East Asia, such as Buddhism, Hinduism and Confucianism, I have to say that these traditions and values are not becoming a dynamic force for the creation of a harmonious society in the coming age. With such a background it is quite understandable that the organisers have titled one of the sessions of the seminar as 'Asian Values—Myth or Reality?' I would like to give my thoughts on this from the Buddhist point of view.

One of the serious problems which society is facing currently is that of relationship with others, including with the environment. There is a strong tendency towards competition rather than co-existence, distrust and hatred instead of trust and friendship, oppression rather than harmony and selfishness instead of selflessness. At the heart of these problems lie the system of education and the structure of society, which produces people who are more capable of competition than humanity. This escalates the competitive tendencies in society.

The Buddhist concept of 'three thousand realms in a single life moment' states that a life in a single moment possesses the phenomenal world of 'three thousand' which includes organic as well as non-organic existence. In other words, life is not mere body and mind but an invisible network of interconnectedness with and among people outside, like parents, brothers, sisters, relatives, friends, society, environment, earth and the universe. This kind of inter-connectedness among people is called 'dependent origination'. This is another important Buddhist concept. Dependent origination holds that all beings and phenomena exist or occur in relation to other beings or phenomena.

Everything is linked in an intricate web of causation and connection and nothing, whether in the realm of human affairs or of natural phenomena, can exist or occur solely of its own accord. In this view, a greater emphasis is placed on the interdependent relationship between individuals.

Human beings should not hurt one another and should not oppress each other because they are a part of our life. They are a part of our own cause and will result in retribution to one's own self. A competitive system will not give happiness and harmony. There is a serious error in that system where competition is used as a means. Therefore the philosophy of co-existence becomes the key to the new century.

In the modern system, either in the individual's activities, in economic activities, in the relationship between societies and in the relationship between nations, the structure of competition is deeply rooted. As a result competition becomes the main stream of society. But development at the cost of destruction or disharmony is not really what we are aiming for. What is most wanted in the 21st century is the philosophy of co-existence, the intellectual ability to care for others, as parts of one's own self.

This philosophy of co-existence derives from Asian traditions and culture. And it is Asian spirituality itself. It is obvious that this Asian spirit is gradually deteriorating due to the influence of the internationalised mass media—satellite broadcasting and the Internet—as well as the globalised commercialisation imposed due to the guidelines of the IMF and the World Bank.

Dr Ikeda proposed inner motivation as the most important key for opening the way to an era of soft power. Over the ages, hard power systems have succeeded by using the established tools of coercion or oppression to move people toward certain goals. What is characterised as soft power, however, is by contrast based on the inner-generated energy deriving from the internal urge that is created through consensus and satisfaction among human beings. The process of soft power, the unleashing of the inner energies of the individual, have since ancient times been considered the proper province of philosophy in the broadest sense, rooted in the spiritual and religious nature of man.

Even the philosophy of co-existence cannot be imposed but it has to be derived from inner motivation. And the flow of inner motivation cannot be creating without re-establishing philosophy among people. What we have to create in the 21st century is not an externally oppressed culture but the culture of inner motivation. Thank you so much.

CONTRIBUTORS

Mr. Akash K. Ouchi is Director of the Institute of Oriental Philosophy, India Centre, and Soka Gakkai International, Japan.

Prof. Bangwei Wang is Professor of Buddhist Studies and President, Academy of Oriental Studies, University of Beijing, China, with specialisation in Sino-Indian cultural relations.

Prof. Brij Tankha is with the Department of Japanese Studies, University of Delhi, Delhi, and Honorary Fellow, Institute of Chinese Studies, Delhi.

Prof. D. Dashpurev a former Member of Parliament, is Director of the Institute of Philosophy, Sociology and Politics, Ulaanbaatar, Mongolia

Prof. D. P. Chattopadhyaya is Chairman, Centre for Studies in Civilizations, Calcutta.

Prof. Geng Yinzeng (Ms) is Professor of History, currently associated with the Institute of Afro-Asian Studies, University of Beijing, China.

Prof. G. P. Deshpande is Director, Institute of Chinese Studies, Delhi, and Professor at the Centre for East Asian Studies, School of International Studies, Jawaharlal Nehru University, New Delhi.

Prof. Hsin-Huang Michael Hsiao is with the Department of Sociology, National Taiwan University, and Director, Program for Southeast Asian Area Studies (PROSEA), Academia Sinica, Taiwan.

Dr. Kapila Vatsyayan President, India International Centre, is also its Founder Trustee. A former Secretary, Department of Arts, Ministry of Human Resource Development, she is an internationally acclaimed authority on the arts, and a widely published author.

Dr. Karan Singh, Member of Parliament, is Founder Trustee of the India International Centre and Chairman of its Asia Project.

Dr. Lokesh Chandra, a former Member of Parliament, is the Director of the Indian Academy of Indian Culture. He is a specialist on Buddhism of East Asia. For two generations he has been working on cultural relations between India and China.

Prof. Ma Keyao is President of the Chinese Research Association of World Medieval History, Vice-President of Beijing History Society, and Professor at the Department of History, University of Beijing, China.

Prof. Manoranjan Mohanty is with the Department of Political Science, Delhi University, and Honorary Fellow, Institute of Chinese Studies, Delhi.

Prof. Man-Young Hwang is Professor of Oriental Painting at the Fine Art College of Mok-Won University, Korea.

Mr. Nobuaki Ito is Deputy Chief of Mission at the Japanese Embassy, New Delhi.

Prof. Philip Leung Yuen-Sang is Director of the Research Institute for the Humanities, Faculty of Arts, The Chinese University of Hong Kong.

Prof. R. R. Krishnan is with the Centre for East Asian Studies, School of International Studies, Jawaharlal Nehru University, New Delhi.

Prof. Satya Bhushan Verma is Professor Emeritus of Japanese at the School of Languages, Jawaharlal Nehru University, New Delhi.

Dr. Tam Wai-Lun is Assistant Professor, Department of Religion at the Chinese University of Hong Kong.

Prof. Tan-Chung is with the Department of Chinese Language and History, Jawaharlal Nehru University, and Honorary Fellow, Institute of Chinese Studies, Delhi. He is the son of the renowned Tan Yun-shan who founded the Cheena Bhavan in Shantiniketan University at the invitation of Rabindranath Tagore.

Prof. Yu. Munkh-Amgalan is Head of Department of Mongolian Linguistics, School of Mongolian Studies, National University of Mongolia.